DA

M

KIND KIT

KIND KIT

AN INFORMAL BIOGRAPHY
OF CHRISTOPHER MARLOWE

Hugh Ross Williamson

London
MICHAEL JOSEPH

To
The Marlowe Society

Contents

CONTENTS

8

Kind Kit Marlowe
                —John Marston

Marlowe, renown'd for his rare art and wit,
Could ne'er attain beyond the name of Kit.
                —Thomas Heywood

Of English blank-verse, one of the few highest forms of verbal harmony or poetic expression, Marlowe was the absolute and divine creator. By mere dint of original and god-like instinct, he discovered and called it into life and at his untimely and unhappy death, more lamentable to us all than any other on record except Shelley's, he left the marvellous instrument of his invention so nearly perfect that Shakespeare first and afterwards Milton came to learn of him.
                —Algernon Charles Swinburne

Behind the poet stands always the Elizabethan man, certainly one of the notable personalities of his age. To his enemies he was a terror and a grisly warning; to his friends 'kind Kit'. The issue is not yet balanced and will never be by force of reason and historical research. Formal biography is, in this instance, more than usually futile.
                Professor C. F. Tucker Brooke

9

PROLOGUE

Deptford: Friday, 1 June 1593: Morning

The Inquest

Prologue: The Inquest

The murdered man's body lay on a chest in the middle of Mistress Bull's dining-room. The head was covered by a cloak because the fatal dagger-thrust through the right eye made it unpleasant for the jurors to look at, though they had, of course, all inspected it before they took their seats.

There were sixteen of them. They formed a special jury because they were concerned with a crime committed 'within the verge', that is to say within twelve miles of the person of the Sovereign. Queen Elizabeth was in residence at her favourite palace of Greenwich, less than a mile down-river from the little port of Deptford where, on Wednesday, 30 May 1593, the murder had been committed. She had accordingly issued instructions to 'our well-beloved William Danby, gentleman, Coroner of our Household' to view the body of Christopher Marlowe 'there lying dead and slain'.

Among the hurriedly empanelled jurors were a local grocer and a carpenter from Chatham, a baker from Limehouse and a farmer from Lewisham, a yeoman from East Greenwich and a husbandman from Bromley as well as three gentlemen from Deptford, of whom one was the owner of a wharf and another the tenant of the Lord Admiral's official residence by the dock-yard. But none of them knew the dead man or recognised the wounded and distorted face.

There had, of course, been plenty of gossip in the thirty-six hours between the murder on the Wednesday evening and the meeting of the jurors on the Friday morning, but most of it was unreliable and contradictory and William Danby, whose duty as Coroner of the Household was to ensure that in the crime and its

13

ramifications there was no hint of hidden danger to the Queen, was at a loss to evaluate the situation. The only official hint he had received was to find, if possible, that the killing had been done in self-defence.

As a well-trained Court official he understood at once that the real object of this directive was to safeguard the freedom of movement of Robert Poley, one of the three men charged with Marlowe's murder; for Poley was a valuable and trusted Government spy and *agent-provocateur* who, on the morning of the murder, had arrived at Deptford from Flushing 'carrying letters for Her Majesty's special and secret affairs'. The other two men involved in the murder, Nicholas Skeres and Ingram Frizer, were of less importance, though Skeres had occasionally acted as jackal to Poley in the spy-service and Frizer was the confidential servant of young Thomas Walsingham, cousin of the late Secretary of State, Sir Francis Walsingham, whose life-work had been to create 'the Service' and make it the most efficient in Europe.

Thus it might seem that the murder of Christopher Marlowe was connected in some way with the secret service—a theory which gained plausibility from the fact that the young poet-dramatist was reputed himself to have been employed, shortly after he had taken his B.A. at Cambridge, by Sir Francis Walsingham.

Yet, as the Coroner turned this over in his mind, he saw certain practical objections. In the first place, why should it have happened publicly at Deptford? Marlowe had been living with young Walsingham at his manor of Scadbury in the parish of Chislehurst. Both Poley and Skeres were *personae gratae* at Scadbury where Frizer was the majordomo. If the three for some reason wished to get rid of Marlowe, they had ample opportunity at Scadbury, where their victim could have been buried in the woods or drowned in the lake without the outside world being any the wiser. With the plague raging as it was, claiming between two and three hundred corpses a week in the London area alone, a sudden disappearance was hardly noted. For Poley, Skeres and Frizer to have murdered Marlowe openly —if indeed it were a state affair—argued considerable, even criminal, carelessness. And although it still seemed most probable that the clue to Marlowe's death lay somewhere in the secret service, the Coroner had to consider that it might, on the other hand, be connected with events in the theatre.

During the previous month, the April of 1593, the citizens of London were on the verge of anti-immigrant riots. The religious wars on the Continent had flooded the capital with refugees, French Huguenots and Dutch Calvinists, who set up their businesses in London where unemployment was already high and, according to the incensed natives, took bread from English mouths. One of the numerous placards which appeared in the City gave a versified warning:

> You strangers that inhabit in this land
> Note this same writing, do it understand;
> > Conceive it well for safeguard of your lives,
> > Your goods, your chattels and your dearest wives!

and proceeded to give them a time-limit to leave.

A Bill was introduced into Parliament 'against Alien Strangers selling by Retail any Foreign Commodities' and in the course of the debate on it mention was made of a previous occasion in the reign of Henry VIII when a riot of apprentices on 'Evil May Day' against foreigners was quelled by the then Sheriff of London, Sir Thomas More. This gave the idea to a group of playwrights, led by Thomas Kyd, of hastily throwing together a topical play, *Sir Thomas More*. The Censor angrily refused to license it. The authorities connected the anti-immigrant placards with the playwrights and Kyd was arrested, his rooms searched and his papers impounded. Among his manuscripts were found a few sheets of Marlowe's, who had been collaborating with him about two years earlier. A week after Kyd's arrest, Marlowe was summoned before the Privy Council as a witness in the case and forbidden to go out of reach of London until all investigations had been completed. That was on May 20, a mere ten days before Marlowe's murder, and he was still bound, at the time of his death, by the Council's restriction.

The Coroner had thus to consider its possible bearing on the death at Deptford. Was Marlowe in any way associated with the censored play or with the offending placards? The Privy Council, under cover of retaining him as witness in the Kyd case, was having his own beliefs investigated. The Coroner knew that gossip in literary circles—as well as his play on the German necromancer, *Doctor Faustus*—associated Marlowe with the Black Art; and it was no secret at Court that he belonged to the intellectual circle devoted to the discussion of such things which revolved round Sir Walter Raleigh. Might it be that Marlowe was guilty of the most heinous offence of all—'diabolical atheism'? *

'Diabolical atheism', at whatever level, was thought of in wider than theological terms. Since the identification of the Church with the State made by Henry VIII, it was the age's most emotive epithet of abuse. It denoted a denial of moral action as well as the negation of religious belief and, indissolubly linked with 'pestilent Machiavellian policy', such 'atheism' was regarded as the major danger to the stability of the state. There was also a subsidiary theological issue which contributed to the unrest of the times. An extreme Puritan sect known as 'Brownists' (after their founder, Robert Browne) had launched an attack on the Anglican bishops in a series of anonymous tracts written by 'Martin Marprelate'. The printer of these tracts, a young man named John Penry who had been Marlowe's contemporary at Cambridge, had been captured and brought to trial the day after Marlowe appeared before the Privy Council. Many believed that Penry was 'Martin Marprelate' himself and he was hanged the day before Marlowe was killed.

Was there, the Coroner asked himself, any connection between the two deaths? Absurd though it was to imagine that the atheistical Marlowe had any sympathy with 'Brownism' with its passionate personal belief in Jesus Christ, there were certain things that must be taken into judicial consideration. To begin with, Deptford was a notorious centre of Brownism where a secret congregation, composed mainly of young shipwrights in their twenties, held their forbidden Gospel services in the surrounding woods. Further, from Deptford Robert Bull crossed regularly to Holland with manuscripts written by the leaders of the movement to be printed at Middleburg and

---

* 'Atheism', as the word was used at the time, meant any form of belief other than official Anglicanism. It was applied indiscriminately to Roman Catholicism and Puritan Nonconformity as well as to the fashionable recrudescence of Arianism— the denial of the divinity of Christ—with which Raleigh's circle was associated.

smuggled back in sheets into England for binding and distribution; also, Marlowe had recently had his translation of Ovid's love poems (at the opposite pole, indeed, to Puritan theology, but equally exasperating to the Archbishop of Canterbury who had them burnt as soon as he could lay his hands on them) printed at Middleburg; also, Poley, in the course of his spy-service, had brought from the Low Countries 'a book in sheets, one of the first, I think, that came out of the press, the subjects chiefly against the religion and government of England', which made it clear that he was countering the Puritan as well as the Catholic attack on the English Establishment; and, finally, Eleanor Bull's house at Deptford was an obvious rendezvous for a variety of activities which would make it a natural meeting-place for Poley and Marlowe on the day of Poley's return from The Hague.

The house provided meals and, if necessary, beds for visitors. Drake's famous ship, *The Golden Hind*, in which he had circumnavigated the world and on which, on his return, he had given a great banquet to the Queen at which she had knighted him, still lay in dock at Deptford, serving now as a tourist attraction and a floating tavern which, under the attention of souvenir-hunters, was falling into decay. Its capacity for entertainment was limited by its size* and enterprising citizens were not slow to take advantage of the situation by providing additional centres of sustenance for sightseers. In Eleanor Bull's house and garden Marlowe had spent the last day of his life with Poley, Skeres and Frizer, talking, walking in the garden, eating, drinking, playing backgammon, quarrelling and arguing—about what? Could the religious issue, the Coroner asked himself, in any way supply the answer.

The questions seemed thus to pose themselves. Was the crime connected with something in the spy-service, which all four men served? Was the root of it religious? What relationship had it with Marlowe's appearance before the Privy Council? Was there, for instance, anyone who feared that Marlowe, were he examined again, might—possibly under torture—make revelations so damning that it was prudent to remove him? Sir Walter Raleigh, for example, who had lost the Queen's favour and whose 'school of atheism' was about to be officially investigated?

* The deck was rather shorter than a cricket-pitch.

Or Mr Thomas Walsingham who might now find his intimacy with Marlowe a bar to the Court favour he was carefully engaged in seeking? Or even Thomas Kyd's powerful patron and protector, Lord Strange, heir of the Earl of Derby and, by some Catholics, regarded as a possible successor to the Crown on Queen Elizabeth's death?

Yet, however acutely the Coroner might try to thread his way through the tangle of Christopher Marlowe's various lives in search of the clue to his death, he was aware that he was only indulging his private curiosity and that none of his conclusions must be allowed to influence his direction to the jury to accept the three defendants' story of 'self-defence'.

BOOK I

Summer 1585:

Marlowe in the Long Vacation

1. The Queen's Service

'And your firm desire is loyally to serve Her Majesty to the best of your ability?'

The Secretary of State suddenly leaned forward and thrust his swarthy face closer to that of Christopher Marlowe. It was a movement which had become second nature to him when he had reached a certain point in the interrogation of prisoners. He had been told that it struck terror into their hearts. But as Marlowe was not a prisoner it had no effect but to cause surprise at Mr Secretary's intensity.

'Of course, sir,' he answered evenly, 'that is why I am here.'

The question struck him as excessively foolish. What else could he have replied? Had he been a conspirator traitorously bent on assassinating Queen Elizabeth what would he have said but 'Of course, sir!'? In any case, mundane words were always misleading. It was their nature. An identical phrase, apparently unambiguous, connoted different things to different people. It was unlikely that 'loyal service' would be construed in the same way by each of them. Christopher Marlowe intended merely to lend the leisure of his Long Vacation to experiment, whereas Sir Francis Walsingham was, he knew from all reliable Cambridge gossip, a fanatic in thrall to an *idée fixe*. 'Loyal service' was his life-work.

In this assessment, Marlowe was not wrong, though neither he nor anyone outside Walsingham's immediate circle understood the extent of the Secretary's dedication. This frail sickly man, of whom the Queen was not particularly fond, had poured out his personal fortune to organise a spy-service for her protection. He kept fifty-three paid agents abroad—in France, in Spain, in Italy, in the Low Countries, in Germany, even in

21

Turkey—as well as a score of well-trained *agents-provocateurs* in England itself.

For greater efficiency he usually employed two spies on any one mission, ensuring that each was ignorant of the other and would report confidentially on him. By this method the dangers inseparable from trusting anyone were minimised. It was, of course, expensive; but Walsingham's favourite maxim was: 'Knowledge is never too dear.'

The driving-force of his actions was his religion—a passionate Protestantism on which he was not prepared to compromise. 'A most sharp maintainer of the purer religion'—that was the phrase Marlowe had heard at Cambridge describing him—Walsingham openly admitted: 'I wish first God's glory and next the Queen's safety'; though to him, in the England of 1585, the two were indivisible. Queen Elizabeth's life was the one barrier against a Catholic offensive which would put Mary Queen of Scots on the English throne. 'So long as that devilish woman lives', Walsingham had proclaimed, 'neither can Her Majesty be assured of continuing in quiet possession of her crown nor we, her faithful servants, in safety of our lives.' And he saw it as his God-given mission somehow to compass the Queen of Scots's death. He already had it in train, but he was under no illusions that it would be a long and complicated operation and, in the machine of excellent cunning he had devised, Marlowe might well be useful as a cog.

'And you would also wish to serve the Church of England?'

'I am, sir, as Master Watson may have told you, intending to take Holy Orders. I am up at Corpus on a Parker scholarship.'

Walsingham, looking at the sensual young face, with its too-full underlip and its intense, smouldering eyes, permitted himself to doubt whether Marlowe would make an ideal parson. But nowadays one had to take what one could get. As the Queen herself had remarked, when the Archbishop of Canterbury had pointed out that the Established Church needed thirteen thousand worthy and competent ministers, 'Jesus! Thirteen thousand? It is not to be looked for!' In any case, Marlowe's ecclesiastical career was not Walsingham's business. He was interested in him merely as a potential spy.

Marlowe, on his side, had deliberately parried Walsingham's question. Tom Watson, before introducing him to Mr Secretary, had warned him to avoid, if possible, any mention of religion as being too dangerous a topic in an atmosphere where every *nuance* was noted and most of them misconstrued. Watson knew that his young friend's main reason for seeking the interview was that he might find some way to avoid taking Holy Orders, which was a condition of Archbishop Parker's scholarship that had already ensured his education at Cambridge for four years and had still two more to run before he would emerge as a Master of Arts and be found a suitable parish.

Four years spent sharing a study with parsons' sons from Norfolk had reduced Marlowe to a state of frustration and fury with the Establishment in which he did not scruple to say that 'Protestants are hypocritical asses' and that 'if there be a God and any sound Religion then it is the Papists' because their service of God is performed with more ceremonies'. When these propositions failed to provoke his room-mates, he would question the credibility of the Biblical account of the Creation and even submit the most sacred narratives in Holy Writ to a realistic treatment which could only be called blasphemous, such as saying that, because Gabriel had 'brought tidings to Mary', the Archangel could be described as, in a sense, 'bawd to the Holy Ghost'. There were other even less acceptable glosses which, for the moment, he kept to himself.

His companions, who were in any case not intellectually equipped to argue with him, contented themselves with asking each other what else one could expect from a cobbler's son. * Marlowe, who had become inured to that sneer when he was a scholar at the King's School, Canterbury (when he was young enough to be hurt by it), retorted that he preferred to be the son of a useful citizen to being the offspring of lazy pedlars of divinity, a study which was 'unpleasant, harsh, contemptible and vile'.

But as even Walsingham's ubiquitous information was unlikely to extend to such negligible matters Marlowe trusted that his reply would be taken inferentially as a proclamation of his quiet, unquestioning orthodoxy.

The Secretary's third question, however, was more testing:

* They all attained a long-lived nonentity, one as vicar of Norton Subcorse and Raveningham and rector of Stokesby; one as vicar of Aylsham and rector of Trunch; one as vicar of Cromer and rector of Sidestrand and one as vicar of Elvedon.

'In your opinion, should Her Majesty strengthen her alliance with the King of France?'

This obviously needed total avoidance.

'Such higher matters are beyond me', said Marlowe, 'and in them I should be guided entirely by Your Lordship's wisdom.' This counted as satisfactory, though the correct answer, as far as Walsingham was concerned, was 'No'.

The 'Moor'—Elizabeth's nickname for Walsingham—stood as far removed from the principles of the Queen's foreign policy as if he had indeed been a Turk assessing the needs of Europe. Whereas Elizabeth assumed that her country's safety lay in maintaining the balance of power, of using France as an ally to counter the enmity of Spain, Walsingham maintained that the fundamental issue was not that between nation and nation but between creed and creed and that Protestant England should make no alliance with any Catholic power. 'How can Christ and Belial agree?' he asked.

The Queen, irritated by such *simpliste* idealism, remonstrated: 'You Puritan! You will never be content until you drive me into war on all sides and bring the King of Spain on to me!' But Walsingham was impervious to argument. His attitude had been crystallised in an emotional experience, thirteen years earlier, when he had been the English Envoy in Paris at the time of the massacre of St Bartholomew. He had never forgotten the horror of it, with its two thousand corpses and the murderous mob yelling for Huguenot blood,* and the English Embassy crowded with Protestant refugees of many nations.

Relating it to the Queen, he had informed her: 'It was not your country which your Embassy protected that night. It was your Faith.'

The episode had affected him also by a certain contrariety. The lesson inculcated, so blindingly clear to him, seemed to have escaped everyone else. Catherine de Medici, the formidable Queen-Mother of France, was completely at a loss to understand why the sanguinary incident in any way formed an obstacle to the Anglo-French alliance: 'You must know, *M. l'Ambassadeur*,' she said, 'that our countries were never closer than when your Mistress's father, King Henry VIII, was forcing his subjects to

---

* See Chapter 20 of *The Florentine Woman* and Chapter 1 of *The Last of the Valois*.

become Protestant and my father-in-law, King Francis I, was burning the heretics.' What the King of France had been 'constrained to permit to his very great regret' could surely not in any way affect the friendship between the nations!

'How is it possible, Your Majesty, for you to come to my Royal Mistress's help if she is attacked on the grounds of religion?'

'What difficulty can there be there?' asked Catherine. 'You can assure her I would come to her aid even if his Catholic Majesty King Philip of Spain himself attacked her for the sake of religion.'

'But', protested Walsingham, 'you allow the Huguenots no chance to exercise their religion.'

'In exactly the same way', retorted Catherine, 'as Queen Elizabeth of England allows no Catholics to exercise their religion. I cannot see the difference.'

'If Admiral Coligny had still been the adviser of your son, the King, Madame, then the Protestant cause would have been indivisible.'

'If you really believe that, *M. l'Ambassadeur*, I can only commiserate with you.' And she handed him a memorandum, which he immediately recognised as in the murdered Coligny's handwriting, warning the King of France that the Queen of England was as great an enemy of the French crown as King Philip of Spain.

Completely taken aback, Walsingham had found nothing to say and soothed his hurt in vituperation to Queen Elizabeth that he had heard new plots were afoot to liberate Mary Queen of Scots (Catherine de Medici's daughter-in-law) and that unless some 'violent remedy' were applied to 'that sore' there would be a 'Bartholomew Breakfast' in England.

The heaviest burden the Ambassador had to bear was his own Queen's apparent indifference. Elizabeth would go through the expected motions of protest, but when it came to the point of action she was as shrewd a political realist as the Queen-Mother of France and at this crisis she even consented to stand godmother to the French king's baby daughter. It was some consolation to Walsingham that her present of a gold font, worth £100,000, was stolen in the Channel by Huguenot pirates, but he felt that he was not the man for any subsequent negotiations and begged to be relieved of service in 'this country so contaminated with innocent blood that the sun cannot look upon it but to prognosticate the wrath and vengeance of God'. Eventually his plea had been granted and he had returned to London determined to organise the best spy-service in Europe to save his Queen in spite of herself.

One of Walsingham's friends in Paris in those traumatic times had been Thomas Watson, then a youth of seventeen, studying in France before proceeding to Italy to read Roman Law. In the summer days before the Massacre Walsingham would spend leisured moments with him on the banks of the Seine, listening to the 'tunes' Watson loved to compose or criticising kindly his Latin verses. In the aftermath of the August blood-letting, the Ambassador found he could always rely on Watson for sympathetic agreement with his point-of-view. Thus a friendship was formed which had survived the years.

Watson's heart was not in the law and though he eventually took his degree in Bologna and was able to sign himself 'Thomas Watsonus I.V. studiosus'—which signified that he was proficient in 'either law' (*I*uris *V*triumque), civil or canon—when he came back to England he found himself disinclined to practise it. His interests were poetry, music and the theatre and his *Passionate Century of Love*, a collection of a hundred sonnets, not only became a best-seller, but set a fashion which other poets followed as well as gaining him the reputation of 'the sweetest singer in England'.*

But, apart from occasional tutoring, he found 'his daily practice and his living' in the theatre. Here, on the one hand, he paid tribute to the classics by translating the *Antigone* of Sophocles from Greek into Latin and, on the other, he made himself master of farcical gags to tickle the fancy of the groundlings so that it was said that 'every balductum† play contained the froth of witty Tom Watson's jests'.

On a visit to Cambridge he had met Marlowe, to whom he was immediately attracted by both his personality and his gifts. He found that the undergraduate, nine years his junior, was

---

* Shakespeare, because of his sonnet-sequence, was known as 'Watson's heir'. Watson's great contemporary reputation is today known only to students of 'Eng. Lit.'—and not always by them.
† Worthless; or, as we might say, 'lowbrow'.

almost his equal as a Latinist and had amused himself, when he ought to have been immersed in theology, in translating Ovid's elegant sensualities, *The Loves*, into English verse. The young man was also trying his hand at a play on Dido, Queen of Carthage, based on Virgil's *Aeneid*. The identity of their interests was such that Watson immediately entered into all Marlowe's hopes and fears and projects and dreams and they determined to live together when Marlowe left Cambridge and went to try his fortune in London.

Meanwhile, Watson suggested, it might be worth while for Kit to visit Sir Francis Walsingham and to offer his services to him for the summer. This would have at least three advantages. It would give him experience of life and travel; it would earn him some money, and, if he were successful in impressing the Secretary, it might gain him a powerful protector who would be able to persuade the Cambridge authorities to give him his Master's degree without insisting on his liability, under the terms of his scholarship, to take Holy Orders.

To Marlowe's inquiry as to why a powerful statesman should trouble to see an unknown scholar, Watson explained that he could give an introduction and that, if necessary, he would himself take him to Walsingham's private mansion in Seething Lane.

In the event, Watson had had the satisfaction of finding that Walsingham, who was tenacious in his friendships, even invited him to remain in the room during the interview.

'Are you constant in your purposes?' was the Secretary's last question to Marlowe.

Kit hesitated. He had enough self-knowledge to be aware that constancy was not in his nature. Life for him was a pageant to be delightedly enjoyed, not an arena for fanatical conflict.

'It is my endeavour to be so, sir,' he replied, 'but all I dare swear to is obedience.'

Unexpectedly Walsingham smiled. 'Such honesty', he said, as much to Watson as to Marlowe, 'demands being put to the test.' He rang a small silver hand-bell. 'The servant will take you to Master Robert Poley, who will give you your instructions. Meanwhile I shall have the too-rare pleasure of talking to Master Watson.'

2. Robert Poley

Robert Poley's room was in the wing of the house occupied by Walsingham's son-in-law, Sir Philip Sidney, in whose service he had been given a temporary post while Sidney was making the final preparations to take up his appointment as Governor of Flushing. It had not yet been decided whether Poley was to attend his master to the Netherlands or whether he was to stay in the household and act as steward to Lady Sidney, Walsingham's only daughter. His position, in either case, gave rise to some speculation. A fellow-spy had written: 'Poley is a Catholic and has been placed to be Sir Philip Sidney's man that he may the more quietly live a Christian life', but as Sidney was an even more bitter anti-Catholic than Walsingham, the remark was generally interpreted as ironical.

Poley, who had been born in the reign of Elizabeth's predecessor, the Catholic Queen Mary married to Philip of Spain, had certainly been baptised and brought up in the old faith and had ostensibly continued in it during Elizabeth's reign when it had become first unfashionable and then illegal. He had insisted on his marriage being performed secretly by a seminary priest and he had spent some time in prison as a recusant. He was in consequence completely trusted by his co-religionists, who were unaware that he had in fact renounced his faith and become Walsingham's most trusted *agent-provocateur*, all the more valuable because of his reputation as a secret Papist. At the moment he was a key character in the elaborate plot on foot to enmesh Mary Queen of Scots to her death. 'Good Robin' was a large, genial man of thirty-two, with fair hair, blue eyes, a frank, open countenance, an infectious laugh and great natural charm—characteristics which deceived the great majority of

28

men who lacked the *savoir vivre* to recognise them as the conventional concomitants of a Judas.

He received Marlowe with his usual calculating affability.

'I understand from Sir Francis that you are still up at Cambridge.'

'Yes. Corpus.'

'I was at Clare. Came down more years ago than I care to remember, so we're not likely to overlap in acquaintances. Except some of the dons. We're still plagued with one of them visiting here. Keeps wanting to talk hexameters with Sir Philip.'

'Gabriel Harvey,' said Marlowe. It was an affirmation rather than a question. No one but Gabriel Harvey would talk hexameters.

'You hit the bull in one.' Poley made it sound congratulatory. 'D'you come across him much?'

'At the moment he is Junior Proctor.'

'So obviously you keep out of his way!' said Poley.

'Except in his lectures on Rhetoric, which I have to attend. He's a pedant and an ass and, since he "discovered" Edmund Spenser at Pembroke, quite insufferable.'

'If he has his way, he won't be at Cambridge much longer. He's trying to get a footing at Court.'

Poley proceeded to tell Marlowe how Harvey, the brilliant son of a Saffron Walden rope-maker, had used his friendship with the poets Edmund Spenser and Sir Philip Sidney to get himself presented to the Queen on one of her Progresses and 'came ruffling it out huffty-tuffty in a suit of velvet and thrust himself into the ranks of the noblemen and the gallants and whatever they were talking about he would interrupt and take the words out of their mouths'. The Queen, when she gave him her hand to kiss, said that he looked like an Italian. This overwhelmed him. He considered it only fitting that thenceforward, on all special occasions, his accent, his deportment and his gestures should become noticeably Italianate.

This self-important pedant was of no relevance in himself, but it was Poley's method of dealing with those he wished to use to concentrate on their interests, whatever they might be, until they were completely at their ease with him. From Watson Walsingham had learned of Marlowe's love of poetry and of his

translations from the Latin and Poley, on receiving the information, naturally decided to utilise it. Himself something of a
scholar, he knew of, though he did not participate in, the academic debate raging fiercely at the moment on the subject of
classical prosody. Should Latin hexameters be faithfully translated into English hexameters?

'Of course not,' said Marlowe. 'An English hexameter is an
unnatural measure, whatever Gabriel Harvey says. I put Ovid's
elegiacs quite simply into pentameters.'

'Could you give me an example?'

> 'Ergo cum silices, cum dens patientis aratri
> Depereant aevo, carmina morte carent

easily becomes

> Therefore when flint and iron wear away
> Verse is immortal and shall ne'er decay.'

'That seems an excellent rendering,' said Poley. 'And what
would you say to Harvey's own hexameters?' He quoted the
beginning of a poem which the egregious Gabriel had composed
in an attempt to demonstrate that the classical measure could
easily be assimilated in native verse.

> 'What might I call this tree? A laurel! O bonny laurel
> Needs to thy boughs will I bow this knee and veil my
>   bonnetto.
> Who but thou the renown of princes and princely poeta!'

'Vile affectation,' said Marlowe.

'How would you have put it?'

'I doubt whether I should have indulged the thought.'

'But if you had,' persisted Poley.

Marlowe paused for a moment, then declaimed:

> 'Laurel I name this Daphne-tree whose leaves
> Compose a crown for poet and for prince
> And doff my cap to it and crook my knee.'

'You leave me in no doubt about your vocation,' said Poley,
'but what still puzzles me is why you wish to take service here.'

'Let us call it curiosity,' said Marlowe. 'I would like to see a
little of the great world before I write about it.'

'An excellent plan which should benefit us all.'

'What will be my duties?'

'To learn to look and listen.'

'And—?'

'No more. Just to look and listen until it becomes second nature.'

'But I already look and listen,' Marlowe protested, thinking: what does this fool suppose that poets are?

'Yes, but only to the people and the things that interest you. In any company of ten you would not be able to report on more than four—and none of the four might be important.'

'I value myself at five.'

'Then you are indeed a treasure. You will be fit for prison the quicker.'

'Prison?'

Poley nodded.

'No wonder the realm is rotten if men are punished for their talents!'

'You should not say that. It is just such a sentence as you must learn to report lest its speaker should verge into treason.'

'I intended no treason, but I should proclaim myself a total lack-wit if I suppose the country well governed.'

'As a student you are permitted that judgment, but if you are entering Sir Francis's service you would do well to forget it and believe that all that he and the Queen do is for the best. In any case, you were speaking carelessly out of ignorance. You would not go to prison for punishment.'

'Then why?'

'As part of your service. It is when you are in prison that you can most easily discover men's secret thoughts as long as they suppose you too are a victim of the law. But before we of the Service come to prison-work we must be adjudged proficient in our ordinary observation.'

'Then you've been to prison?' There was a note of genuine interest in the question. Marlowe was glimpsing the outlines of a new world.

'Of course,' said Poley proudly. 'I left the Marshalsea about a year ago, after a fifteen-month spell.'*

* He was committed by Walsingham about Shrovetide (February 12) 1583 and released on 10 May 1584.

'And it was successful?'

'Very. I was able to denounce four secret priests.'

'I think I should hate to lose my liberty.'

'You have the "liberty of the house". Sir Francis pays for that.'

Poley did not mention that in his sojourn in the Marshalsea the 'liberty of the house' included prolonged visits from his mistress and frequent 'fine banquets' in his chamber, beside sufficient money to present a large 'silver bowl double-gilt' to her husband as a kind of consolation prize. The imprisonment had also had the advantage that his keeper could prevent visits from his own wife, who repeatedly and clamorously tried to see him. Indeed, for amorous convenience, the Marshalsea had been a distinct improvement on the arrangement Poley had had to make after his release, when he was forced to use the house of his mistress's mother, and found it the focus of unfortunate notoriety on account of the old lady's sudden death.

In the words of the coroner who investigated it, 'one, Mr Poley lay in her house and her daughter coming to her house to dry clothes she found her sitting upon the said Poley's knee, the sight whereof did so strike to her heart that she prayed to God to cut her off very quickly for fear she should be a bawd unto her own daughter; and her prayer was quickly answered for the Monday following she was departed and ready to be carried to the church to be buried'.

That unfortunate occurrence had taken place only a few months ago and partly explained Poley's presence in Walsingham's house. The Secretary had been so incensed both as a politician and as a Puritan at the publicity and the cause of it that he had ordered the agent immediately to leave his own house, 'the Garden', just outside the city walls by the Bishop's Gate, and take up his residence in Seething Lane where Sir Philip Sidney could keep some check on him. There were indeed moments when Walsingham regretted that he had no means of disciplining Poley, who had tended to become a law unto himself. But he was both too valuable and too knowledgeable. At Walsingham's last attempt to reprimand him for a misdemeanour of which both were quite aware, the Secretary had asked him how he dared deny what both knew was true.

'Marry, sir,' said Poley insolently, 'I am prepared to forswear myself to any limit rather than accuse myself. Would you have it otherwise in any of us of the Service?'

Walsingham did not answer but—according to Poley—'fell into such a heat that he looked out of the window and grinned like a dog'.

The memory of this incident was not absent from the agent's thoughts when he assured Marlowe: 'If you want liberty you can best gain it by knowledge, which is power.'

'It seems to me that it will take too many years.'

'You are refusing the service?'

'No. Having gone so far, I will sample it; but I do not promise to persevere in it. Who am I to report on?'

'As yet, no one in particular. We shall, of course, study any information you wish to send and by it we shall gauge your ability. In this first trial, you are asked only to observe anyone you judge worth observing.'

'When do I start?'

'As far as anything is settled, you will cross with me to France about midsummer. I have work to do in Paris. You will go on to Rheims and apply to enter the English College there.'

'You mean I am not to go back to Cambridge?'

'Indeed you are to go back. But there is plenty of time before the beginning of the Michaelmas Term. At Rheims you will merely talk of entering. That will give you all the opportunity you need to use your wits.'

'Do I pretend to be a Papist?'

'It would be safer not to unless you know something about it. Do you?'

'By reading only.'

'That ranks as ignorance. I was brought up a Catholic so, when I am among Catholics, I can use the right catch-words at the right time to escape suspicion. You would be seen through at once. Especially at Rheims.'

The choice of Rheims for his testing was sufficient to convey to Marlowe that he was to be used in the forefront of the religious struggle. This coronation city of the Kings of France had, for the past seven years, given hospitality to the English College of Douai when its scholars had been driven out of the Netherlands by William of Orange. Douai University had been founded in 1561—three years before Marlowe's birth—by King

Philip of Spain in an effort to combat the growing Protestantism of his Dutch subjects. The English College at the University opened in 1568 under the charge of a dedicated Lancashire priest, Father William Allen, with the object of providing a university education for young English Catholics who, by Elizabeth's penal legislation, were forbidden to attend either Oxford or Cambridge.* Its special mission was to train priests who would dare to return to England, in spite of the penalty of being hanged, drawn and quartered for saying Mass, to keep the Catholic faith alive there. When the Pope endowed the College with a grant of a hundred golden crowns a month there were, according to one of its professors, 'swarms of candidates for Holy Orders daily coming to the college on the mere report of such magnificent liberality'.

The visitors, however, were by no means confined to Catholics. Tom Watson, in his travels, had attended the lectures on Canon Law and Marlowe knew from him how 'gentlemen's sons, studying the humanities, philosophy or jurisprudence, had been moved by the fame of the university to visit it as well as travellers on their way to France, Italy and Brabant, most of them without any religion, who would turn aside to see the seminary'.

After its removal to Rheims, the College became even more renowned as a religious and political centre. There was an increase of students apostolically dedicated to daring martyrdom to restore England to the Faith and eschewing, as the Church insisted they should, any entanglement with politics; but there were also those prepared to attempt to assassinate Elizabeth on the grounds that 'that guilty woman of England is the cause of so much injury to the Catholic faith and the loss of so many million souls that whosoever sends her out of the world with the pious intention of doing God service not only does not sin but gains merit'. And, between these two positions, there was a body of intellectuals not in the least interested in any practical action but delighting to spend their time and show their philosophical, theological and political skills in endlessly debating the rival theories.

Father Allen's avowed purpose was 'to train Catholics to be plainly and openly Catholic; to be men who will always refuse

* This was still in force as late as 1828.

every kind of spiritual commerce with heretics', and the result, in spite of the plotters and the indifferents, was to transform the English situation. Walsingham complained bitterly: 'Nothing in the world grieves me more than to see Her Majesty believe this increase of papists in her realm can be of no great danger' and began to look on 'Rheims' as only a little less of a menace than the Armada which Philip of Spain was said to be preparing for the invasion of England. To counteract the apparent indifference of the Queen (who, in fact, was at the moment more concerned with the growth of extreme Puritanism which was, in its theories, threatening to disrupt both Church and State) Walsingham multiplied his spies in Rheims, even making use of university students, and an addition was made to the Prayer Book imploring the Almighty 'to permit our gracious Queen still to reign in despite of Rome and Rheims and Spain and Hell'.

'Am I to attend any lectures at Rheims?' Marlowe asked Poley.

'Surely I have made it plain', said Poley, 'that you are left to your own discretion. Any other questions you can ask Sir Francis.'

And, without more ado, he led the way back to Walsingham's study.

3. At First Sight

Throughout the interviews with Walsingham and Poley Marlowe had remained commendably calm. However daunting it had seemed in prospect to face the great of the land and to become involved, even peripherally, in affairs of state, he found that the actual meeting did not disturb him. He was protected not only by the natural arrogance of youth but by his special pride in his poet-hood. In his translation of Ovid's elegy addressed to 'those who envy Poets their Eternity of Fame', from which he had already quoted two lines to Poley, was another couplet which was constantly in his mind.

> Thy scope is mortal, mine eternal, fame
> That all the world may ever chant my name.

In common with all poets at all times, he accepted this as a simple fact of nature with an unconcern more maddening than belligerent affirmation would have been. He agreed with the claims which had been made by poets for themselves through the centuries and, could he have foreseen it, would have accepted the judgment of one who was to be much in his debt: * 'The final cause and consummation of all natural and human activity is dramatic poetry.'

At the moment the champion of poets was Sir Philip Sidney. In his *Defence of Poesie*, which Marlowe had read with delighted approval when it circulated in manuscript in Cambridge,† Sidney had written: 'Only the poet, lifted up by the vigour of his

---

* Goethe.
† *The Defence of Poesie* was not printed till 1595, but it had a wide circulation in MS from 1580 onwards.

own invention, goeth hand in hand with nature, not enclosed within the narrow warrant of her gifts but freely ranging only in the zodiac of his own wit. Nature never set forth the earth in so rich a tapestry as divers poets have done. Her world is brazen; the poets only deliver a golden.'

And the circumstance that Marlowe was in Sidney's house, that Poley, for all his earthiness, was Sidney's servant and that a poet so well regarded as Tom Watson had effected the introduction increased the young poet's confidence. He would not have been unduly impressed—indeed he would have regarded it as only fitting—if in a corridor or in the hall or at the turn of a stair he had seen Sir Philip himself.

But the chance meeting that took place as he and Poley neared Walsingham's study was of a very different nature and left Marlowe defenceless and disturbed. It was a boy of seventeen, whose golden hair fell to his shoulders in a fashionable love-lock; whose slim body, straight as a wand, moved with a dancer's grace; whose insolent eyes and slack, half-open mouth seemed to invite mastery. The effect on Marlowe was immediate. Whoever loved that loved not at first sight?

And love for Marlowe at twenty-one wore an exclusively masculine habit. His realisation of this trait in himself had been gradual. He had assimilated his early experiences as a choir-boy at Canterbury, regarding them at first with surprise and curiosity, then with occasional enjoyment and finally with a kind of bored resignation, but it had never occurred to him to connect them in any way with love. Love was for girls and his instinctive aversion to them, whether they were the friends of his sisters or visitors to his father's shop or those accompanying their mothers on good works connected with the cathedral, convinced him that love was not for him.

Only when he got to Cambridge and began to soak himself in the classics did he excitedly discover different definitions, from Plato's teaching that the highest form of love is, exclusively, that between two men and that the love of women is an inferior emotion belonging only to the 'Venus of the market-place' to Homer's epic celebrating the love of Achilles and Patroclus and to the warp and woof of popular mythology, where Adonis was the beloved of Apollo and Ioläus of Hercules and Ganymede of Jupiter himself.

The undergraduate's sense of release was such that he allowed his enthusiasm to outrun his discretion. He opened his play on Dido with a love-scene between Jupiter and Ganymede. Marlowe intended the work for the Children of the Chapel and in Ganymede's coy

> I would have a jewel for mine ear
> And a fine brooch to put upon my hat
> And then I'll hug with you a hundred times

he portrayed with exactitude an ordinary acquisitive choirboy with his 'gentleman', but at the same time he considerably lessened the play's chances of production.*

In his conversation he gradually became foolishly reckless. He was prepared to defend the proposition that 'all who were not lovers of boys were fools' and was even indiscreet enough to scandalise his theological companions by blasphemously suggesting that the sixteen-year-old John, 'the disciple whom Jesus loved', was the Beloved in the Platonic sense.

Yet Marlowe's self-awareness had given him no practical happiness. Brief encounters, whether with fellow-undergraduates or with youths from the town, increased his restlessness. He would risk the penalty imposed by the Archbishop of Canterbury, John Whitgift, when he was Vice-Chancellor of the University—that if any scholar should go into any river or pool to wash or swim, by day or night, he should be sharply and severely whipped in the College Hall before the assembled members; and the day following whipped openly by the Proctor in the school which he attended. This had not deterred Marlowe and his friends from hot summer night expeditions to bathe at Grantchester any more than other stringent regulations had prevented him from mixing with the townspeople at the bull-baiting exhibitions at Great Chesterton or at the 'pernicious and unhonest games' organised on the Gogs or in the week-long saturnalia of Midsummer Fair.

But each transient relationship, momentarily bright with promise and possibilities, was abandoned in disillusion almost before it had begun. And Marlowe was quite aware of the

---

* The play was not printed until after Marlowe's death and there is no evidence that it was acted in his lifetime. It may have been the *Dido* which was acted in the June of 1607 as a court amusement of James I, who was prone to Ganymedes.

disintegration it caused. He adopted as his motto: *Quod me nutrit me destruit*, what feeds me destroys me.

The academic curriculum still preserved the pattern of the great mediaeval idea of education. Grammar, Logic and Rhetoric formed the basis of it—the Trivium. In Grammar was learnt the language which was the common instrument of thought; in Logic, the student was taught to think correctly; in Rhetoric, to convey his thoughts persuasively to others. These things mastered and Latin, the common language, making communication possible between educated men of every nation, the Quadrivium was undertaken. Mathematics exercised the student's capacity for abstract reasoning; Natural Philosophy taught him the laws of Nature; Moral Philosophy the laws of human nature and society and Metaphysics the laws of being. So the student was equipped for the business of living. Or should have been. But there were too many omissions. Philosophy, said Marlowe, if not as bad as Divinity, was 'odious and obscure'. Eros had empery.

> Lo! I confess I am thy captive, I,
> And hold my conquer'd hands for thee to tie.

So, when suddenly the young poet came face to face with the golden boy in Walsingham's house, he surrendered at a glance. For an instant Marlowe had the wild hope that he would stop to greet Poley and that thus he would be introduced to him. But he merely smiled and passed on.

'Who is that?' said Marlowe when he was out of earshot.

'Someone of less importance than he imagines himself.'

'That might describe most of us,' Marlowe snapped in sudden irritation.

'*Touché*,' said Poley amiably. 'And to do him justice his birth gives him some importance. He's Sir Francis's young cousin, Thomas Walsingham. He's occasionally used in the Service to give him occupation. His father died last year and the estate went to the elder son, Edmund. He's only thirty-two. So young Thomas isn't likely to inherit anything. But he gives himself all the airs in the world.'

'His father left him nothing?'

'An annuity of £75 a year or so. The estate naturally went to the heir; but his brother's very good to him and when he's not on a mission, Thomas spends most of his time at Scadbury.'

Then, as Poley suspected that Mr Secretary intended to use his young cousin to report on Marlowe in Rheims, he said, as they reached the door of Walsingham's study: 'It would be as well not to mention that you have seen him.'

4. Theatre

Watson's lodgings, to which he took Marlowe after Mr Secretary had dismissed them, were at the corner of Bishopsgate Street and Hog Lane in the Liberty* of Norton Folgate, within a few minutes' walk of London's two theatres, *The Theatre* and *The Curtain*.

The Theatre had been built when Marlowe was twelve—in 1576—by James Burbage, a master-carpenter who in his youth had been an actor in the Earl of Leicester's company of players and who retained a passion for the theatre. In the liberty of Holywell to the east of Finsbury Fields Burbage leased five tenements and a dilapidated barn and on the empty piece of ground bounded by the barn, a horse-pond and the back-garden of one of the tenements he built *The Theatre*. It was of wood and of his own original design which combined the open circularity of a bear-baiting pit with the raised platform and the ample 'penny-public' standing room of the inn-yards where theatrical performances were accustomed to take place. He planned *The Theatre* so that it would be large enough to house a crowd of Londoners on a holiday afternoon and the venture was so successful that, within a year, a second house, *The Curtain*, was built on the other side of Holywell as an 'easer' to *The Theatre*.

The advent of the theatres was disliked by the City Fathers

---

* A 'Liberty' lay outside the jurisdiction of the City of London and its officers were answerable not to the Lord Mayor but to the justices of Middlesex. Such a district was, therefore, as Mark Eccles puts it in *Christopher Marlowe in London* 'a good place of residence for players and others who had reason to be shy of sheriff's officers'. Other liberties included Holywell, which housed *The Theatre* and *The Curtain*; the Clink, in which the *Globe*, the *Hope* and the *Rose* theatres were eventually built; the Liberty of the Rolls in Chancery Lane and the Liberty of the Duchy of Lancaster outside Temple Bar.

and detested by the clergy. The Lord Mayor and Aldermen pointed out to the Privy Council that the plays were 'a special cause of corrupting their youth, containing nothing but unchaste matters, lascivious devices, shifts of cozenage and other lewd and ungodly practices, being so that they impress the very corruption of manners which they represent'; that the two houses were 'the ordinary places for vagrant persons, masterless men, thieves, horse-stealers, whoremongers, cozeners, coney-catchers, contrivers of treason and other idle and dangerous men to meet' and that the theatrical profession attracted 'such persons as have no vocation and draw apprentices and other servants from their ordinary works'.

The preachers were even more bitter and not, perhaps, altogether impartial. 'Will not a filthy play, with the blast of a trumpet, sooner call thither a thousand, than an hour's tolling of a bell bring to the sermon an hundred? If you resort to *The Theatre* or *The Curtain* you shall on the Lord's Day have those places so full as possible they can throng. I know not how I might with the godly learned discommend the gorgeous playing-place erected in the fields than to term it, as they please to have it called a Theatre—that is after the manner of the old heathenish theatre at Rome, a show-place of all beastly and filthy matters. Do they not maintain bawdry, insinuate foolery and renew the remembrance of heathen idolatry? Do they not induce whoredom and uncleanness? Nay, are they not rather plain devourers of maidenly virginity and chastity? For proof whereof but mark the flocking and running to Theatres and Curtains, daily and hourly, night and day, time and tide, to see plays and interludes where such wanton gestures, such bawdy speeches, such laughing and fleering, such kissing and bussing, such clipping and culling, such winking and glancing of wanton eyes and the like is used as is wonderful to behold. Then these goodly pageants being ended every mate sorts to his mate, every one brings another homeward of their way very friendly and in their secret conclaves they play the sodomites. And these be the fruits of plays and interludes for the most part.'

The most bitter enemies of the stage did not, however, deny its financial attractiveness. 'By playing but once a week (whereas many times they play twice or sometimes thrice) it amounteth to two thousand pounds by the year.'

To James Burbage, however, financial success seemed by no means so assured. He might play to crammed houses on Sunday afternoons, when the swarming audience made a beaten track through the fields, but on ordinary days the size of *The Theatre* ensured that there were many empty seats. Also he had spent all his savings in acquiring the lease of the land and the money for the timber and the plaster and the nails, to say nothing of the workmen's wages, had to be found elsewhere.

Fortunately, Burbage's wife's brother, a wealthy grocer named John Brayne, was at the outset only too pleased to invest liberally in what seemed to be a most profitable enterprise, though when difficult times came he complained bitterly that he had been ruined and that, as a result of his vast expenditure, *The Theatre* properly belonged to him. His financial stringency was in fact due to his speculation in a soap-works in Whitechapel, and now, in this year 1585, the family feud had reached such proportions that the Burbages and the Braynes were about to embark on legal action against each other.

Tom Watson, much against his will, had become involved in the quarrel by the mere fact that he was on the point of marrying the sister of the lawyer, Hugh Swift, who was acting for Burbage. Since Watson's living depended mainly on writing for the theatre, it was necessary for him to remain on good terms with as many as possible and in his conversation in the taverns frequented by theatrical people he resembled no one so much as the fool who tried to please everybody.

To avoid any argument which might be embarrassing in the presence of Marlowe, Watson selected with some care the tavern to which to take his guest. He chose the *Unicorn* down the road in Bishopsgate Street, just within the city walls, of which the landlord was John Alleyn, the elder brother of the actor, Edward Alleyn, who, at nineteen, had recently leapt to sensational stardom at *The Theatre* in a play called *The Spanish Tragedy*.

It was unlikely that in such an atmosphere the anti-Burbage faction would be present in any strength and, since the landlord was renowned for keeping a careful eye on his customers, there was little likelihood of a brawl.

Tom Watson was reassured in his choice by the sight of two notorious trouble-makers leaving the *Unicorn* as he and

Marlowe entered it. He pointed them out to his guest. One of them, the shorter of the two, powerful in physique and garish in dress, was William Bradley, the good-for-nothing son of an innkeeper in Holborn; the other, his boon-companion, George Orwell, 'a most desperate rake-hell as ever lived', tall, thin and taut who 'held his neck awry'. They were both twenty-one, the same age as Marlowe, and usually confined their activities to the taverns of Holborn and Temple Bar and Fleet Street. Recently, however, they had moved into the theatrical district partly, at least, because the landlords whose business they disrupted had threatened Bradley's father, the elder William who kept the *Bishop's Head* at the corner of Holborn and Gray's Inn Road, with reprisals unless he kept his son away from local houses.

Their favourite mode of operation was to carry a pair of false dice which, at an appropriate moment, they surreptitiously used when playing tables* and then complained to the landlord for providing them. Brushing aside his protests, they loudly demanded compensation and if this were refused started a brawl which resulted in those customers sober enough to move hurriedly leaving the inn for safety's sake.

The circumstance that they had on this occasion left the *Unicorn* peaceably suggested that John Alleyn had offered them some financial inducement to do so—a fact which he later confirmed in conversation with Tom Watson and Marlowe. Watson, whose friendly conversation with Sir Francis Walsingham had confirmed his good opinion of himself as one able to pontificate equally in the worlds of art and politics, attempted to offer advice on the foolishness of paying blackmail; but John Alleyn promptly rejected it.

'You're but a customer and an important one, Master Watson. You're free to spend your money wherever you choose. But I'm a landlord and therefore a prisoner. Willy-nilly I must stay here, doing my best to make it a tavern worth your choosing. If I care to lend William Bradley a groat or two to make sure my other customers are not disturbed, it's no more than my way of accounting.'

---

* Backgammon. A common form of false dice used was known as 'barred cater-trays' which never turned up the four (quatre) or the three (trois). The three can be a very useful throw in backgammon, especially for those who like to play safe.

'I understand that well enough, John,' said Watson. 'Diplomacy's a game with the same rules at all levels. I'm only warning you as a friend and a man of some experience that a groat or two today might well be a pound or two tomorrow.'

'And to show you I appreciate your concern and take no offence at it I will ask you and your friend to have your first drink on the house. What shall it be?'

'Sherris-sack for me,' said Watson.

'Beer,' said Marlowe, who thought it best to remain on a drink with whose effects he was familiar.

The landlord poured him out a large double-beer and asked his name.

'Marlowe. Christopher Marlowe. They call me Kit. I'm studying for Holy Orders at Cambridge.'

'More to the point', interposed Watson, 'is that he's bent on writing plays and from what I've read of his first efforts he'll probably succeed."

'He must meet Ned,' said John Alleyn. Then to Marlowe he explained: 'My brother Edward's always looking for new plays. If he comes in you must talk to him.'

A man of about thirty, with a rasping voice and a discontented face, who, with his back to them, had been listening to the conversation, turned round suddenly and said: 'And I can assure you, young Kit—if that's what you like to be called—that as you're from Cambridge Ned Alleyn will welcome you with open arms.'

Before Marlowe could reply, Tom Watson said: 'Ungenerously spoken. You must be careful, Master Kyd, that the chip you carry on your shoulder does not become a block to crush you.' Then to Marlowe: 'This, Christopher, is Thomas Kyd, our greatest playwright, who cannot cease complaining that he was never at a university.'

The epitome was not altogether unfair. Thomas Kyd, the son of a scrivener, had been educated at the Merchant Taylors' school in East Smithfield, but he had not, like Edmund Spenser, another old boy of the school, gone on to a university. At Merchant Taylors', however, under its first headmaster, Richard Mulcaster, Kyd had become absorbed in acting and the drama, for Mulcaster produced the boys in various plays with such effect that the general public crowded to see them (until the governors decided that it was undignified) and they were eventually selected by the Lord Chamberlain to perform at Court before the Queen.

A year or two after Kyd left school, Burbage built *The Theatre* and the young man, earning his living in his father's profession as a noverint,* copying letters and documents in an exquisite Italian hand, spent all his spare time in trying to write plays. His competitors, mainly 'University Wits' just down from Oxford and Cambridge, sneered at him for his supposed lack of learning. 'It is a common practice', wrote one of the more malicious, 'now-a-days amongst a sort of shifting companions, that run through every art and thrive by none, to leave the trade of a Noverint, whereto they were born, and busy themselves with the endeavours of art, that could scarcely Latinise their neck verse if they should have need;† yet English Seneca read by candlelight yields many good sentences, as *Blood is a beggar* and so forth, and if you entreat him, he will afford you whole handfuls of tragical speeches.'

Kyd, though actually he was as proficient in Latin as Mulcaster could make him, had indeed pored over the recently-published English translation of Seneca's ten tragedies and was far ahead of his academically-cultured rivals in realising how to adapt for the young English stage the Roman philosopher's concoctions of blood and horror, based on the most revolting of the classical myths. For whereas they strove to be 'right Senecal', accepting as sacrosanct the Latin structure—chorus, unities of time and place, long and ornate descriptive passages and all—Kyd took some of the horrors which Seneca had merely described in decorative verse as taking place off-stage and put them into action as realistic as possible on-stage. Audiences at his *The Spanish Tragedy*, which was an instantaneous success, could watch murders, suicides, stabbings, hangings, the preparations for burning at the stake, a display of instruments of torture, a distracted mother 'running lunatic' and an old man 'biting out his tongue', so that something of the blood-lust of the bear-pit was injected into the theatre and added to an appreciation of the verse and an interest in the tale of revenge.

* The technical name for a scrivener, deriving from the phrase at the head of documents: *Noverint universi per praesentes* (Let all men know by these presents).
† i.e. could not save himself from hanging by quoting a Latin verse from the Bible.

For good measure and in part as a reply to his critics, Kyd put a few unimportant speeches into simple Latin, which flattered groundling and gentleman alike.

Yet, despite his acknowledged triumph, Kyd remained morose and unsatisfied. His scrivenership was a perpetual irritant and in Marlowe, who had had to endure the 'cobbler's son' sneer, he found a University man who gave him an instinctive sympathy. On his side, Marlowe was overwhelmed in admiration. The unexpected meeting with the playwright added another dimension to the morning interviews with Walsingham and Poley.

Marlowe's sense of the supremacy of poetry which had enabled him arrogantly to discount any greatness the vulgar might attach to the rôle of statesman became curiously modified. Sir Francis Walsingham as patron, Sir Philip Sidney as practitioner might, he realised, share his own view of poetry and concede, at least privately, his scale of value. The supremacy of 'divine Poesy' was not in dispute and even Sir Walter Raleigh, Queen Elizabeth's reigning favourite, did not disdain recognition as a poet. But the stage was an altogether different matter. Of the theatre, even Sidney in his *Defence of Poesie* had written, in disapprobation of its 'gross absurdities', how all its plays were 'neither right tragedies nor right comedies, mixing kings and clowns with neither decency nor discretion so that we have nothing but scurrility or extreme show of doltishness'. The stage, in fact, was an instrument to devalue poetry which, by it, was 'pitifully abused' and 'like an unmannerly daughter shewing a bad education causes her mother's honesty to be called in question'.

But now Marlowe, as he talked excitedly to Kyd, realised that he was surrendering to the despised theatre, that it was the stage itself that was captivating him, entangling his ambition and claiming his service; and as anecdote succeeded argument and tales of personalities displaced discussions of plots and prosody, he knew he would choose to live with its paupers and lechers and spendthrifts and rogues and vagabonds and cheats and poseurs and braggarts in preference to any kind of Government employment.

Impatiently he awaited the entrance of Edward Alleyn. But though other players from Burbage's company made brief appearances and Tom Watson, realising Marlowe's eagerness, delayed leaving the *Unicorn* until the last moment before the city gates were closed, the great actor did not make an appearance.

5. The Best Hated Man in England

One reason for the success of Kyd's *The Spanish Tragedy* was the topicality of its background of a war between Spain and Portugal. Kyd, aware of the popular value of discreet instruction, had even introduced a short dramatised history lesson reminding spectators of three English interventions in the affairs of the Peninsula.

First, there

> Was English Robert, Earl of Gloucester,
> Who, when King Stephen bore sway in Albion,
> Arriv'd with five and twenty thousand men
> In Portingal, and by success of war
> Enforc'd the king, then but a Saracen,
> To bear the yoke of th' English monarchy.

Secondly,

> Was Edmond, Earl of Kent in Albion,
> When English Richard wore the diadem.
> He came likewise and razéd Lisbon's walls,
> And took the King of Portingal in fight.

And last

> Was, as the rest, a valiant Englishman,
> Brave John of Gaunt, the Duke of Lancaster.
> He with a puissant army came to Spain
> And took the King of Castile prisoner.

The audience needed no reminder that contemporary events in Spain and Portugal were not without their effect on England.

The death of the last member of the reigning house of Portugal had prompted Philip II of Spain to claim the throne. He had invaded Portugal, defeated the Portuguese pretender, Don Antonio, and made himself master of, in addition to the seaports and seamen of Portugal, the rich Portuguese possessions overseas. As soon as he had assimilated his new conquests it was obvious that Philip would turn his attention in earnest to the long-projected attack on the English pirates under Sir Francis Drake, who were disrupting the Spanish trade-routes, capturing the treasure-ships and burning and pillaging the Spanish settlements in the New World.

But Portugal, though less dangerous, also demanded attention, and Sir Walter Raleigh had received a commission to clear the sea of Don Antonio's privateers which had become a general nuisance.

Raleigh's main care, however, was the expedition to Virginia which he was organising. Bernadino de Mendoza, the Spanish Ambassador in Paris who, since his removal from the embassy in London had continued to keep a wary eye on English affairs, informed King Philip: 'The Queen has knighted Raleigh, her favourite, and has given him a ship of 180 tons burden, with five pieces of ordnance on each side, and two culverins in the bows. Raleigh has also bought two Dutch flyboats of 120 tons each to carry stores, and two other boats of 40 tons, in addition to which he is having built two pinnaces of 20 to 30 tons each. Altogether Raleigh will fit out no fewer than 16 vessels, in which he intends to convey 400 men. The Queen has assured him that if he will refrain from going himself she will defray all the expenses.'

And at the same time—the spring of 1585—the Reverend Richard Hakluyt, chaplain to the English Ambassador in Paris, wrote to Sir Francis Walsingham: 'The rumours of Raleigh's fleet so vexes the Spaniard that I hope, if the voyage be stayed, the rumour of it be continued.'

But the expedition was not stayed and now, a month later, England was awaiting news of it. Raleigh himself was not with it—the Queen allowed him everything but his freedom and his cousin, Sir Richard Grenville, went in his place—but to be his eyes and ears and brain he sent the twenty-five-year-old Thomas Hariot whom he had taken into his household as mathematical tutor to aid him in making new designs for his privateering vessels and in instructing his sea-captains.

Hariot was destined to be one of the greatest scientists of the age—to anticipate Galileo in the use of the telescope, to be the first to observe Halley's comet, to give algebra its modern form, to make discoveries in pure mathematics far in advance of his time—though, as he refused to publish during his lifetime, others subsequently gained credit for what were in fact his discoveries. He was to correspond with Keppler and from him Descartes himself was to learn. But, at the moment, he was content with the humbler task of applying his precision of observation to the New World and writing *A Brief and True Report on the New-Found Land of Virginia*, a survey of the crops, merchandise, flora, fauna and minerals of the country, so that Raleigh might know the colony he had founded but was never to see.

Raleigh's career had started when at the age of sixteen he had gone with a regiment of Devon volunteers, many of whom were his relatives, to fight on the Huguenot side in France. He had served under the Calvinist leader, Montgomery (a relation of his by marriage), in the bitter campaign in the south,* one incident of which—the smoking-out of some Catholics from the caves of Languedoc—he left on record: 'We knew not how to enter by any ladder or engine till at last, by certain bundles of straw let down by an iron chain with a weighty stone in the midst, those that defended it were so smothered that they surrendered themselves with their plate, money and other goods therein hidden; or they must have died like bees that are smoked out of their hives.'

Raleigh's apprenticeship to life was thus served in a bitter civil war whose realities were bloodshed and plunder, hatred and 'no quarter' which gave to his courage an edge of ruthlessness it was never to lose. And it fed a kind of contempt for religion in whose name atrocities could be done. Yet, when he left France, he volunteered for a yet more bitter strife.

Ireland was on the verge of rebellion. For years there had been smouldering hostilities, as the Irish tried to drive out the English colonists who, seeking their fortunes there, regarded the

---

* For another incident in the campaign—the first 'massacre of St Bartholomew'— see *The Florentine Woman* p. 182.

natives in the light of vermin to be exterminated. Raleigh, as captain of a band of soldiers who were determined to carve a new Devon out of Ireland, landed in the August of 1580 and was immediately commissioned to try the brother of the Earl of Desmond, the Irish leader, who had fallen into English hands. The prisoner was immediately, without proper trial, hanged, drawn and quartered.

As Raleigh began, so he proceeded. He was responsible, in November, for a massacre at Smerwick where men, women and children were indiscriminately slain, so that about six hundred stripped bodies—'as goodly and gallant personages as ever were beheld' according to Lord Grey, the Deputy of Ireland—were laid out on the sands. Grey had his own opinion of Raleigh. He admitted frankly: 'I like neither his carriage nor his company.'

When Raleigh's company was disbanded the following year he returned to London to complain to the Earl of Leicester, who had procured him his captaincy: 'I have spent some time under the Deputy in such poor place that, were it not that I know him to be one of yours, I would disdain it as much as to keep sheep.'

The moment of Raleigh's arrival at Court coincided with the last months of the visit of 'Monsieur', the French king's brother, with whom Elizabeth, for diplomatic reasons, was carrying on marriage negotiations. * No one, with the possible exception of Anjou, took the marriage project seriously, though everyone had to pretend to. Its political importance was that, because of Monsieur's claim to the Netherlands, Elizabeth could use him in her diplomatic struggle against Spain. When, in the February of 1582, he left England for the Low Countries to be invested as Duke of Brabant, the Queen herself accompanied him as far as Canterbury and on parting tearfully assured him that she lived only for his prompt return and begged him to write to her every day as his wife. On the Channel crossing, he was accompanied by Leicester, who carried the Queen's secret instructions to the Prince of Orange to keep Monsieur in the Netherlands at any cost and never to let him, under any pretext whatever, return to England.

In Leicester's train of nobles and gentlemen went Raleigh, part of whose duty was to establish personal contact with

* See *The Last of the Valois* Chapters 16 and 17.

William of Orange. He remained after Leicester's return to London, partly to ensure that Monsieur did not leave the Low Countries (his knowledge of the secret gave him his first insight into diplomacy at the highest level) and partly to establish a privateering business under cover of a commission from the Prince of Orange.

On his return to London, Raleigh, at thirty-one, astonished everyone by his meteoric rise to favour. The two dominant figures at Court were Leicester and Burleigh—Leicester, who had grown up with Elizabeth and was so enduringly powerful in her affections that many believed that she was secretly married to him, and William Cecil, Lord Burleigh, who had guided her since girlhood and whom, as architect of her policy, she trusted as surely as she loved Leicester. The reigning favourite was an inconsiderable little man, Sir Christopher Hatton, whose skill in dancing had brought him to her notice—one who 'came to the Court by the galliard, a mere vegetable of the Court that sprung up by night'. She called him her 'skipping sheep'.

Such royal nicknames were the order of the day. Burleigh was her 'spirit', Leicester her 'eyes', Monsieur (who was small and hunchbacked as well as French) her 'frog'. Raleigh, because of his seafaring background and the usual pronounciation of his Christian name, became, obviously enough, 'water'. He improved on it, in a typically grandiose fashion, to 'ocean'* though the Court preferred to refer to him as 'the Bucket'.

Certainly into him enough favours were poured. The year he returned—1583—already wealthy from his piratical exploits he was granted the farm of wines, which meant in practice he had the right to collect £1 a year from every vintner in the country. The same year the Queen gave him the use of Durham House in the Strand where he kept forty men and horses in attendance on him and used as his study 'a little turret that looked into and over the Thames and had a prospect which was as pleasant as any in the world'. In 1584 he was granted the monopoly of the export of woollen broadcloth—more lucrative even than the wine licence—was knighted and became Member of Parliament for Devonshire. Now, in 1585, he was made Lord Warden of the Stannaries, that is to say governor of the Devon and Cornwall

* In which form it still lives in English literature in Raleigh's great poem to Elizabeth, *The Ocean's Love to Cynthia*.

tin-miners, a community of about 13,000 with laws of its own.

Against this appointment a protest was made to Burleigh that 'no man is more hated than him: none more cursed daily of the poor, of whom in truth numbers are brought to extreme poverty through the gift of the cloths to him: his pride is intolerable, without regard for any, as the world knows'; but in spite of this he was given, in addition to the Wardenship, the Lieutenancy of the County of Cornwall and the Admiralship of Devon and Cornwall.

Such was Raleigh at thirty-three, 'the best hated man in the world, in Court, city and country'—and the most remarkable. Six feet tall, with a swarthy complexion and long melancholy face, pointed beard and heavily-lidded eyes, he outdistanced every fashion. His jewelled shoes were said to be worth more than 6,600 gold pieces, his hat-band of pearls, his ear-rings, the silks and damasks he wore and the ornaments with which he bedecked himself were worth a king's ransom. And he had the pride of the peacock he emulated. In his broad Devonshire accent, which always amused Elizabeth and which, in consequence, he was careful to cultivate, he would utter witticisms which wounded and insults none dared challenge. He knew what men said of him and treated it with contempt. 'If any man accuseth me to my face, I will answer him with my mouth but my arse is good enough to return an answer to such as traduceth me behind my back.'

The ballad-mongers sang:

> Raleigh doth time bestride,
> He sits 'twixt wind and tide,
> Yet uphill he cannot ride
> For all his bloody pride.
> He seeks taxes in the tin,
> He polls the poor to the skin
> Yet he vows 'tis no sin,
> Lord, for thy pity!

But this was only the hate of envy. There seemed nothing to prevent him riding as high as he wished. 'The Queen took him for a kind of oracle which nettled them all.'

And the Queen was not disposed to tolerate criticism. When

the leading comic actor, Richard Tarlton, to whom she or-
dinarily allowed the widest privileges of a jester, pointed at
Raleigh in attendance on her and remarked: 'See, the Knave
commands the Queen!', he 'was corrected by a frown from Her
Majesty'.

The previous year, Marlowe had had a momentary glimpse of
Raleigh in Cambridge. The Vice-Chancellor of the University
had contested Raleigh's right to license the vintners on the
grounds that such privilege pertained to the University and
could not be alienated at the whim of the monarch. When
Raleigh's agent, one Brown, rescinded the licence of one publi-
can and appointed another in his place, the undergraduates,
additionally exhilarated at being, for once, on the side of lawful
authority, beat up the intruder and nearly frightened his wife to
death. The Vice-Chancellor co-operated by sending Brown to
jail and ignoring three protesting letters from Raleigh.

Eventually the favourite, suspecting (as it transpired only too
cogently) that his agent was dishonest, determined to visit
Cambridge to investigate for himself. He wisely decided to
remain *incognito*. To make an official examination was beneath
his dignity. Also, by giving warning, he would make it easier to
tamper with accounts. So when Marlowe met him in the *Eagle*,
just across the road from Corpus, all the undergraduate saw was
a tall, saturnine soldier whose imperious bearing was at odds
with his rough clothes and whose thick Devon accent contradicted his occasional elegancies of conversation. Effortlessly
Raleigh established himself as the centre of the room, holding
the older of his auditors with his anecdotes of warfare and
flattering the sprinkling of undergraduates by inquiring about
their studies in a tone which suggested that he was genuinely
interested.

'I am studying Divinity, sir,' Marlowe replied when he was
questioned, 'as most of us at Corpus are.'

'And do you find that you progress with your studies?'

'Tolerably well, sir, when I apply myself to them.'

'I do not make myself clear. I mean, do you advance? Do you
go forward?'

'How else can one progress?'

'Most of the clerics I have met have an affinity for the circle. They go round and round and imagine themselves to be going straight forward. How, for example, would you define the soul?'

Marlowe gave the conventional definition: 'A spiritual and immortal substance breathed into man by God.'

'Yes, yes,' said Raleigh, 'but what *is* this spiritual and immortal substance?'

'The soul,' said Marlowe.

'You give me my point,' said Raleigh, 'or rather my circle.'

'All arguments from first principles', answered Marlowe, 'have to proceed in circles.'

'Which make them interminable and inconclusive—and far too long to indulge in now. But are you kind?'

'Kind?' Marlowe repeated, puzzled at the turn of the argument. 'I do not catch your drift.'

'Kind. Doing good to those who treat you badly. Forgiving till seventy times seven. Loving your enemies. Turning the other cheek. You do this? It's what you're supposed to do.'

'I find it too hard,' Marlowe admitted.

'I find it altogether impossible,' said Raleigh. 'But then it's not my profession. It *is* yours.'

'Doubtless I shall come to it in time.'

'If you do, I will find you a good living in Devonshire. You will be a nine-days wonder. Your name, young sir?'

'Christopher Marlowe.'

'I will not forget,' Raleigh laughed. 'Kind Kit.'

'And how shall I find you, sir?'

'When you come to London ask the first passer-by the whereabouts of the ocean,' said Raleigh and turned away to talk to another undergraduate.

Marlowe, feeling snubbed, left the *Eagle* without any further attempt at conversation and it was not until some months later that, having related the episode to Tom Watson, he received immediate enlightenment: 'Ocean? It must have been Raleigh, of course.'

6. Meeting at Rheims

Marlowe had little difficulty in adapting himself to life at Rheims where he arrived in the July of 1585. For one thing, as the pattern of university preoccupations differs little at any centre of learning, Cambridge had prepared him for it. For another, the special constitution of Rheims itself was deliberately directed to accommodating all sorts and conditions of men. Its founder had laid it down that everyone of whatever belief who visited the college 'is to be pressed to remain a few days with us and, if they are poor, to be kept at the common expense for thirty days'.

Marlowe, following Poley's advice not to pretend to be a Catholic because he would be unable to sustain the rôle, thus found his Protestantism no obstacle to general acceptance. He was indeed telling the literal truth when he explained that he was a theological student whose study had bred doubts about the truth of Anglican tenets and who in consequence was seeking wider experience and deeper knowledge before he finally committed himself to taking Holy Orders according to the rite of the Church of England. Also, as he was genuinely impressed by the unfamiliar splendour of the High Masses which he attended regularly in the cathedral, it was natural for his companions to suppose that his inquiries and his inclination were leading him in the Catholic direction.

This impression was confirmed by the fact that he seemed to spend much of his time in the cathedral. The habit originated because of his initial loneliness in a foreign land. By reason of his birth and boyhood at Canterbury he was, inescapably, a cathedral child. Living in the shadow and shelter of the majestic building with its proportioned space and patterned ceiling, its straight stone avenues between the great pillars, its soaring arches, its windows like jewels, he found that it insensibly added a special dimension to life. It had been part of a daily experience lacking at Cambridge but now welcomed again, in its essentials, at Rheims.

An additional fascination of Rheims Cathedral for Marlowe was that it had not suffered the spoliation which the Protestant Reformers had inflicted on Canterbury. The altars and the chantries and the saints in their niches still stood; the shrine was unpillaged; the lingering scent of incense was a reminder of prayer; the Blessed Sacrament still reigned from the tabernacle. As a result, the character of the men and women who frequented the cathedral differed. At Canterbury, Marlowe had been accustomed to see those who went, as he himself went, to particular services at certain set times; at Rheims, people of every age and class visited the cathedral throughout the day for longer or shorter periods, some of them certainly interested in sightseeing but most to say their prayers or to make their confessions or to pay homage to Christ in the Sacrament.

It so happened that by observing these visitors Marlowe was led to his first political discovery. He noticed among those who paid regular visits to the Blessed Sacrament a tall, dark-eyed and dark-bearded man in his early thirties, resplendent in a gold-laced cape and scarlet doublet studded with silver buttons whom he had occasionally met among the English residents and who was known as Captain 'Foscue'—the French approximation to Fortescue.

As far as Marlowe understood from snatches of tavern gossip, the Captain was serving in the war in the Netherlands and was now on his way back to England to raise his own regiment. With him, as a constant companion, was John Savage, a large, lazily good-humoured young man in his early twenties who had also fought in the Netherlands but who had now decided against a military career and, having attended some lectures at Rheims, was returning to London to take up seriously the study of law at Barnard's Inn.

A third Englishman who was often with them was a young seminarian named Gilbert Gifford, the member of a long-established and much respected Catholic family in Staffordshire but who himself had lived almost entirely abroad and had now, after an unsettled and unsatisfactory youth, entered the college at Rheims to train for the priesthood. Had it been Gilbert Gifford who had frequently visited the cathedral, Marlowe would have considered it unremarkable. Even the presence of Savage, Protestant though he was, would not have surprised him, for Savage, despite his placid appearance, was at odds with himself. Scholar and soldier, he hovered perpetually undecided between philosophy and adventure, between thought and action. To such a nature a spell of meditation in the numinous atmosphere of the cathedral might well afford relief. But Captain Foscue was a very different matter. It was difficult to imagine him with his flamboyance, his simple-minded enjoyment of life, his careless generosity which suggested an absence of all financial cares (in contrast to Savage's chronic impecuniosity), his eupeptic good humour, paying anything but formal lip-service to religion—and, as he was raising a company to fight the Spaniards in the Netherlands, certainly not before a Catholic altar. There was a lack of congruity.

Consequently Marlowe applied himself to cultivating the Captain's acquaintance in the taverns and other special haunts of the English colony, but though he found that Fortescue, as an old Caius man, was delighted to discuss with him the differences between the Cambridge of today and the Cambridge of ten years ago, the conversation was otherwise confined to the most general of topics and offered no confirmation of Marlowe's suspicions. Yet they persisted and, as the Captain announced his intention of returning to England to conduct his recruiting there at the end of August, Marlowe decided to be in London before him in order to inform Poley that he might be worth watching.

In this he was undoubtedly right, though he could not know that Poley and Walsingham were quite aware that the gallant Captain Fortescue was in fact Father John Ballard, one of the priests who, at the risk of their lives, ministered secretly to the persecuted Catholics in England, saying Mass, hearing confessions, reconciling the lapsed, strengthening the timid.

Poley also knew more about Gilbert Gifford than Marlowe could have guessed, for Gifford was one of the reasons for Poley's present visit to Paris. Walsingham's grand strategy at the moment was to bring about the death of Mary Queen of

Scots by involving her in a situation in which she could be considered an accessory to the attempted murder of Queen Elizabeth. His most important secret agent was Thomas Morgan, the Queen of Scots's completely trusted Secretary who was now in France. In this particular scheme Gilbert Gifford was hardly less valuable. His youthful appearance—he looked still in his teens—and his air of wide-eyed innocence, reinforced by his open preparation for the Catholic priesthood, successfully masked his true nature, whose dominant passion was to betray and destroy. Under his aliases of 'Mr Coleredin', 'Cornelys' and 'Pietro', he had already rendered good service in France and Italy, but his crucial assignment was now to be in England where his family's estates were in the neighbourhood of Mary Queen of Scots's place of imprisonment.

The object of Poley's visit to Paris had been to get Morgan to provide a letter of introduction for Gifford which would induce Mary to trust him and Morgan had immediately supplied it: 'Gilbert Gifford, a Catholic gentleman well known to me, is returning to England. His father is John Gifford, a Staffordshire man, a gentleman of good house and well friended in that county, but at present a prisoner for our religion in London. I thought it my duty for the increase of your servants to deal with Gilbert and I hope he will show his good-will and diligence. He has asked for a letter to give him credit with Your Majesty and I give him these few lines, in assurance of his faith and honesty.' This letter Poley would give to Gifford when he arrived in London whenever that might be.

Gifford however could not cross the Channel until John Savage had preceded him and taken up his law studies at Barnard's Inn; for it was Savage who was Gifford's present responsibility. He had persuaded him to take an oath to attempt to assassinate Queen Elizabeth and he intended to see that the young lawyer fulfilled it.

The day Savage had confided to Gifford that he too intended to train for the Catholic priesthood, Gifford, instead of welcoming the decision, said emphatically: 'There is a better service you could render the Faith' and explained that, as Queen Elizabeth was a usurper and excommunicate and her continued existence was the one obstacle to the restoration of Catholicism in England, to kill her would be a deed meritorious in itself and, to a soldier like Savage, a far better service than the study of divinity.

Savage objected that the College had actually published an official treatise condemning those who upheld the lawfulness of regicide and 'inveighing against such as should seek Her Majesty's death'.

Gifford retorted that the treatise was merely a blind to put the Privy Council off its guard and that the best ecclesiastical authorities considered the assassination legal—as, by the accepted standards of law in view of the excommunication, it was.

Savage pondered the matter for several weeks and eventually became convinced—or managed to convince himself—that Gifford was right. He took a solemn oath to perform the deed and from that moment became an essential factor in the plot against the Queen of Scots. Parliament, a few months earlier, had enacted the death penalty for anyone in whose favour any move against Queen Elizabeth was undertaken. Thus, if it could be established that a conspiracy or rising had as its object the placing of Mary Queen of Scots on the throne, then, even though Mary were totally ignorant of the plans on her behalf, she could be legally put to death. *

To encourage such an attempt at the earliest possible opportunity had been Walsingham's policy during the seven months since the Act was passed and now Savage, manipulated by Gifford under the general direction of Poley, was to be the unwitting 'Instrument'—the centre of a manufactured 'plot' which should involve idealistic young Catholics, with more enthusiasm than intelligence, determined to right the wrongs they and their co-religionists suffered in Elizabeth's England.

The plan, though complex in its details and requiring infinite patience and secrecy to carry out, was in essence simple enough. Mary Queen of Scots's captivity was to be made so strict that she was completely cut off from the outside world and from the usual diplomatic courtesies of communication with her Ambassador in France. When she was reduced to a sufficient degree of

---

* The Protestant historian, Sir John Neale, has described the Act as 'the declaration of lynch law aimed at Mary Queen of Scots' and the Catholic historian, Philip Hughes, has called the Act 'the bloodiest ever passed by a legislature whose members made any pretence of Christian ideals'.

misery and frustration, her post was not only to be restored to her, but Gifford was to arrange some way for the delivery of secret letters. These, from, it was hoped, Savage and his associates among others, were all to be deciphered by Walsingham's brilliant forger, Phillips (with whom Gifford was to lodge), who would also forge additions if considered necessary.

Marlowe, by his suspicion of 'Captain Fortescue', had thus accidentally stumbled on Walsingham's master-plan. Naturally he could not guess the nature and scope of it or suppose that the easygoing, undecided John Savage was inflexibly committed to regicide and that the ingenuous Catholic student, Gilbert Gifford, was really an ingenious Protestant spy. But his perception in the case of the Captain convinced Poley, when he reported it on his return to London, that Marlowe was material worth training and he gave him five pounds.

Marlowe, returning to Cambridge for the Michaelmas Term, reflected that five pounds was likely to be his yearly stipend as a parson* and, though he was by no means certain that he wanted to enter Walsingham's service, he was more determined than ever at all costs to avoid taking Holy Orders.

---

* In this year 1585 the Archbishop of Canterbury complained that less than 600 benefices offered a stipend worthy of a scholar, that half the parishes of England paid less than £10 a year and a third only £5 and under.

BOOK II

September 1585 to November 1587:
Master of Arts

7. Changing Perspectives

When, in that stifling, parched autumn of 1585—already known as 'the Year of Drought'—Marlowe returned to Corpus Christi for the Michaelmas Term, he found more perspectives changed than his increasing dislike of Divinity. The very weather, accentuating the always-deadening climate of Cambridge, seemed to reflect the aridity of the academic atmosphere. The prescribed debates in the schools, which in his days as a freshman he had found exciting and in which his gift of words made him occasionally excel, seemed now drearily irrelevant. He had argued—and while preparing for his M.A. would have to continue to argue—such propositions as 'whether the lower bodies are ruled by the higher', 'whether the moon causes the ebb and flow of the sea', 'whether Aristotle should have included a wife among the goods of a philosopher', 'whether gold can be manufactured from inferior metals'. He had disputed, either as *oppugnant* or as *propugnant*, 'which is the more difficult to withstand, anger or desire', 'whether there be any power in incantations', 'whether all things exist as only in the imagination', 'whether he can be a good citizen who is not a good man' and 'whether government by the best law is better than government by the best king'.

But these questions, as far as they verged on practical politics, seemed to him completely removed from reality now that he had glimpsed, if only in a small way, the actualities of power. A 'good citizen' was one who believed implicitly whatever lies the Government chose to tell him. A 'good law' was whatever the Government chose to enact to maintain its power. He was 'good' in so far as he allowed himself to be trained to spy and betray in the Government service. He would be equally 'good', if not

better, if he became an official exponent—at £5 or so a year—
of unproved and dubious supernatural sanctions against the 'bad'
opponents of the Government.

His visit to Rheims had been, as well as a practical introduction to the lower reaches of statecraft, an occasion of deepening
his knowledge of Machiavelli. He had, of course, read a version
of *The Prince* at Cambridge, for Simon Patricke's English
translation of Gentillet's *Contre-Machiavel* had been published
not long before he went up to Corpus and had swept through
the University. 'You cannot step into an undergraduate's
study', complained the officious don, Gabriel Harvey, 'but (ten
to one) you shall likely find open a certain parlous book called
Il Principe by Nicolo Machiavelli.'

But in those days of his adolescence, Kit had accepted *The Prince*
at the valuation his elders and betters put upon it—a handbook,
an alphabet even, of devilish principles, which made 'Machiavel'
a name to inspire terror and loathing as an epitome of ruthless
wickedness. If, as he grew wiser, the undergraduate argued on
behalf of certain of Machiavelli's postulates, it had been due to
his temperamental impatience with convention, like his baiting
of his clerical fellow-students, rather than to any serious con-
viction.

Now, however, the maxims of *The Prince* suddenly made
sense. Their truth was so obvious that he could not understand
why he had ever been blind to it and he saw the rage of those
who piously rejected it as fury at being unmasked. The diabolical honesty of Machiavelli betrayed their organised duplicity.

Once it was pointed out, it was plain enough that 'men in
general are ungrateful, fickle, false, cowardly, covetous, but as
long as you are successful they are yours entirely'. To rule them,
through force, and severity in using it, is the ultimate sanction—
'that there were no dissensions in Hannibal's army was due to
his inhuman cruelty'—dissimulation can accomplish much. The
ruler 'must appear altogether merciful, faithful, humane, upright and religious, though there is no need for him to be any of
these things'. The most important quality is devotion to
religion and he must support even what he knows to be false in
religion if it serves his turn. 'Nothing is more important than to
appear pious, for everyone sees what you appear to be while
few know what you really are and those few will not dare to

oppose the opinion of the many. Ordinary men are always taken in by what seems to be and by what comes of it and in the world there are only the vulgar, for the few find a place only when the many have no ground to rest on.'

So it was that Marlowe on his return from France, where Machiavellianism was openly accepted—*Il Principe* was known as 'the Queen-Mother's Bible'—and its exercise taken for granted, became an unquestioning devotee of the Italian writer and amused himself by composing a simple soliloquy which might have been spoken by his ghost:

> To some perhaps my name is odious;
> But such as love me guard me from their tongues
> And let them know that I am Machiavel
> And weigh not men and, therefore, not men's words.
> Admir'd I am of those that hate me most.
> Though some speak openly against my books,
> Yet they will read me and thereby attain
> To Peter's chair; and, when they cast me off,
> Are poison'd by my climbing followers.
> I count religion but a childish toy
> And hold there is no sin but ignorance.
> Birds of the air will tell of murders past?
> I am ashamed to hear such fooleries!
> Many will talk of title to a crown.
> What right had Caesar to the empery?
> Might first made kings and laws were then most sure
> When, like the Draco's, they were writ in blood.
> Hence comes it that a strong-built citadel
> Commands much more than letters can import.

Machiavelli's key to the understanding of men and their motives had liberated Marlowe's thought, but the exhilaration of release was tempered by an accompanying gloom, for he was too honest to try to except himself from the general judgment. He, like everyone else, was driven by a desire for power and would struggle for it by all means at his disposal.

But what kind of power and what means had he? Military glory was out of the question. He knew he was no soldier. Indeed the only possible advantage he had seen in a career in the church was that he would not be expected to be a swordsman. 'Kind

Kit' had wounded by its accuracy. His imagination might run riot among scenes of blood and cruelty and violence such as Raleigh would actually perpetrate without a second thought, but in action Marlowe was too considerate—or was it too cowardly?—to hurt anyone. In his play on Dido he had characterised himself in two lines he had invented for Juno to speak:

> Tut, I am simple without mind to hurt
> And have no gall at all to grieve my foes.

But in the same play he had also departed from what was in essentials a translation of Virgil to interpolate in Aeneas's account of the sack of Troy:

> Frighted with this confused noise, I rose
> And, looking from a turret, could behold
> Young children swimming in their parents' blood,
> Headless carcasses piled up in heaps,
> Virgins half-dead, dragg'd by their golden hair
> And with main force flung on a ring of pikes;
> Old men with swords thrust through their aged sides,
> Kneeling for mercy to a Greekish lad
> Who with steel pole-axes dash'd out their brains.

If the classic way to power—the murderous competence of the *condottiere*—was temperamentally closed to him, Marlowe had to recognise that the other two main roads, eminence in the church or influence in the Government, were equally impossible, the first because of his passion for truth, the second because of his respect for morals. There was left to him as a driving force only the need to vindicate his egoistic belief in the primacy of poetry and by wedding it with the theatre to command that popularity which could be reckoned as power of a sort. He was encouraged by the thought that Machiavelli himself was a dramatist who put more value on his play *Mandragola* than on his treatise *The Prince*. Marlowe would, however, for the moment continue his studies since a Cambridge M.A. gave him status. He would also hold himself at Walsingham's occasional disposal since Government service gave him money.

He was to be used by the Government again sooner than he had expected. Towards the end of November, when the Michaelmas Term was nearly over, Poley decided to send him to Paris to try to trace Gilbert Gifford. By then Savage, the self-appointed regicide, was already in London, quietly studying law at Barnard's Inn and quite unsuspicious that he was under rigid surveillance by Walsingham's spies. Gifford's presence in France was thus no longer necessary, whereas he was urgently required in England because without him the construction of the plan to ensnare the Queen of Scots could not be begun. The rumour was that Gifford, who tended to be a law unto himself, had gone to Paris to consult at first hand Thomas Morgan, the trusted Secretary of Mary Queen of Scots. This precaution, in Poley's opinion, was quite unnecessary, as he himself had the requisite letter of introduction from Morgan which Gifford was to present to the Scottish Queen.

It was possible, of course, that Gifford was already on his way to London and Poley had no wish to waste a valuable man on what might turn out to be a wild-goose chase. The occasion was thus obviously one for using the Cambridge student and, without entrusting him with any actual secret, for initiating him a little more fully into the Service. Marlowe was given a letter to deliver to Gifford if he could find him in Paris. If he could not discover him within a week, he was to return to England, leaving the letter with Nicholas Berdon, *alias* Beard, one of Walsingham's regular agents.

Marlowe, having accepted the arrangement and received his instructions, decided to visit his family at Canterbury on his way to Dover. He had not seen them since his birthday in February, when he came of age. He could now make the excuse to himself that, before he visited Paris for the first time, it would be wise to inquire something about the city from the Priments, a French family he had known since they came as Huguenot refugees to settle in Canterbury when he was ten. From M. Vincent Priment, who set up as 'a teacher of youth', he had learnt a little French before he went to the King's School, and M. Priment's son, Pierre, who was his own age, had become his playfellow and companion. Whether or not he really supposed he would gain any useful information from expatriates who had left their country eleven years ago and continued to see everything in terms of the Massacre of St Bartholomew was doubtful.

He had, in any case, heard their stories so often (at each repetition slightly modified or embellished to suit the particular audience) that he could have told them better himself. But the idea of getting first-hand information not only appealed to his self-importance but also masked the simple sentimentality which had actually prompted the visit. He wanted to show his mother his new doublet.

The doublet was of black velvet, profusely slitted to show the gold silk beneath, and ornamented with thirty patterned silver buttons. The collar was of the ultra-fashionable cobweb lawn in place of the conventional ruff. Kit hoped she would approve of it. From her he had first learned to take a delight in stuffs and materials. About the house there had always been a sufficiency of taffeta cushions of many colours, coverings of silk and damask, hangings and embroideries carefully chosen for their congruous designs and shades. Along the top of the carefully polished old chest in the dining-room was the fine runner which was the housewife's particular pride, the gift of a grateful refugee weaver—a flowered brocade made of raw silk from Turkey and 'thrown'* silk from Italy, with gold and silver threads intertwined.

When Kit thought of his mother, he always associated with her her favourite ring with a 'double posy' of tiny jewelled flowers. This had been to him a kind of talisman. Looked at in the light of comparisons he was now able to make, it seemed quite ordinary and not particularly valuable, yet for him it never lost the childhood magic suggesting the fabled riches of fairyland. At the very least it suggested its possessor as an arbiter of taste. He found himself wearing his new doublet with an added certainty—not to say arrogance—once his mother had approved it.

Though she was Kit's main reason for visiting his family, he was also fraternally interested in his young sisters' love-affairs. The eldest, Margaret, at twenty, was growing increasingly impatient with her fiancé, a tailor, for not bringing matters to their conclusion. She had been additionally exacerbated by the marriage of one of her younger sisters, Joan, two years ago when she was only thirteen, to their father's leading apprentice, John Moore, who had now set up for himself as a shoemaker.

* Twisted.

The two other girls, Anne and Dorothy, aged fourteen and twelve, were showing incipient interest in the youngest of the present apprentices, which was acidly discouraged by Margaret and secretly abetted by Joan.

Their father, John Marlowe, had what might be termed a professional interest in marriage in general. Having himself married for love while he was still an apprentice, he appreciated some of the difficulties of the young and would occasionally act as surety for impecunious couples seeking marriage licences. Usually they were simple yeomen or husbandmen and, though John Marlowe was sufficiently established for his bond of £100 to be unquestioningly accepted, he was not one of the professional bondsmen who had degraded a personal security into a trade. In his own trade as shoemaker and tanner he was successful enough. When Christopher was ten, the family had moved from the old house at the corner of St George's Street and St George's Lane where all the children had been born* to a better house in the very centre of Canterbury, near the Bull-Stake. The move, which was in a sense forced on him, was reluctantly undertaken after the Queen's memorable fortnight's visit to Canterbury to celebrate her fortieth birthday and to meet the two French Ambassadors† who had come to open negotiations for her marriage to the Duc d'Alençon, the French King's youngest brother.

On that occasion Queen Elizabeth had stayed in the palace which Henry VIII had built from the pillaged ruins of St Augustine's Abbey outside the East Gate. As it was less than three minutes away from the Marlowe house in St George's Street, Kit and his sisters were able to watch at close quarters the daily tide of magnificence which flowed past the door—courtiers and officials, the English nobility and the French visitors and, from time to time, most splendid of all, the Queen herself—and its vividness made it an indelible memory.

The Queen's official host was the Archbishop of Canterbury, who played—or overplayed—his part so expansively, entertaining all and sundry at his palace for the entire fortnight, that

---

* The house was destroyed by enemy action on the night of 1 June 1942.
† Two Ambassadors, because one, Retz, was sent by the Queen-Mother, Catherine de Medici, and the other, Maisonfleur, by Alençon. They were usually at cross-purposes. See *The Last of the Valois* pp. 31–4.

serious inroads were made into ecclesiastical finances and the Archbishop of York was moved to write reprovingly: 'It will be hard indeed for any of our cloth to do the like for a hundred years and how long after God knoweth.' And at the birthday-feast itself (when the Archbishop presented the Queen with an agate salt-cellar, garnished with a great diamond inset, with a golden ship in full sail on the cover and containing six golden pieces of Portugal, and to every other lady a commentary on the Book of Ecclesiastes, in English, bound in tooled leather) the ordinary citizens of Canterbury pressed into the room until it was uncomfortably crowded and before long the royal voice was heard even above the music peremptorily commanding everyone to stand aside so that she might have an uninterrupted view of the guests actually seated at her table.

One of the matters on which the French Ambassadors were in complete agreement was an insistence, as one of the pre-conditions of the marriage, that some definite measures be taken against the Huguenot refugees in Kent, where the immigration problem had assumed a complexion of its own. At Sandwich, for example, the 'Strangers', who now constituted a third of the population, organised themselves into companies of 'free-booters' and made piratical attacks on French shipping in the Channel. As a practical solution the Queen promised that the 'Strangers' should be forbidden access to ports and harbours and be redistributed among inland towns at some distance from the seaboard. Canterbury should set an example. The Mayor was ordered to make provision for a hundred immigrant families and the Archbishop to assign to them the crypt of the cathedral as 'a competent church' where they could worship as they chose. *

In spite of the city's protests, dwindling eventually to requests that the imposed influx 'may not be of the meanest sort', Mid-summer Day 1575 was officially appointed for their arrival, protected by a special enactment that only the Queen and the Privy Council had the authority to order their expulsion, so that they had complete security of tenure and could buy or rent what property they chose.

* It held comfortably from 2,000 to 2,500 worshippers, and as 'families' included dependants, servants and employees, it was by no means too large. They had soon set up over 1,000 looms and were employing poor English women, boys and girls to work for them.

Thus John Marlowe realised that Midsummer 1575 was the latest date at which he would have the chance to establish himself in the centre of the city. In common with his fellow-Canterburians he foresaw that the Strangers would probably take over the riverside parishes where they could have the use of the water of the Stour for their industries. For himself he chose St Andrew's at the very hub of the shopping district and during the ten years that had followed the move he had managed to hold his own though not to increase his business at a rate commensurate with the higher rent he had to pay. The advent of the Strangers, though extremely beneficial to themselves, was no advantage to the natives, because the newcomers brought with them, as part of their quota, their own bakers, tailors, carpenters and cobblers whom they naturally patronised.

So now, in 1585, John Marlowe, after several summonses for non-payment of rent, had to move again, this time into cheaper premises in the neighbouring parish of St Mary's. Inspection of the new house was in fact another reason for Kit's visit. It seemed to him cramped and the change became a symbol of the final severance with his youth. He doubted if he would come back to Canterbury.

The day before he left an accidental circumstance arose to emphasise his adulthood. A family friend, John Benchkyn, called to say that his mother had been suddenly taken ill and was anxious to make a new will. John Marlowe, his wife's brother, Thomas, and his son-in-law, Joan's husband, were at the shop and, so, immediately available. But who would make the necessary fourth witness?

'Why cannot I?' asked Kit. 'I am of age now.'

'Of course,' said his father and, by way of atoning for his tactlessness, he suggested, when the will was duly drawn up, that his son should read it aloud, slowly and carefully as a scholar could, to old Mistress Benchkyn so that she could make her mark of approval, in the presence of the witnesses, before her son threw the old will into the fire.*

Before Kit finally left Canterbury to embark for France, he called on the Priments for a farewell visit to ask if there were any private messages he could deliver to their cousins in Paris.

* The will was discovered only in 1939 and contains the only known signature by Marlowe. It is now in the Maidstone Public Record Office.

On the way back, as he was crossing the bridge in Westgate Street near Allhallows, he noticed two men in front of him and his pulses suddenly raced. Though the dark russet cloak was unfamiliar, the erect back, the graceful carriage, the curled love-lock could belong to only one person. Tom Walsingham—for it must be he—was accompanied by an older man who was slightly lame. In spite of his limp he managed to walk at a good pace and though Marlowe quickened his own in an effort to overtake them, they had turned into a narrow passage between two of the houses bordering the Cathedral Close before he could draw level with them.

He was about to follow them when his courage failed him. Supposing he were mistaken? And even supposing he were not, what was there to say? Never had the gap between imagination and action been more unbridgeable.

He paused for a moment to catch his breath and then went slowly home.

8. Paris Encounters

The house to which Marlowe made his way in Paris stood in the little winding street connecting the rue du Champ Fleury with the rue du Coq in the overcrowded and unsalubrious area between the Louvre and the rue St Honoré. Walsingham had provided it for the use of his agents and entrusted the overseeing of it to Nicholas Berdon, his senior man in Paris.

The tall narrow house with its peaked roof and projecting gable, harboured as strange a collection of humanity as could be found in any one dwelling. Because of its nearness to the English Embassy in the rue St Honoré it was occasionally used by Sir Edward Stafford, the English Ambassador, to put up relatively unimportant guests when the Embassy was too full to entertain them. Two of the rooms were furnished in some style. On the other hand the attics, which were occasionally required for criminals or beggars who had rendered a passing service and had to be temporarily protected from the police, had nothing but straw in the place of beds. Between the extremes was adequate, if not overcomfortable, accommodation for the stream of spies, informers, messengers, *agents-provocateurs* and renegade priests who made it their base for a longer or a shorter time. Marlowe, whom Berdon after a shrewd appraising glance classified as unimportant, was given a small back room beneath the attics.

'You will be here for a week?'

'At most,' said Marlowe. 'Master Poley said I was to return in a week if I could not find Gilbert Gifford. You are quite certain he has not been here?'

Berdon looked at him with some disdain. 'Unless I had certainty in such matters, it is unlikely that *I* should be here,' he said. 'Though in Paris, Gilbert is usually known as M.

Coleredin, just as in London I am Master Beard. You know him?'

'I met him in Rheims in the summer.'

'And what was your name?'

'I have told you. Christopher Marlowe.'

'But that is your real name. I mean your name in the Service.'

Kit was surprised at the depth of his distaste. 'I neither have nor wish to have any name but my own,' he said.

In the absence of Gilbert Gifford, there was nothing for Marlowe to do but to wait. He found Paris itself a fascinating enough city to explore though he was at first a little intimidated by its size— eight times as large as London with ten times as many inhabitants. 'Paris', as one traveller had remarked, 'is not a town; it is a world.' And it was a world distracted by rival loyalties, rent by internecine feuds, smouldering on the edge of a civil war, whose political climate made London seem by comparison an abode of ordered peace.

The day after his arrival Marlowe went over to the university quarter on the Left Bank in search of the Priments. Even if his official mission were to be frustrated, he could at least discharge a simple domestic duty. He found the Huguenot family living in the shadow of the Church of St Séverin, whose *curé*, Jean Prévost, was the most notorious of the anti-Huguenot preachers and had set up in his churchyard an enormous painting of Queen Elizabeth presiding over the tortures and deaths of the Catholic martyrs, Edmund Campion and his companions, four years ago in London. It was intended as a warning to all good Parisians of what might be expected in Paris if Henry of Navarre, the Huguenot leader and heir-apparent to the French throne, should ever wear the crown.

The matter was urgently topical. Seven weeks earlier the Pope had excommunicated Henry of Navarre and proclaimed him incapable of succeeding, because of his heresy, to the diadem of St Louis. The King of France, Henri III, had on the advice of his mother, Catherine de Medici, issued an edict declaring that henceforth only Catholicism would be tolerated in France and that the exercise of the *religion prétendue réformée* was forbidden. To enforce this, the King had to rely on the League which was, according to the first article of its constitution, 'an association of Catholic princes, lords and gentlemen for the upholding of the sole supremacy of the Catholic, Apostolic, Roman Church'. During the last few years the League had so grown in strength that it now controlled Champagne, Picardy, Burgundy, Berri, Dauphiné, Brittany and a considerable part of Normandy and had complete control of Paris itself where its chief, Henry, Duke of Guise, was the idol of the Parisians. France was thus on the verge of a bitter civil war, already being talked of as 'the War of the Three Henries'—Henri III, Henry of Navarre and Henry of Guise—the result of which was unpredictable but from which many hoped and more feared that the Duke of Guise, leading the army of the League, might emerge as the eventual King of France. *

This general situation Marlowe, of course, knew well enough from his stay in Rheims earlier in the year. Though Henry of Navarre's excommunication had not in fact taken place until after Marlowe's return to England, it was generally anticipated and its possible consequences had loomed large in the academic arguments about the lawfulness of killing an excommunicated sovereign. And though in Rheims he had twice caught sight of the Duke of Guise's youngest brother who was its Cardinal-Archbishop, his attitude had been one of detached interest. He remained an outside observer.

But now in Paris he was made by the Priments' friends to see everything through Huguenot eyes. An emotional torrent of fear and hatred was unleashed at the mention of the Queen-Mother and the Duke of Guise. Scripture was invoked for parallels. Catherine de Medici was a blend of Jezebel, Herodias and the scarlet-clad woman, 'the mother of harlots and abominations, drunken with the blood of the saints and the martyrs of Jesus'; Guise was a combination of Cain, Pharaoh, Herod and the Prince of Darkness himself. Fortunately, so the Huguenots believed, vengeance was imminent. God would strengthen the arm of His heroic servant, Henry of Navarre, and before long dogs would lick the Queen-Mother's blood as once they had licked Jezebel's when she was thrown to death from an upper window of her palace. As far as Guise was concerned, Marlowe

* For the personalities, policies and events of this period in detail see *Paris is Worth a Mass*.

as an Englishman, so the Priments told him, should join with them in praying that a well-directed dagger-thrust should find his heart before he gained the French crown and invaded England to put his cousin, Mary Queen of Scots, on Queen Elizabeth's throne.

Kit at length ventured to ask what would happen if God failed to defend the right.

'Then we shall have to follow our cousins to your Canterbury,' they said.

It so happened that, two days later, Marlowe caught a glimpse of Guise himself. The Duke, wishing to test the temper of Paris, had ridden up from Châlons-sur-Marne, which was the headquarters of the League, to meet *the Sixteen*—the representatives of each of the *arrondissements* of the city who were bound to each other by oath to support the League and to do all in their power to suppress the Huguenots. They were mainly merchants and lawyers and had a certain democratic and self-governing tendency of which Guise did not altogether approve, though it was inaccurate to say, as his enemies said, that he had 'put himself in the hands of the *canaille* of Paris'. He had put himself in no one's hands and, rightly, never doubted that he could control the wildest mob and enforce order were it necessary. What he could not do was to prevent *the Sixteen*, in his absence, making plans of their own.

His swift visit to Paris, on this occasion, was made in secret and he arrived in the darkness of the early morning at his Paris mansion, the Hôtel de Guise in the rue St Honoré; but the rumour of his presence soon spread and by the time that Marlowe, about ten o'clock, started on his daily exploration of the city, the crowd round the Hôtel was already dense and steadily increasing. When at last the Duke emerged, his reception was of a wild, hysterical, enthusiasm such as Marlowe had never even imagined, let alone experienced. He heard himself, though crushed almost to breathlessness, yet mustering enough breath to shout compulsively *Vive Guise! Vive Guise!* with the rest and then marvelling at himself as he watched the Duke, with an arrogant courtesy, doff his green-plumed hat to the mob.

Instead of continuing on his way, Kit returned to his lodging and asked Berdon if he could provide him with some paper, a quill and an ink-pot.

'You have found matter for a despatch?' asked Berdon, not hiding his curiosity.

'Yes,' Marlowe answered curtly and with the writing materials ran up to his attic.

But what he wrote was not a despatch or even a letter. The playwright in him had seen in the Duke a perfect Machiavellian hero, such as he could use in a contemporary, instead of a classical, play. While the experience was still hot on him, he would put it into words, endeavour to capture the character of 'King of Paris' as it had stamped itself on his consciousness.

> What glory is there in a common good
> That hangs for every peasant to achieve?

he wrote.

> That I like best that flies beyond my reach.
> Set me to scale the high Pyramides,
> And thereon set the diadem of France;
> I'll either rend it with my nails to naught,
> Or mount the top with my aspiring wings,
> Although my downfall be the deepest Hell.
> For this I wake, when others think I sleep;
> For this I wait that scorn attendance else;
> For this, my quenchless thirst, whereon I build,
> Hath often pleaded kindred to the king;
> For this, this head, this heart, this hand, this sword,
> Contrives, imagines, fully executes,
> Matters of import aiméd at by many,
> Yet understood by none.
> For this hath Heaven engender'd me of earth;
> For this, this earth sustains this body's weight,
> And with this weight I'll counterpoise a crown
> Or with seditions weary all the world.
> Then, Guise, since all cards are within thy hands
> To shuffle or to cut, take this as surest thing
> That, right or wrong, thou deal thyself a king.

The day before Marlowe's week of waiting ended and there was still no sign of Gilbert Gifford, new visitors arrived at the house. That they were of some importance was evident from the fact that Berdon was having the best rooms cleaned and prepared for them.

'They wish to see you before you leave,' Berdon informed Kit.

'Why?'

'Orders from Master Poley, probably.'

'Do I know them?'

'How should I know? They are Master Francis and Master Williamson—Theobald Williamson, of course: Nicholas is in the Gatehouse.'

Marlowe had never heard of Francis or of either Williamson and certainly had no information that one of them was in prison. Berdon obviously attributed to him more importance in the counsels of Poley than he had or was ever likely to have, so he merely nodded as sagely as he could to confirm the impression. Nothing more was said and he was unprepared for the shock of finding that 'Theobald Williamson' was Tom Walsingham and 'Francis' the man who had been with him at Canterbury, Ingram Frizer.

Frizer, a family servant of the Walsinghams, had known Tom from childhood. At Scadbury, the seat of Sir Thomas Walsingham, Sheriff of Kent, he had watched the two boys, Edmund and Thomas, grow up and he had come to dote on the younger as a nurse on her favourite charge. In all the natural boyhood quarrels and rivalries of the brothers, Frizer had supported Tom when most of the servants sided sycophantically with the heir and his undiscriminating vehemence had at first wounded and then infuriated Edmund to such an extent that when Sir Thomas's sudden and unexpected death left him as Lord of the Manor his first act had been to dismiss Frizer and warn him never to show his face at Scadbury again.

Frizer had then devoted his life to looking after 'Master Tom', not only becoming his unpaid personal servant but augmenting his small annuity with his own savings and what money he could procure by the exercise of his wits. He was in process of negotiating the purchase of the *Angel Inn* in his native town of Basingstoke as a property which would assure him and his young master a regular income of sorts.

If Ingram Frizer's devotion to Tom Walsingham had in it a loyalty not altogether unadmirable, its total effect on the youth had been to produce the characteristic symptoms of a spoilt child—instability, weakness and ingratitude—so that Tom's usual attitude to him in public was an arrogant discourtesy. That Frizer could endure it without any sign of resentment was due to the strain in him which made him a natural servitor. He was one of those unfortunates who need a master for their own survival. Servility was second nature to him. He was born cringing.

It was this aspect of him, an aura of obsequiousness which clung to him like a physical emanation, which made Marlowe take an instant dislike to him, even before he knew who he was. Their antithetical temperaments clashed at the deepest level and their mutual antagonism was altogether independent of Tom Walsingham, whose existence, however, soon added to the hatred the more rational motive of jealousy.

They were all scrupulously courteous on their meeting.

Kit said: 'I understand from our host that you wish to see me.'

'If you are indeed Master Christopher Marlowe,' said Tom.

'That, Master Thomas Walsingham, is my only name.'

Kit was surprised at himself. He had often enough imagined and sometimes even rehearsed the first words he would say if Eros should ever be compassionate enough to grant him a meeting with his love. He had invented arresting sentences he might have used had he had the courage to carry to its conclusion the pursuit at Canterbury. He had even wondered whether he might not be too tongue-tied to say anything at all. But never had he considered it within the bounds of possibility to speak as he was now speaking.

Frizer said angrily: 'Berdon had no right to give you any name for my master but Williamson. It might lead him into some danger.'

'He gave me that name, so he is not to blame. It chanced that I know the true one.'

'Have we then met before, Master Marlowe?' asked Tom. 'I must confess I cannot remember it.'

'Why should you? I am hardly memorable. And it was only a moment's passing in your cousin's, Sir Francis's, mansion in Seething Lane.'

Thomas looked at him more carefully. As their eyes met, Kit

gained great comfort. He was certain that his interest was returned. Tom's next words confirmed it.

'Yes, yes, of course. It was in the summer and you were with Robin Poley. I was going to Philip Sidney's apartments. I hoped Robin would stop and make us acquainted.'

Kit's voice betrayed more than he intended as he answered, 'So did I.'

Frizer said: 'I remember the occasion.'

'You weren't there,' snapped Tom, 'so you can't possibly remember it.'

'But you told me of it at once,' said Frizer smoothly. 'You said that you had seen Poley with a young man wearing a cobweb-lawn collar and that it was a miracle to see anything so fashionable in the Seething Lane house.' He turned to Marlowe and explained: 'Master Thomas has a rare eye for the fashions whoever wears them—a most rare eye.'

'What business is it that you wish to see me on, Master Walsingham?' said Kit.

'To give you Robin Poley's message that there is no need for you to leave the letter to Gilbert Gifford with Berdon, as I shall be here to make any arrangements. I gather you have not seen Gifford?'

'No. I have found no trace of him. Does Master Poley want the letter back?'

'He did not say so.'

As Marlowe drew the letter from his doublet, Frizer, holding out his hand, said: 'Nevertheless it would probably be wiser if we kept it to avoid any misunderstanding.'

Marlowe pushed past him, tore the letter in half and threw it in the fire.

9. The Triumph of Sir Francis Walsingham

Marlowe decided to leave Paris immediately now that his mission, such as it was, was ended rather than accomplished. He was uncertain what kind of reception he could expect from Poley and, for the moment, he did not greatly care. 'The Service' had lost any appeal it might ever have had and, for the first time, he was anxious to get back to the routine of Cambridge. The disciplines of the mind, pedantic and constricting as they might be, offered a respite from the unpredictable interplay of political 'practising'. Though he was still adamant against ordination, he was prepared to study unremittingly for his Master's degree.

Next morning he had packed his few possessions and was on the point of going downstairs to return the borrowed inkstand when there was a knock at his attic door. It was Tom Walsingham, who said: 'I'm glad I've caught you before you go.'

Fighting to preserve a nonchalance of tone, Kit said: 'Is there some service I can render you in England? It would give me much pleasure if I could do so. I was overhasty yesterday.'

'In what way?'

'Burning the letter.'

'Why should you think that matters?'

'I suppose it could be called a state document. I am still not sufficiently versed in these things to have a proper understanding of them; but I should not wish to cause you any inconvenience and if there is anything I can explain to Master Poley—'

Laughingly, Tom broke through the barrier of the curiously stilted speech: 'My dear Kit, it's of no consequence whatever. You mustn't take Robin Poley's little scheme so ridiculously seriously. No, I came to say that I hope we can meet again in England. Will you visit me?'

'Of course, if you invite me.'

'And one other thing. It was not because of your collar that I remembered you. That was an invention of Ingram's. Though the collar is fine enough.'

As he fingered the delicate lawn, Marlowe bent his head so that his cheek rested on the slim hand. The pressure was returned and the two young men fell into each other's arms.

Poley, when Marlowe reported to him on his return to London, questioned him closely about Gilbert Gifford. Had anyone seen him? Were there any rumours of his whereabouts? What was Berdon's latest information about him? Had Marlowe himself taken any particular steps to find him? Poley's urgency was due to the fact that Sir Philip Sidney had crossed to the Netherlands to take up his Governorship at Flushing and written home complaining to his father-in-law: 'I am here among the worst-humoured people in a garrison no more able to command Flushing than the Tower is to answer for London. I can in no way answer for anything unless I be increased by at least 400 men.' His personal staff was new and inexperienced and he would have welcomed Poley's organising ability even more than a regiment of recruits. But until the indispensable Gifford had set the Great Design in motion Walsingham would not allow Poley to leave England in any circumstances whatever.

As Poley was now questioning Marlowe, he privately blamed him for not having made more intensive efforts to trace Gifford. It was true that he had given him no specific instructions to do so, but anyone worth his place in the Service would have taken it for granted. He revised his original judgment of his potential value. He carefully gave Kit two crowns, told him to work hard at Cambridge next term and made a resolve never to employ him again on any but the simplest utilitarian occasions.

Gilbert Gifford eventually arrived in London a few days before Christmas and went immediately, as had been arranged, to lodge in Leadenhall Market with Thomas Phillips, an expert forger, fluent in French and Italian and with the rare gift of being able to break almost any cipher. He was about thirty, small and pockmarked, and entirely loyal to Walsingham.

Gifford's first visit was to the French Embassy to present various letters of credit (including one from Morgan, Mary Queen of Scots's treacherous secretary),* testifying to his honesty and fidelity and his devotion to the Catholic religion and the Queen of Scots. The French Ambassador, though at first suspicious, eventually accepted Gifford's account of himself— that he had been sent to England by the Queen's servants and friends in Paris and that he had undertaken, solely *à cause de la religion*, to organise a secret post by which the Queen could communicate with the outside world again.

Gifford next resumed his friendship with the pledged regicides, Savage, studying at Barnard's Inn, and Father Ballard who, as Captain Fortescue, had become as well-known and flamboyant a figure in the tavern life of London as he had been in Rheims. Gilbert rallied them a little sadly on their tardiness in removing Queen Elizabeth and promised to discuss ways and means with them when he returned from a short visit he was about to make to his family's estates in the Midlands.

Finally he visited his father, old John Gifford of Chillington, who was still in prison for his Catholicism, to tell him that he was about to enter the priesthood and to beg his blessing and his aid in the scheme he had afoot to aid the Queen of Scots. His father, overjoyed, wrote to his friends and tenants on his Staffordshire estate which adjoined Chartley, where Mary Queen of Scots was imprisoned, asking them to give Gilbert any assistance he might need.† He arranged with the steward of the Chartley estate, one Newport, to let him lodge with him to facilitate arrangements.

A brewer from Burton was induced—for a consideration—to include in his delivery of the beer to the Queen of Scots's household any letters which Gifford should deliver him. He would

---

* Morgan's treachery, though long suspected by historians, was finally established only in 1964 in a work of monumental scholarship *An Elizabethan Problem* by Leo Hicks.
† When he eventually discovered Gilbert's real purpose he wrote broken-heartedly: 'I would to God he had never been born. I may well say: "Happy is the barren that hath no child." '

enclose them in a corked tube and slip it through the bung-hole of one of the casks. In the same way, when he collected his empties, he was to look for the tube and deliver it to Gifford or a deputy who would be in the neighbourhood.

Everything was thus reduced to an efficient simplicity. Mary Queen of Scots's correspondence was known in every detail to Sir Francis Walsingham long before the recipients of her letters received them. The brewer, meaning no evil, delivered the tube containing them to Gifford who passed them on immediately to Phillips who deciphered them and sent a copy *en clair* to Walsingham. The letters were then resealed by Arthur Gregory, Walsingham's expert in that particular art, and taken by Gifford to the French Embassy whence they were distributed under diplomatic immunity. Incoming letters were similarly treated in the interval between Gifford's collection of them from the French Embassy and his delivery of them to the 'honest man' —as they called him, not altogether in irony—the brewer. The trap was perfect and Gifford, as if to atone for his delay in arrival, worked so quickly that it was completed by the end of the second week in January.

The only untoward circumstance was that, by the end of April, there was still nothing in any of the letters which could possibly be twisted to serve Walsingham's purpose. There was no suggestion of any plot or plan against Queen Elizabeth. There was, indeed, nothing which could not have been openly shown to her. Ambassadorial protocol was scrupulously observed. It was clear that, if the Grand Design were to succeed, some new correspondents must be found. Walsingham sent Gifford back to Paris to ask Morgan who among English Catholics would be the most useful for his purpose. In the middle of May Gifford returned with the name of Anthony Babington.

Babington, who was twenty-five, was a Derbyshire gentleman 'of enchanting manners and wit' and a reasonable fortune. His seat was at Dethick, two miles from Matlock, and he owned considerable property in several Midland counties as well as a mansion in the Barbican in London. He had once been a page in the household of the Earl of Shrewsbury, the gaoler of Mary Queen of Scots, and he had never lost his boyish romantic devotion to the Queen. When, a few years later, he was visiting Paris, Morgan (who had been Shrewsbury's secretary at the same time as Babington had been his page) asked him to find some way of delivering certain letters to Mary Queen of Scots and Babington, through friends in Shrewsbury's household, had managed to do so. When, however, Mary was removed from Shrewsbury's charge to another and stricter imprisonment at Chartley and all her correspondence cut off, further service was impossible.

Babington had then undertaken to serve the Faith in another capacity—to aid the priests who at the risk of their lives still secretly administered the sacraments to Catholics. 'Without priests', as he put it, 'we desire not to live, holding them more necessary to our souls than food to our bodies.' Babington and a few Catholic friends of his own age therefore devoted themselves to serving them, providing funds, helping them to find places of refuge, conveying them in secret from one part of the country to another. Having his own coach and travelling constantly between London and the Midlands, he found this not difficult, though it was dangerous enough, since 'the entertainment and accompaniment of Catholic priests' involved the penalties for high treason.

In this way Babington had come to know Father Ballard, meeting him—as 'Captain Foscue'—openly enough, dining at the *King's Head* in Fish Street or drinking at the *Plough* tavern by Temple Bar. When Ballard had taken him partly into his confidence and suggested that an attack on England by the King of Spain and the Duke of Guise for the freeing of Mary Queen of Scots would give English Catholics the opportunity of rising for the Faith Babington was sceptical and said that very few English Catholics were likely to respond. 'Most of us', he said, 'would rather be dragged by the heels to Tyburn for our religion than have the realm reformed by strangers.'

'But if the Pope should once more pronounce Queen Elizabeth excommunicate?'

'It would make no difference. The State is so well settled that as long as she is alive, nothing can be looked for.'

'That difficulty', said the priest, 'will be taken away. The means are already made. Her life can be no hindrance.'

But when he took him into his confidence and revealed the oath Savage had taken Babington recoiled in horror and refused to have anything to do with it, though, after some days of agonised consideration, he did not oppose outright the idea of kidnapping Queen Elizabeth and making the release of Mary Queen of Scots and the toleration of Catholicism the condition for freeing her. And, should such a desperate enterprise be decided on, he reserved for himself the main point of danger, whatever that might be.

Yet the more he considered it the more impossible the whole situation seemed, and he began to think seriously of going to live abroad. He would visit France again and go on to Italy where, if all the good things he had heard about Italy were true, he would settle, dedicating himself to study and relinquishing all idea of meddling in affairs of state. Some of his friends would certainly come with him, provided they could get a licence to travel, which he had no reason to suppose would be refused. He applied to Sir Francis Walsingham, as the Secretary of State responsible for these matters, and in due course received an invitation to call on him.

Babington was received by Robert Poley whom he knew only by his reputation as being secretly a good practising Catholic who heard Mass in private whenever possible and was well regarded by all Catholics on account of his extravagant, almost importunate, generosity to Catholic priests. Poley showed himself the soul of sympathetic understanding and admitted that he would himself have liked to accompany Babington abroad were it not that, as a Catholic under some suspicion, he was bound with two sureties to present himself every twenty days at the court.

Babington, returning charm with charm, suggested that, if money were at the root of Poley's inability to travel, he would be only too delighted to advance him £50 immediately and further sums as he might need them.

For a little while they talked as one Catholic to another before Babington asked Poley to advise him on his wisest approach to Sir Francis.

'Be completely open with him,' said Poley. 'He knows you by repute as a loyal Catholic who pays the recusancy fines. It might ease matters if you offered to show your loyalty by reporting any events in the countries of your travels which you feel he ought to know for England's sake.'

Babington followed this advice and found Walsingham surprisingly amenable. The Secretary promised to look into the matter as speedily as he could. Poley on his part offered to do his utmost to expedite the licence; and Babington returned in high spirits to his new lodgings in Hern's Rents, Holborn, close to the London house of his aunt, Lady Darcy.

He found a visitor awaiting him—a young man who introduced himself as Gilbert Gifford and explained that he had just returned from a visit to Paris where Thomas Morgan had given him Babington's name as a loyal Catholic who in the past had rendered certain services to the Queen of Scots, and might be prepared to do so again.

Babington answered that he was on the point of leaving the country as he saw no chance of a Catholic being able to live a tolerable life or to practise his religion in England. As far as Mary Queen of Scots was concerned, he had in the past managed to get some letters delivered on her behalf, but now under the conditions of her new and stricter imprisonment such a service was impossible.

'But I can assure you', said Gifford, 'that will all be changed soon enough.'

'How?' asked Babington.

'I am not yet at liberty to tell you,' answered Gifford, 'but I beg you not to leave the country in despair until you receive some proof of what I say.'

The 'proof' arrived a few days later—a letter from Mary Queen of Scots, addressed to 'Master Anthony Babington dwelling most in Derbyshire in a house of his own' and informing him that she had been advised by Thomas Morgan in Paris that it was possible for him to communicate with her again. 'I pray you therefore', she wrote, 'from henceforth to write unto me as often as you can of all occurrences which you may judge in any wise important to the good of my affairs.'

With his answer accepting the charge Babington enclosed a note to the Queen's French Secretary, Nau: 'I would gladly understand what opinion you hold of one Robert Poley, whom I find to have intelligence of Her Majesty's occasions. I am private with the man and by means thereof know somewhat.'

Though Babington was more and more impressed by Robin Poley the more he saw of him he felt it necessary to check with higher authority now it was possible and he was relieved when Nau replied that 'there is great assurance given of Mr Poley's faithful serving of Her Majesty and by his own letters he hath vowed and promised the same. As yet Her Majesty's experience of him is not so great as I dare embolden you to trust him much. Let me know plainly what you understand of him.'

Things were obviously left to his own discretion and in this matter he had no doubt Robin Poley, no less than himself and Gilbert Gifford and Father Ballard, would die, if need be, for the Faith. All that was needed was for Babington to recruit from his own Catholic friends, especially those who, as Gentlemen Pensioners, had easy access to Queen Elizabeth, half a dozen 'of stout courage', reckless enough to seize her royal person and hold it 'in some strong place' against the release of Mary Queen of Scots.

During June and July they all discussed the matter interminably, not as conspirators meeting secretly, but showing themselves openly, as carefree gallants, at the taverns they had always been accustomed to patronise—the *Three Tuns* in Newgate Market, the *Plough* and the *Rose* near Temple Bar, the *Castle* near the Exchange (this was 'Captain Foscue's' favourite haunt, 'most safe' because 'it hath two doors')—and at the barber's just outside Bishopsgate where Babington's portrait was hung as an indication that the shop was worthy to be patronised by the *élite*. In an expansive moment, Babington had had it inscribed with the heroic verse: *Hi mihi sunt comites quos ipsa pericula iungunt.** But though this might be interpreted as a wittily ironical allusion to the dangers of the razor, Poley suggested it was foolish to run any risk by even a recondite clue and Babington changed it to *Quorsum haec alia properantibus?†* The barber's shop was a convenient rendezvous for Poley's own residence, 'The Garden', about three minutes' walk away, where, when secrecy was considered advisable, the conspirators foregathered.

At length, after detailed discussion and contrary counsels, much quoting of ecclesiastical sanctions and weighing of political

* My comrades these whom very peril draws.
† To what purpose these things to those departing hence?

90

possibilities, they reduced their courses of action to three—to rouse the Catholics of the country to support a possible invasion by the Duke of Guise aided by Philip of Spain for the liberation of Mary Queen of Scots; for a picked band of Catholic gentlemen to surprise and abduct Queen Elizabeth; or themselves, if the necessary permit could be obtained from Walsingham, to leave England. Poley and Father Ballard, vehemently supported by Gilbert Gifford, were in favour of a combination of the first and second, though Savage was still prepared to fulfil his vow and substitute for abduction the assassination of Queen Elizabeth, and Babington and his personal friends, who wished to delay any decisive action until the foreign situation became clearer,* were easily overborne. The only point they gained was that no action should be taken until they had consulted Mary Queen of Scots.

Babington therefore wrote to her, telling her that he had intended to emigrate when 'standing upon my departure, there was addressed to me from parts beyond the seas a man of virtue and learning and of singular zeal to the Catholic cause who informed me of great preparation by the Christian Princes (Your Majesty's allies) for the deliverance of our country from the miserable state wherein it hath too long lain'. The result of Gifford's visit and information was to make Babington 'consider by what means, with the hazard of my life and friends in general, I might do your sacred Majesty one good day's service'. The considerations he put down for the carrying-out of 'the last hope ever to recover the faith of our forefathers and to redeem ourselves from the servitude and bondage which heresy has imposed on us with the loss of thousands of souls' were

'First, assuring of invasion, sufficient strength in the invader;
Ports to arrive at appointed, with a strong party at every place to join with them and warrant their landing;
The deliverance of Your Majesty;
The dispatch of the usurping Competitor.'

* Gifford had been assured in France that the invasion was about to take place and there is no reason to suppose that he did not himself believe it. Though the Spanish Armada did not in fact sail for another two years—the July of 1588—King Philip had completed his plans for it and many people (including Walsingham) were convinced that an invasion in this July 1586 was a possibility.

These matters had been taken care of. He himself with ten gentlemen and a hundred followers would undertake to release her from Chartley, while 'the usurping Competitor' would be dealt with by 'six noble gentlemen, all my private friends'.

'Forasmuch as delay is extreme dangerous, may it please your most excellent Majesty', asked Babington, 'by your wisdom to direct us and by your princely authority to enable such as may to advance the affair.'

This curious, indiscreet letter, written under the influence of the enthusiasm of Gifford and Poley, Babington duly delivered for forwarding at the French Embassy, where the next day Gifford secretly collected it, took it to Phillips to decipher and copy, presented the copy to Poley to give to Walsingham and delivered the original to the 'honest man', the brewer, to pass in, in the usual manner, to the Queen of Scots.

When, in the absence of Babington, Gifford and Poley read it over, they indulged in some self-congratulatory laughter that their work had been so well and quickly accomplished. The letter, establishing a plot against Queen Elizabeth on Mary's behalf, could, whatever Mary might reply, be used under the new Act as the Queen of Scots' death-warrant. Gilbert Gifford had only one more duty to perform—to collect Mary Queen of Scots' reply from Chartley and to deliver it to Phillips. This he did and the same night, without taking any farewells, crossed to France and was never seen in England again. He knew too well the unkind fate which, in Walsingham's world, was apt to overtake those whose knowledge was considerable but whose utility was at an end. *

Poley, contemplating the next few weeks, saw increasing complications looming. It was, in any case, difficult enough to keep a plot of this magnitude going smoothly until the moment was ripe to 'discover' it. Some of the victims might become suspicious and make their escape. Some well-intentioned magistrate might accidentally blunder on to part of it and make an arrest—a secret priest, for instance—which would give the

---

* The rest of his career was short. He managed to get himself priested but shortly after his ordination was arrested in a brothel and died in prison, still under thirty. The papers found when his lodgings were searched caused the English Ambassador to write to Walsingham: 'They have letters which prove that he was the setter-on of the gentlemen in the late enterprise; and that he was engaged for this by you with Her Majesty's knowledge.'

alarm and ruin everything. The maximum number of Walsingham's agents was required to shepherd the 'conspirators' smoothly to their doom. Berdon, for one, had been sent for from Paris; but his presence did not really compensate for Gifford's absence. Moreover, the Court had just removed to Richmond, more difficult of access than Greenwich, and as the Queen insisted on being informed of every move and Walsingham had developed a painful boil on his leg which made movement difficult, Poley foresaw that more responsibility than he cared for would be laid on him. He would need all the help he could get and, in spite of his recent resolve, might have to use Marlowe again.

It was Babington, however, who was the most affected by the writing of the letter most of which he realised when he considered it coolly in retrospect was simply not true. The 'ten gentlemen' and the 'hundred our followers' existed only in his optimistic imagination and of the 'six gentlemen' ready to remove 'the usurping competitor' there was only the oath-bound Savage, Gifford (who was no longer available) and one Anthony Tuichenor, one of Sir Walter Raleigh's circle who had volunteered, provided that Queen Elizabeth was in no way harmed, to arrange for conveying her to a safe place of keeping —a place, so he let it be understood, that Raleigh himself would assist in providing.

The position of Sir Walter Raleigh was equivocal. In the spring he had been involved with Mendoza, the Spanish Ambassador in Paris, whom he had known well when he had been Ambassador in London, about a pension from Spain. 'I signified to him', Mendoza wrote to King Philip, 'how wise it would be for him to offer his services to Your Majesty, as the Queen's favour to him could not last long. If he would attend sincerely to Your Majesty's interests in England, apart from the direct reward he would receive Your Majesty's support when occasion arose that might prevent him from falling.'

There was nothing particularly strange in such an arrangement—the English Ambassador in Paris, Sir Edward Stafford, was deep in King Philip's pay—and it would, by its nature, be the most secret of arrangements, but when Raleigh proposed openly to sell to Spain two of his excellent privateering vessels at 5,000 crowns apiece—at a time when the two countries were preparing for war—King Philip became both sceptical and suspicious. Though Mendoza assured him that 'Raleigh is much more desirous of sending to Spain his own two ships for sale than to use them for robbery', the King replied: 'It is out of the question. It is not improbable that this is some kind of trick.'

Raleigh was desperate for money and as much as he could get. The expedition he had sent to Virginia was on the verge of collapsing unless he could provide supplies and reinforcements. At first everything had gone well enough and the colonists had regarded the island where Sir Richard Grenville had put them ashore in the summer of 1585 somewhat in the nature of an earthly paradise. It was, so the Governor, Ralph Lane, had written, 'so abounding with sweet trees which bring such sundry rich and pleasant gums, grapes of such greatness, yet wild, as France, Spain nor Italy have no greater; so many sorts of apothecary drugs; such several kinds of flax and one kind like silk and sundry other rich commodities that, were this goodliest and most pleasing territory in the world once inhabited by Englishmen, no realm in Christendom were comparable with it'.

The exploitation of these resources would take time and the Indians, friendly at first, had watched with growing apprehension the settlers' exploration of their coast. Instead of aiding and trading, the natives started either to harass them or to withdraw and leave them without the means of getting food. The winter was a hard one. Fighting broke out. An Indian chieftain was killed and each side feared an attempt at extermination by the other.

When Sir Francis Drake in the course of one of his plundering expeditions in the Spanish Main called at the island to see how his fellow-Devonians were faring, they thankfully accepted his offer to get them home and 'for fear that they should be left behind they left all things confusedly, as if they had been chased from thence by a mighty army; and no doubt so they were, for the hand of God came upon them for the cruelty and outrages committed by some of them against the native inhabitants'.

The unsuccessful colonists in the *Bark Bonner*, which Drake had lent them, put in at Portsmouth at the end of July in the wake of Drake's own gold-crammed vessels and, half-starved

and despairing, offered an instructive illustration of the comparative rewards of hard work and ruthless robbery.

Yet Raleigh discovered, as he greeted Hariot on that July 29,
that they had brought him gold of a sort—the leaves of 'a herb
which is sowed apart by itself and is called by the natives
Uppawaoc. In the West Indies it has different names according
to the several places where it grows. The Spaniards generally
call it Tobacco and its medicinal virtues alone would require a
volume to narrate.' Hariot assured Raleigh that he had, in his
report on Virginia, not neglected its praises and would do his
utmost to popularise it, so that something might be saved from
the failure of the expedition.

On the same day that tobacco made its first appearance in
England, the final touch was added to Walsingham's Grand
Design. Mary Queen of Scots' reply was delivered to Babington.
It was not exactly the reply Mary Queen of Scots had written.
Although the mere reception of Babington's letter made her
mortally guilty and the very existence of a reply, confirming the
reception, justified Phillips in triumphantly drawing a gallows
on it, from the point of view of Queen Elizabeth, it left something to be desired. She wished to be able to represent to foreign
courts that Mary herself had taken a personal interest in the
arrangements. And of this Mary's letter afforded no evidence.
Elizabeth therefore suggested to Walsingham that Phillips
should forge a postscript which would put the question of
Mary's active complicity beyond doubt.

'I would be glad to know', the forged postscript ran, 'the
names and qualities of the six gentlemen which are to accomplish
the designment, for it may be that I shall be able, upon knowledge of the parties, to give you some further advice necessary
to be followed therein, as also from time to time particularly how
you proceed, and as soon as you may (for the same purpose) who
be already, and how far, everyone is privy hereunto.'

There was now no reason why all the conspirators should not
be arrested immediately, but Queen Elizabeth insisted, much to
Walsingham's annoyance, that nothing should be done until
Babington's answer to the Queen of Scots was safely in Government hands. This involved an indefinite delay during which

surveillance would have to be stretched to its limits and Poley, even more exasperated than Walsingham, tried to arrange for meetings of the conspirators to be held as far as possible at his own house.

Marlowe obeyed Poley's summons somewhat reluctantly. He was prepared to refuse another assignment abroad because he had planned to spend most of the Long Vacation in London staying with Tom Watson, making further acquaintance with men and things theatrical. Once in Poley's presence, however, his resolve weakened and as soon as he understood that he would be required for no more than a week—if, indeed, so long—and that the sphere of his service would be London, he accepted without demur.

'It will be easier than last time,' said Poley, smiling. 'Then you had to find someone. Now all you have to do is not to lose someone.'

He proceeded to explain that a young and valued friend of his named Anthony Babington was engaged in a project which needed much consultation. In this Babington had come to rely so much on Poley that he did not care to act without him.

'But as it happens, I have other duties,' said Poley. 'With the Court at Richmond and Sir Francis indisposed, I cannot spend all my time with Anthony. I may have to visit Her Majesty in Sir Francis's place. There are a hundred and one matters which may crop up unexpectedly. So to reassure Master Babington and to relieve any anxiety, I shall leave you in my place.'

'I appreciate the honour,' said Marlowe, 'but I cannot cozen myself into supposing that I can do him the service or give him the counsel that you can.'

'Naturally. But that is not required. All that is necessary is for me to leave you with knowledge of my whereabouts so that you can send a messenger if there is anything of urgency needing consultation. And if there is anyone else he wishes to see, you can go with him.'

'So,' thought Marlowe, 'I am to act as gaoler to this Babington, whoever he may be!' But aloud he said: 'And if he does not wish for my company, I am still not to lose him?'

'Precisely,' said Poley.

'When am I to meet him?'

'Tonight. We are having a little supper for six at the *Castle*. Do you know it?'

'No. I don't think so.'

'It's a good tavern near the Exchange.'

'No. In that case I'm sure I don't know it. Who are the other three?'

'You have met them before. Berdon you stayed with in Paris. Captain Fortescue and John Savage you showed your intelligence about and rendered us good service by it in Rheims.'

'Berdon, I suppose, is Thomas Beard,' said Marlowe intending to impress Poley by airing his knowledge of Berdon's *alias* in England.

'No,' said Poley, quite unimpressed, 'at the moment he is using "Thomas Rogers". You, by the way, are "Christopher Thornborough", interested in the supply of hides for shoe-making. You should know enough of that to be able to make some conversation on the subject if necessary.'

'Yes, provided I am not pressed too far. But Savage and the Captain know me a student of theology and by my own name, so might it not be—'

'That is of no consequence whatever,' Poley interrupted. 'The important thing is that Babington does not. The last thing I want is any talk of theology. It is dangerous these days. And if Babington knew you were instructed in it, he would never leave the subject.'

'I will do my best to behave like a merchant.'

Poley softened. 'You will do excellently, I am sure. All that matters is that you are a secret Catholic who, like the rest of us, would give your life for your faith. Talk as little as possible. And I promise you that on other occasions I will let you keep your own name, since you set such store by it.'

'I do not remember saying that to you.'

'Of course not, since you did not say it to me.'

'Then how—'

'You said it to Berdon in Paris.'

The supper passed off without any mischance. Marlowe was particularly impressed by Babington's dependence on Poley. He seemed unable to reach any conclusion on any subject without having first ascertained Poley's judgment. 'What is your opinion, Robin?' ran through the conversation like a refrain.

For Marlowe it was an object lesson. He wondered how far he himself had surrendered to Poley's charm and strength and whether, should he ever wish to escape from 'the Service', he would be able to should it come to a clash of wills.

Babington Marlowe found himself gradually disliking. Not only was he weak; he was over-talkative. A man endowed by nature and by circumstances with great gifts, he was unable to put them to their full use. Whatever 'project' he might have in hand—and to this the conversation had given Marlowe no clue—it would be likely to miscarry if he had the responsibility for it.

Obeying Poley's instructions, Kit spoke very little, though he wanted to get Berdon to talk of Tom Walsingham and to know whether he had managed to meet Gilbert Gifford in Paris; but a question by the Captain to the company in general about the present whereabouts of Gifford had produced so curiously strained an atmosphere that he judged it wiser to keep silent.

In the days that followed there were other meetings either at the *Castle* or the *Rose* near Temple Bar (which was Savage's favourite tavern as the *Castle* was the 'Captain's') or at Poley's house or at Babington's lodgings. The company changed, but Babington, Poley and Marlowe remained the constant and the conversation ranged over such a variety of subjects that by the Wednesday Marlowe found himself able safely to speak of poetry. On this occasion the other two persons present were Anthony Tuichenor, a Gentleman Pensioner and an intimate of Sir Walter Raleigh, and Chidiock Tichborne, Babington's closest friend, who was himself a poet. The sad return of Raleigh's expedition from the West Indies was the topic of the hour and, discussing Raleigh's protean personality, Tuichenor mentioned Sir Walter's latest lines on the mutability of life and the tyranny of Time:

> Even such is Time, which takes in trust
> Our youth, our joys, our all we have,
> And pays us but with age and dust;
> Who in the dark and silent grave

> When we have wandered all our ways,
> Shuts up the story of our days.

This gave Marlowe an opportunity to cap it with a verse of Tom Watson's poem on Time:

> Time wasteth years and months and hours,
>   Time doth consume fame, honour, wit and strength,
> Time kills the greenest herbs and sweetest flowers
>   Time wears out youth and beauty's looks at
>   length.
>   Time doth convey to ground both foe and friend,
>   And each thing else but love which hath no end.

'Yes,' said Chidiock Tichborne, 'I remember liking that when I read it* but now I prefer Raleigh's.'

'And what', asked Poley, 'are your favourite lines on the subject?'

'Those that I am writing,' said Chidiock Tichborne. 'Every poet really believes his own most recent poem is the best, though few have my honesty in admitting it.'

The others laughed and Babington asked: 'May we hear it?'

'When it is finished,' said Chidiock Tichborne.

'And you, Robin?' asked Babington.

'For me, Virgil has said everything,' answered Poley, 'here as in other things: *Sed fugit interea, fugit irreparabile tempus.'* †

There were moments when Poley experienced something like pity for his dupes. 'Or you could epitomise everything with *Sunt lachrymae rerum,'* he said softly, almost to himself.

That same evening a copy of Babington's reply to the Queen of Scots, deciphered in the usual way by Phillips, had reached Walsingham. It made the Secretary the more angry that he had been forced to wait for it, since it contained no answer to the forged postscript inquiring the names of the 'six gentlemen' but indulged in such pious generalities as: 'It is God's cause, the Church's and Your Majesty's, an enterprise honourable to God and man, undertaken in zeal and devotion, free from all ambition and temporal regard and therefore no doubt will succeed

* It had been published in Watson's best-selling *Hekatompathia* four years earlier— in 1582.
† Meanwhile Time is flying, flying relentlessly.

happily.' Walsingham decided to act immediately and gave Poley his final instructions.

On the Thursday morning Poley called on Babington at ten o'clock and found him still in bed. Hysterically he gave him the news that 'the Captain' had been arrested. It was the work, Poley thought, of an officious, priest-hunting magistrate who had discovered that 'Captain Fortescue' was in fact Father Ballard and had proceeded to hold him in custody, as he had the right—and even the duty—to do on his own initiative. It was an isolated action, Poley thought, and though unfortunate was not to be taken to mean that everything was discovered. Nevertheless, to ascertain the exact circumstances, Poley would go immediately to Court to consult Walsingham and on his return from Richmond would report to Babington at the *Grapes*, a tavern which was not one of their known haunts. Further to avert suspicion, it would be as well if Babington's companions were none of their fellow-conspirators. Poley had therefore arranged for one of Sir Francis's own confidential secretaries, John Scudamore, and Christopher Thornborough, the pleasant young dealer in hides, to keep him company while waiting at the *Grapes*.

As soon as Poley had left for Richmond Babington became a prey to every kind of anxiety. His first fear was that he had betrayed Poley and his other associates to their deaths. In the far background of his thoughts was a scarcely-admitted suspicion that everything was not what it seemed. Denied action, he found some relief in writing a letter to Poley to be delivered he had not considered where or when.

'Robin,
    Sollicitae non possunt curae mutare aranei stamina fusi!*
I am ready to endure whatsoever shall be inflicted—*Et facere et pati Romanorum est.*†
    What my course hath been towards Mr Secretary you can witness; what my love towards you, yourself can best tell.

---

* Father Pollen translates this: 'Nor care nor cautel ever mends Of spiders' webs the broken ends.'
† Both to dare and to suffer is worthy of Romans.

I am the same I always pretended. I pray God you be and ever so remain towards me. Take heed to your own part, lest of these my misfortunes you bear the blame.

Est exilium inter malos vivere! *

Farewell, sweet Robin, if as I take thee, true to me.

If not, Adieu—*omnium bipedum nequissimus.*†

The furnace is prepared wherein our faith must be tried.

Farewell till we meet, which God knows when.

Thine, how far thou knowest,
Anthony Babington.'

That evening at the *Grapes*, Babington, 'Thornborough' and Scudamore eventually started their meal without waiting for Poley. According to Scudamore, the vagaries of Court were such that approximation to punctuality was never to be expected. He recalled an occasion when Sir Francis Walsingham himself had been kept waiting over eight hours for an appointed audience with Her Majesty. Poley might not be back till midnight, if then. There was no point in them all going hungry and, speaking for himself, Scudamore, who had had nothing to eat since early morning, was ravenous. Babington, though he had no appetite whatever, showed himself the perfect host he prided himself on being and ordered a liberal repast.

They were still at table when a messenger arrived with a note for Scudamore who, after glancing at it, informed the others that things were indeed as he suspected and that Poley was detained at Richmond till next day. Babington surreptitiously glanced at the note and happened to catch sight of his own name. It was all he needed. Rising casually to his feet, he announced with perfect *insouciance* that he would 'pay the reckoning'. His cloak and sword were on the back of his chair. Leaving them there, he strolled at a leisurely pace to the bar and, the moment he was out of sight from where the two men were sitting, took to his heels and ran like one pursued by the Furies.

When he did not return to the table Marlowe said: 'Ought we not to go and see what has happened to our host?'

'There is no need,' said Scudamore. 'Sir Francis's men are

* To live among the wicked, what an exile!

† Of all two-footed creatures the wickedest.

posted outside and they will follow him if he tries to go far. I shall finish my supper. By the way, Poley himself is under arrest and being sent to the Tower.'

'But this is—'

'Come, come, Master *Marlowe*,' said Scudamore, 'we are alone now, so there is no need for further pretence. I would take any wager that when Robin Poley introduced you to the Service he told you that it may always be necessary to go to prison to give colour to an action.'

'Then, since you seem to know everything, Master Scudamore—if that is your name—what am I to do?'

'Whatever you like, I imagine. Robin left no instructions. You are not yet of sufficient importance to be particularly prescribed for. At the moment, let us finish this excellent meal.'

'You can have my portion,' said Marlowe and left him.

He went straight to Thomas Watson's lodgings in Norton Folgate to beg a night or two's hospitality, secretly hoping to be offered more. He was not disappointed. The ebullient poet welcomed him enthusiastically and asked him to stay until the beginning of the Michaelmas Term called him back to his final year at Cambridge.

So it was that Marlowe watched from the outside the culmination of the Grand Design in which he had played his part, however small and even negligible, on the inside—the final triumph of Sir Francis Walsingham in unmasking 'the Babington Plot' and so rousing the people of England to a sense of their country's dire peril from the wicked Papists who, at the bidding of the infamous Queen of Scots, were attempting to murder Queen Elizabeth. For good measure, to impress the ordinary thinking citizen, several other charges were added. The 'wicked and devilish youths' set on by 'devilish priests, the ministers of the Pope' had planned to sack the city of London, 'to rob and destroy all the wealthy subjects of this realm and to kill divers of the Privy Council' (including Sir Francis Walsingham), to set the navy on fire and to 'cloy all the great ordnance'.

The effect on Londoners was most gratifying. It was as if England had escaped a new St Bartholomew. The citizens rang their bells, marched about with pipe and tabor, alternately sang psalms and danced in the streets, and shouted *Long live the Queen* till 'the air rang withal'. After the trial and execution of thirteen of the 'hellish plotters', headed by Babington and Father Ballard, there was a spate of pamphlets, ballads and rhymes 'so that what by one mean and what by another all England was made acquainted with this horrible conspiracy'.

One of these anthologies, *Verses of Praise and Joy,* was put together by Thomas Kyd who came to consult Watson and Marlowe about a difficult decision he had to make. He had managed to procure a poem which one of the conspirators was said to have written the night before his execution. Would the inclusion of it damage the sales of the book?

'What is the quality of it?' asked Watson.

Kyd read it to them:

> My prime of youth is but a frost of cares,
>   My feast of joy is but a dish of pain,
> My field of corn is but a crop of tares,
>   And all my good is but vain hope of gain.
>   The day is past and yet I saw no sun,
>   And now I live and now my life is done.
>
> My tale was heard and yet it was not told,
>   My fruit is fallen and yet my leaves are green,
> My youth is spent and yet I am not old,
>   I saw the world and yet I was not seen.
>   My thread is cut and yet it is not spun,
>   And now I live and now my life is done.
>
> I sought my death and found it in my womb,
>   I looked for life and saw it was a shade,
> I trod the earth and knew it was my tomb,
>   And now I die and now I was but made.
>   My glass is full and now my glass is run,
>   And now I live and now my life is done.

'It seems to me to have no great merit,' said Watson. 'Who wrote it?'

'Chidiock Tichborne.'

Watson shrugged disapprovingly.

Kyd turned to Marlowe: 'Then you must give the casting vote!'

Vehemently, choking back his tears, Kit said yes.

10. The World to Conquer

Babington, on the night before his death, had prevailed on Anthony Tuichenor to visit Sir Walter Raleigh on his behalf and give him £1,000 to intercede with the Queen for his life. He made this choice because he knew that both Tuichenor and Raleigh had personal knowledge that Babington had opposed any plan to harm Elizabeth and that the official accusation that he had urged her assassination was as false as the Spanish information that her murder had been undertaken by 'one close to Sir Walter Raleigh'.

Raleigh naturally accepted the £1,000 but made no plea to his royal mistress to spare Babington and his conversation on the matter was generally presumed to have been of a somewhat different nature when it was announced that the Queen had given Raleigh all Babington's estates and, to ensure that her generosity should benefit her favourite to the greatest extent, had additionally directed that the grant should pass the Great Seal without fee.

Raleigh was now busying himself in promoting the popularity of his newly-discovered monopoly, Virginian tobacco. With his long silver pipe and his gold tobacco box, he set a fashion which the courtiers were not slow to follow. The Earl of Northumberland became an enthusiast and the possessor of scores of pipes, many of which he designed himself. In one form or another, Thomas Hariot's advertisement for it in his *Brief and True Report on the New-Found of Virginia* was disseminated and discussed: 'The leaves being dried and brought into powder, the inhabitants of Virginia take the smoke thereof by sucking it through pipes made of clay into their stomach and head from whence it purgeth superfluous phlegm and other gross humours, openeth all the pores and passages of the body and not only preserveth the body from obstructions but, if they have been of too long continuance, in short time breaketh them; whereby their bodies are notably preserved in health and know not many grievous diseases wherewith we in England are often times afflicted. We ourselves, while we were there, used to suck it after their fashion, as also since our return, and have had many rare and wonderful experiences of its virtues, as have some learned physicians also.'

Raleigh interested the Queen in it. One day he bragged to her that he understood tobacco so well that he could even tell what the smoke weighed. Elizabeth challenged him with a wager. Raleigh accepted, weighed a quantity of tobacco, smoked it and then weighed the ashes. The Queen, who had expected an easy victory, did not deny 'what was wanting in the prime weight of the tobacco to have been evaporated in smoke', but paid her losses with the remark that 'many labourers in the fire she had heard of turned their gold into smoke, but Sir Walter was the first who had turned smoke into gold'.

Not everyone, however, adopted the new fashion but agreed rather with James of Scotland's verdict that it was 'a custom loathsome to the eye, hateful to the nose, harmful to the brain, dangerous to the lungs and in the black stinking fume thereos nearest resembling the horrible Stygian smoke of the pit that if bottomless'. And the smoker did not escape the pen of the satirists:

> In a tobacco-shop resembling Hell—
> Fire, stink and smoke must be where devils dwell—
> He sits (you cannot see his face for vapour)
> Offering to Pluto with a tallow taper.

Raleigh therefore availed himself of the most certain means of influencing the public—the theatre. He hired an attorney's clerk named Anthony Chute who supplemented his slender earnings by hack-work for the stage. Chute went to work and soon 'kneaded and daubed up a comedy, escutcheoned with the heraldic arms of the Smoky Society' entitled *The Transformation of the King of Trinidadoes' two daughters, Madame Panacea and the Nymph Tobacco.*

*

At Watson's suggestion, Marlowe visited Raleigh.

'If my memory serves me', said Watson, 'you told me that when you met him in the inn in Cambridge he invited you to call on him.'

'Yes, but he is not likely to remember it. And in any case I was to go to him on church matters. He might offer me a living in Devonshire.'

'Well?'

'Well, I can think of nothing I should detest more than to be a parson in Devonshire. Except possibly', he added, thinking of his room-mates in Corpus, 'to be a parson in Norfolk. And, as you know quite well, I have no intention of being a parson anywhere.'

'By the way, have you told the Master yet?'

'I am not that much of a fool. It will be time enough to let the Babysnatcher know when he has safely given me my degree.'

He answered Watson's puzzled look by explaining that the Master of Corpus Christi, John Copcot, was for obvious philological reasons known as 'the Babysnatcher'.

'Then, my dear Kit, surely you can see that there is no need to let Raleigh know. You are not bound to take a living even if he offers it, but it would be the height of foolishness to throw away a chance of meeting him on familiar terms.'

'Even though he will have forgotten my existence—an unknown undergraduate in a tavern?'

'He will pretend to know you. And there's your *entrée* if you've the wit to use it.'

Raleigh, however, much to Marlowe's surprise, not only remembered him, but greeted him with: 'And what service can I render "Kind Kit"?'

Completely taken aback, Kit could only stammer confusedly: 'Sir Walter, I did not think . . . the greatest presumption . . . how could I imagine . . . a poor scholar . . .'

For a moment or two Raleigh amusedly watched him flounder before, holding out his pipe to him, he said: 'You appear *boulversé*; let me offer you some soothing medicine.'

'What do I . . . how do I . . . ?'

Raleigh took a long pull and exhaled the smoke through mouth and nose. 'It is quite simple,' he said, handing the pipe to Marlowe, who was immediately reduced to a coughing, spluttering helplessness, gasping for breath.

'Like all good things', said Raleigh, 'it needs practice. You will soon feel the benefit of it.'

In an unexpected manner, this proved true. The physical contretemps had the effect of breaking down the barriers of formality. The conversation became as relaxed as if it had been a continuation of the talk in the *Eagle* and Raleigh eventually offered Marlowe a place in the new expedition to Virginia he was sending out under Captain John White the following year.

'Hariot will not be with it. You could go in his stead and have the kindness to see it for me.'

'Thomas Hariot is devoted to the natural sciences and he sees precisely with his eyes. I am a poor poet and see with my mind and imagination. You might not recognise my descriptions. Nor would they be necessary to you, for you are a greater poet than I shall ever be.'

'Then, if you will not go venturing, how can I help you, Kit? Unless you want that living we spoke of at Cambridge. You are still hell-bent for the church?'

Marlowe, now that it had come to a direct question, found himself unable to lie.

'No, Sir Walter,' he said, 'though I should be much beholden to you if you would be silent on that matter should so little a thing ever be mentioned in your hearing.'

'You may rely on me, though I should be grateful for a reason.'

'I do not wish to imperil my Mastership.'

'I must look at you with new eyes,' said Raleigh.

'Why so, sir?'

'You know the proverb?'

'No.'

'I thought it was current jargon. "A Royston horse and a Cambridge Master of Arts are a couple of creatures that will give way to no one."* So that is to be your pride?'

'Would you grudge me the only eminence within my reach?'

'Now you are under-valuing yourself. At your age, you have the world to conquer if your will holds. But you must not be too

* Royston, a few miles from Cambridge, was noted for its malt which was taken to London on heavily-burdened horses which could not easily give way on the road.

proud to accept help when it is offered. If you have no mind for exploring beyond the seas or piloting the way to Heaven, have you a turn for simple land business? If you have, I could let you try a prentice hand at it. Her Majesty has been gracious enough to grant me some estates in the Midlands. They will need attention.'

'No,' said Marlowe, decisively. 'I want nothing from you, Sir Walter, but permission to call on you sometimes when I am in London so that I may learn from your wisdom in the ways of the world.'

Raleigh, missing the ironical undertone, assented with genuine enthusiasm. 'I shall look forward to your return, Kit. And here is a passport for you.' He went to a desk and from a collection of long clay pipes carefully selected one which he gave to Marlowe. 'When you see me again, you will inhale the miraculous leaf without coughing.'

'I will certainly endeavour to master that art.'

'Hariot who is devoted to clay tells me that a little wax on the end protects the lips.'

Back at his lodgings, Marlowe practised assiduously, but was unable to induce either Watson or Kyd to follow his example, even when he tried to provoke them by announcing magisterially: 'All who do not love boys and tobacco are fools.'

To have met the reigning Favourite and to have engaged his interest was, as Kyd said with his usual bitterness, a stroke of great good fortune, adding 'reserved of course for University wits'. Marlowe, accustomed as he had become to Kyd's mono-mania, took issue with him and retorted that, as he had originally met Raleigh at the *Eagle*, an ordinary tavern in which anyone in Cambridge was entitled to drink, it had no more connection with his scholastic status than had his meeting with Kyd himself at the *Unicorn*.

'And did you consider that an occasion of importance?'

'In that I had the great good fortune to meet you, of course. But it had its disappointment also in that I did not meet Edward Alleyn.'

'That shall be remedied, my dear Kit,' said Kyd. 'Next

Thursday is Ned Alleyn's birthday—he's twenty—and of course he's playing my *Hieronimo** that afternoon. Afterwards his brother's giving a special party for him at the *Unicorn*. You must come as my guest.'

Alleyn's performance that afternoon, overwhelming in its power, was for Marlowe a never-to-be-forgotten experience which he came to look upon as one of the turning-points of his life. It had seemed impossible that so young a man as Alleyn could convincingly play the old Hieronimo, Marshal of Spain, driven to revenge and despair by the murder of his son Horatio —a part played by a popular actor, ten years older than Alleyn. But no sooner had Hieronimo made the awaited entrance, suddenly awakened from sleep by cries from the garden where his son's body was hanged in an arbour, than a tense silence fell on the audience, in which Alleyn's magnificent voice, ranging from a whisper to a shriek of despair, held the theatre spellbound

> What outcries pluck me from my naked bed
> And chill my throbbing heart with trembling fear,
> Which never danger yet could daunt before?
> But stay what murd'rous spectacle is this?
> A man hang'd up and all the murd'rers gone!
> And in my bower to lay the guilt on me!
> This place was made for pleasure, not for death.
> Those garments that he wears I oft have seen—
> Alas, it is Horatio, my sweet son!
> O no, but he that whilom was my son.
> O, was it thou who calledst me from my bed?
> O speak if any spark of life remain.
> I am thy father. Who hath slain my son?
> What savage monster, not of human kind,
> Hath here been glutted with thy harmless blood,
> And left thy bloody corpse dishonoured here,
> For me, amidst these dark and deathful shades,
> To drown thee with an ocean of tears?

Alleyn's sweeping gestures, his commanding carriage, his majestic stride were muted as became one slowed by age, yet without losing the natural imperiousness of the Marshal of

* Kyd's *The Spanish Tragedy* was popularly known as *Hieronimo*.

Spain. The savage strength of the sword-blow with which he cut down the hanging body was combined with the natural weakness which made him suddenly stagger as he received the dead-weight of it. His joints were stiff as he knelt to kiss the lifeless face. Alleyn, by the perfection of detail, created a coherent world and, at the climax of his speech, he defined the nature of it:

> O, eyes! no eyes, but fountains fraught with tears;
> O, life! no life, but lively form of death;
> O, world! no world, but mass of public wrongs,
> Confus'd and fill'd with murder and misdeeds.

Kyd's words, in themselves simple enough, were endowed with that enchantment which is the prerogative of the theatre alone. By their placing and their delivery, they assumed an oracular importance. They were both an epitome and a verdict, defining the world Marlowe knew with a finality from which there was no appeal—the world where religion was but an illusory comfort to the weak and where only the Machiavellian walked safely, the world where it was a courteous gesture for Raleigh to offer Marlowe the stewardship of Babington's ancestral home, the world of Walsingham.

On another plane, Marlowe also saw that in art the primacy of creation which he had been accustomed to claim for poetry belonged in fact to drama; and from that moment he asked no other destiny than to be a master playwright. His ambition had narrowed—or expanded—to the ability to create a world which mirrored and illuminated the world, using human beings as materials as the musician used sounds and the writer words and the sculptor marble and the painter colours. And the human being Marlowe was determined to make the pivot of his art was Edward Alleyn.

In the *Unicorn* that evening, his behaviour reflected his changed attitude. The surroundings contributed to his own understanding of the crucial shift in his vision. Here, just a year ago he had first sensed the strange attraction of the professional world of the theatre as he talked with and listened to some of its strange denizens. It was here that he had originally met Kyd and had been introduced by Tom Watson to the landlord, Ned Alleyn's elder brother, as a Cambridge man interested in trying to write for the stage. And here he had known the disappointment and frustration of waiting for Ned Alleyn, who did not arrive.

Now that Ned was present and the introduction had been effected, Marlowe responded very differently from his intentions on that occasion. Apart from an obviously sincere tribute to the actor's Hieronimo, he avoided talking of the theatre. Though Alleyn adopted the usual attitude of established actors to untried playwrights—a compound of encouragement lest they should miss a 'winner' and remoteness to protect themselves against a deluge of rubbish—Marlowe's response was anything but conventional now that he saw the actor as his instrument. Consequently he neither mentioned that he had already written a play and invited Alleyn to read it, nor did he offer to write one and discuss a suitable topic. His instinctive silence was logical enough. In the first place *Dido*, however suitable for boy players, was no vehicle for Alleyn. Secondly, Marlowe did not wish to appear to Kyd, jealously evaluating the conversation, as a possible rival. Finally, and most importantly, he had no idea of a subject. He only knew that, whatever it eventually turned out to be, it must be incontrovertibly the right one. Here, if anywhere, proverbial wisdom must be obeyed: it was the first step that counted.

Marlowe's failure to make the expected gambit forced Alleyn on to the offensive. If the writer did not offer, the actor must ask. Alleyn was too seasoned a professional to let any opportunity slip. Though he was only twenty—two years and four months younger than Marlowe—he was a hardened man of business, who had had to make his own way in the world. His father had died when he was four and his mother had then married an unsympathetic haberdasher. When he was barely sixteen, Ned had had to take a most difficult decision. He had served his theatrical apprenticeship and been given his training as a boy actor in the company of William Somerset, Earl of Worcester. At fifteen he was made a junior member of the company and was by custom expected to serve for a year or two with Worcester's Men. But he came to the conclusion that, as they performed mainly in the provinces and had no outstanding player among them, it would be as well for him to leave them immediately and, at sixteen, he applied for and was accepted by the Lord Admiral's Company which was fast rivalling the Earl of Leicester's and even the Queen's.*

Alleyn's business sense had been fostered and sharpened by the interest taken in him by Philip Henslowe, a thirty-year-old citizen of Southwark, dedicated to the amassing of money. Henslowe had started life in the leather trade as apprentice to a Master Woodward and, on Woodward's death, had in the approved manner of the 'good apprentice' married his widow. He invested his assets shrewdly, buying a dye-works and a starch-works, and added to them a large pawnbroking establishment and a string of brothels. Looking round for more, his eyes naturally fell on the theatre as the money-spinner of the moment.

Philip Henslowe was almost the antithesis of James Burbage, whose love of the theatre for itself was such that he had for over twelve years now warred for it, protecting it from the encroachments of creditors—in particular his grocer brother-in-law—and mortgage-holders and the London Council and splenetic ecclesiastics and any other force which might threaten the object of his devotion. Burbage was an actor, with the stage in his bones; Henslowe was a businessman, regarding the theatre merely as another commodity like his brothels and his pawn-broking and his dye-works. And, because of this, Henslowe was able to see the more clearly where his profit lay.

What had become London's theatre district, the liberty of Holywell northeast of the city walls, where The Theatre and The Curtain were, was not an ideal situation. It was more than a mile from the centre of the city's amusements, the Bankside across the river in Southwark, with its bull-ring and its brothels and its bear-pit; and Henslowe foresaw larger audiences for the new craze of the theatre if it could be transplanted to the already popular venue. To acquaint himself thoroughly with the practical conditions of the entertainment industry, he bought a part-share in the bear-pit and at the same time acquired a large rose-gar-

---

* All the acting companies were rigidly licensed under an Act of Parliament. To avoid being listed as rogues and vagabonds, each company operated under someone's patronage, the smaller groups under local dignitaries or incorporated towns, the larger under prominent Court officials. The 'Worcester's men' to which Alleyn belonged operated mainly at Norwich and Leicester, where, according to the town records, they made themselves a nuisance. The more famous Worcester's Men, which produced, among other plays, Heywood's *A Woman killed with Kindness*, belonged to William Somerset's son, Charles, the fourth Earl, at the beginning of the next century.

den, about a hundred yards away from it, on which in due course he could build a theatre which by its position, its size and its up-to-date improvements in design, would far out-rival *The Theatre* and *The Curtain*.

Henslowe also saw the necessity of a player who could draw the town. *The Rose*—as he intended to call his new house—should not be merely a playhouse where the various companies could be seen. It should be famous, if it were possible to arrange it, for the regular appearance of some outstanding actor.

After seeing Alleyn's performance as Hieronimo, Henslowe was satisfied that he had found his man and he set himself to bind Alleyn to him by every available tie from the flattery of seeking his advice on the design of his proposed theatre to encouraging the actor's manifest interest in his adolescent step-daughter, Joan Woodward. The strongest bond between the two men, however, was the similarity of their temperaments—the single-minded practicality with which they both sought money and success. Neither the theatre of Marlowe's vision nor the lotus-land of Bohemia which sufficed the born 'rogues and vagabonds' came within their purview.

So now as Alleyn talked to Marlowe, his questions had the cogency which Henslowe himself might have given them. 'If you ever decide to try your hand at a play,' he said, 'I would ask you to let no one read it until you have given me the chance of buying it, if I should find it suitable.'

'Certainly,' said Marlowe. 'I should consider that an honour.'

'But you are firm in your intention to write nothing at the moment?'

'Yes. Until next March I must give all my time to my studies at Cambridge. Then, once I have my Mastership I shall be at your service.'

Alleyn, who knew enough about playwrights to disbelieve Marlowe's denial that he had some subject in mind, continued to press him on the matter until Kit admitted that his glimpse of the Duke of Guise in Paris had suggested him as a possible protagonist. Alleyn was shocked and explained as to a child that such a thing was not to be thought of. A figure so vehemently hated—and rightly hated—by all good Englishmen could, if used at all, only be represented as the diabolic villain he was and shown meeting with a terrible and deserved end. And how could this be when the latest news from France was that Guise was flourishing like the proverbial green bay tree, high in the good graces of the French King? That was the drawback of using a contemporary theme. History, not the dramatist, determined the plot.

'You have not started such a play?'

'No. I made notes for one soliloquy while I was in Paris.'

'May I hear it?'

'I am not sure of my memory.'

'A line or two?'

Noticing with relief that Kyd was out of earshot, Marlowe began diffidently:

> Oft have I levell'd and at last have learn'd
> That peril is the chiefest way to happiness
> And resolution is honour's fairest aim.
> What glory is there in a common good
> That hangs for—

Alleyn interrupted: 'Not "happiness", "fame". And "fairest" is unnecessary.' He declaimed it impressively:

> That peril is the chiefest way to fame
> And resolution* is honour's aim.

'That sounds well enough,' said Marlowe, 'but I meant it for a different scansion.' And he repeated his twelve-syllabled lines as he had written them.

Alleyn shook his head. 'No. Mine's the better. Trust me. I know, for I can say it the easier.'

'But the meaning is twisted. Fame is not happiness.'

'Near enough for most. Go on.'

'I fear I have forgotten the rest,' said Marlowe. 'And, in any case, we are agreed that it would be foolish to write the play.'

Alleyn, chilled, exerted all his charm, reiterated: 'But when you find a fit subject, I am to be the first to read it?'

'Of course.'

'Give me your hand on it.'

With a ritual solemnity, they clasped hands.

*

* This would naturally be pronounced as five syllables.

It was in the course of his final studies at Cambridge that Kit eventually got an idea for a play suitable for Alleyn. He had chosen as the thesis for his qualifying disputation in the schools that 'dominion cannot suffer partnership'. As it was a Quodlibetic* he took the liberty of announcing it in English, though none but his intimates realised it was his own translation of

omnisque potestas
Impatiens consortis erat

—lines from Lucan's epic poem on the civil war between Pompey and Caesar, *De Bello Civili*, the first book of which Marlowe had 'Englished line for line' as a self-imposed exercise.

In developing the argument for his disputation, Marlowe naturally took as his central example the two Roman civil wars, in the first of which the two partners in dominion, Pompey and Caesar, had to fight to the death for the single, supreme power, as in the later war after Caesar's death had Antony and Augustus.

Marlowe, as was to be expected, accepted Machiavelli's dictum: 'The kingdoms known to history have been governed in two ways: either by a prince and his servants, who, as ministers by his grace and permission assist him in governing the realm; or by a prince and by barons who hold their positions not by favour of the ruler, but by antiquity of blood, such barons having states and subjects of their own. Examples of these two kinds of government in our own time are the Turk and the King of France.'

The French example Marlowe naturally laid stress on was the Duke of Guise and the general threat to the Valois of the House of Lorraine. For the Turkish he chose the defeat of Bajazet I at Ankara in 1402 by Timur—the Scythian shepherd whose dream was to restore the eastern world-empire, stretching from the Black Sea to the Pacific, of Genghiz Khan, and who had become a half-legendary character as Tamburlaine. The selection of this particular point in Turkish history was because it so well illustrated Machiavelli's paradox that, though the Turkish

---

* The regular Analytics, which concerned itself with the analysis of some aspect of Aristotelian philosophy, was supplemented by Quodlibetics in which the candidate had the liberty to choose his own subject in order to demonstrate his own particular interests outside the set curriculum.

model of a tyrannical dictatorship made for the internal stability of a state in peace and its united strength in war, yet, were it defeated, the defeat would be total. 'It would be difficult to acquire the state of the Turk,' Machiavelli had written, 'but having conquered it, it would be very easy to hold it. It is sufficient to kill the family of the ruler.'

Machiavelli's own historical example of this was the ease with which 'Alexander the Great became master of Asia, for the nature of the kingdom of Darius being similar to that of the Turk, Darius being dead the state remained secure to Alexander'. To the classical example, Marlowe added the overthrow of Bajazet by Tamburlaine, a suitable parallel, and pointed out that Tamburlaine's own subsequent way to empire rested on his ruthless refusal to suffer partnership.

As he was preparing his thesis, Marlowe became aware that what he had chosen as an incidental illustration had provided him unexpectedly but irresistibly with an ideal subject for Alleyn. He read all he could find at Cambridge on things Turkish, which was the easier because the fashion for Machiavelli in the University had brought in its train an interest in them and the formation of—in Gabriel Harvey's words—'an odd crew or two as learned in certain gallant Turkish discourses' as in Machiavelli's *Il Principe* itself. In Philip Lonicer's recent two volumes of *Turkish Chronicles* and in a *Life of Tamerlane the Great* which had been included in an English translation of *Turkish Histories* only the previous year, he learnt enough to confirm him in his choice. Only in one circumstance would he have to make a crucial alteration. Tamburlaine was lame. It was part of his legend— 'Tamburlaine who was lame, yet conquered the world.' But Alleyn would most certainly refuse to appear lame. Nor would Marlowe wish him to. As Hieronimo, the actor had had to simulate age and weakness. It was of the essence of the new play that he should move with his natural striding magnificence. The lameness must be abandoned. To make it clear beyond doubt to Alleyn, when he should discuss the matter with him, Marlowe wrote a description which he could show him at their next meeting:

Of stature tall and straightly fashioned
Like his desire, lift upwards and divine;

So large of limbs, his joints so strongly knit,
Such breadth of shoulders as might mainly bear
Old Atlas' burden; eyes, circles of fire
That guide his steps and actions to the throne;
Pale of complexion, wrought in him with passion,
Thirsting with sovereignty and love of arms;
His lofty brows in folds do figure death,
And in their smoothness amity and life;
About them hangs a knot of amber hair,
Wrapped in curls, as fierce Achilles' was,
On which the breath of heaven delights to play
Making it dance with wanton majesty;
His arms and fingers long and sinewy,
Betokening valour and excess of strength;
In every part proportion'd like a man.

Alleyn, he was certain, would approve the portrait.

Marlowe, however, in spite of temptation did no work on the play. His will was sufficiently strong to make him devote himself to his set studies as he had sworn to do. From his return to Cambridge at the beginning of the Michaelmas Term to the end of the Christmas Term on Lady Day, 25 March 1587, he was in continuous residence at Corpus and, having fulfilled all academic requirements, made his formal *Supplicat* to the authorities to be allowed his M.A. at the next Commencement, July 4.

Once only had he visited London when he had gone to participate in what was almost an obligatory national occasion, the funeral of Sir Philip Sidney.

Sidney had accompanied his uncle Leicester in the course of his campaign in the Netherlands on a reconnoitring expedition in the neighbourhood of Zutphen. On 2 October 1586, he was wounded. Noticing that the veteran Lord Marshal was not wearing his thigh pieces, Sidney, in emulation, had thrown away his own and a musket ball had struck his defenceless thigh, three inches above the knee. He was carried from the field and, when the doctors and surgeons had done their worst, died, after a fortnight's pain and increasing weakness, on October 17. The

Netherlanders begged for the honour of burying him on Dutch soil and pledged themselves 'to erect to his memory a fair and royal monument, yea, though it should cost half-a-ton of gold in the building' but a burial outside England was unthinkable. As Governor of Flushing, his body lay in official state there for eight days, after which it was embarked on his own ship *The Black Pinnace* which arrived in England, sailing up the Thames to Tower Wharf, on November 5, to a London in full mourning. Parliament had just assembled, bringing into the capital the notables from the country and 'it was accounted a sin for any gentleman of quality for many months after to appear in any light or gaudy apparel'. The story of his conduct as he lay wounded at Zutphen had preceded his homecoming and had epitomised the character of one who, for the ordinary citizen, had always been the pattern of true knighthood. Even before Sidney's body had arrived at the Tower, it had become an indelible part of the annals of England how 'being thirsty with excess of bleeding, he called for drink, which was immediately brought him; but, as he was putting the bottle to his mouth, he saw a poor soldier carried along, ghastly casting up his eyes at the bottle, which Sir Philip perceiving took it from his hand before he drank and delivered it to the poor man with these words "Thy necessity is yet greater than mine." '

Sidney's funeral, however, was—unaccountably from the public point of view—delayed. His will authorised his brother and heir, Robert Sidney, and his father-in-law, Sir Francis Walsingham, to sell as much land as was necessary for the discharge of his debts and 'to proceed with all possible speed that his creditors might be paid'.

Unfortunately Walsingham had to confess to Leicester: 'Sir Philip hath left a great number of poor creditors. I have paid and must pay for him above £6,000 which, I do assure your Lordship, hath brought me into a hard and most desperate state. It doth greatly afflict me that a gentleman that hath lived so unspotted a reputation and had so great a care to see all men satisfied should be exposed to the outcry of his creditors. His goods will not serve to satisfy a third part of the debts already known.'

Walsingham saw nothing for it but to postpone the funeral for three months: 'I do not see how the same can be performed with the solemnity that appertaineth without the utter undoing of his creditors, which is to be weighed in conscience.' When the date for the ceremony was finally fixed for 16 February 1587 there was ample time for arrangements to be made for attendance from all over the country.

The weeks of waiting taxed Walsingham in more than his finances, for the final outcome of his Grand Design was still precariously in the balance, and he could not rest. The execution of Babington and his companions was of no importance as long as the object for which he had engineered it, the death of Mary Queen of Scots, was unrealised. In October, Mary had been brought to a secret 'trial' at Fotheringhay which, as Walsingham knew better than anyone, was in international law a farce—for Mary, as an anointed sovereign ruler, was subject to no foreign jurisdiction—and in English law was dependent entirely on the recently framed Act of Association, aided by a forgery.

The news that the death-sentence had been passed on Mary was made known to the public on December 3 and loyal Londoners welcomed it with another bout of bell-ringing, bonfire-lighting and psalm-singing. But this, gratifying as it was to Walsingham, was no compensation for Queen Elizabeth's stubborn refusal to sign her cousin's death-warrant. She was quite aware of the odium this would bring her in the eyes of Europe.

Walsingham suggested a secret assassination. Elizabeth agreed and instructed him to write to Mary's gaoler, a Puritan of Walsingham's own persuasion, to propose it. But the gaoler's religion, however bigoted he was against Mary's Catholicism, was genuine and he wrote back in indignation: 'I am so unhappy to have lived to see this unhappy day by which I am required by direction from my Most Gracious Sovereign to do an act which God and the law forbiddeth. God forbid that I should make so foul a shipwreck of my conscience or leave so great a blot on my poor posterity as to shed blood without law or warrant.'

Elizabeth raged at his 'daintiness' and the 'niceness of those precise fellows' but the fact remained that in January 1587 the death-warrant was still unsigned and Walsingham, at his wits' end, decided that another 'plot' was imperative. There was obviously no time for another masterpiece like the last one. The essentials were now effectiveness and speed. Even credibility could be largely dispensed with. He ordered Phillips to provide him with carefully forged documents which could be presented to him by two of his agents to prove that they had been bribed by the French Ambassador to tie a bag of gunpowder under Queen Elizabeth's bed. This had the double purpose of immobilising the French Ambassador, who was immediately put under house-arrest pending investigation, so that he could not deliver personally the King of France's urgent pleas for the life of Mary, his sister-in-law, and of rousing the country to a patriotic fever-pitch of concern for Elizabeth's safety. *

Rumours started by Walsingham's agents swept the country —the Queen of Scots had escaped from her imprisonment, London was to be set on fire, thousands of Spaniards had already landed in Wales. Roads to the capital were guarded by local levies in arms. When on February 1, Elizabeth at last consented to sign the death-warrant, the action took on something of the character of a national necessity. Walsingham, because of his illness, was unable to be at Greenwich but as soon as she had signed the Queen sent the second Secretary, who was deputising for him, to his house at Barn Elms to give him the news. 'The grief thereof', she blazed with scorching irony, 'will go near to kill him outright.'

Mary Queen of Scots was executed in great secrecy at Fotheringhay at sunrise on February 8, having been given only fifteen hours' warning. Elizabeth immediately closed all the English ports to prevent the news reaching the Continent and the French knew nothing of it for three weeks.† But in London the citizens were told immediately and acclamations in the conventional manner reached their zenith. The repercussions of the 'des Trappes plot' intruded when Londoners asked the French Ambassador to give them wood for their bonfires and,

* This, the co-called 'des Trappes plot', is studiously ignored by most English historians, because it is the key to the real, as opposed to the fictitious propaganda, situation and because it is an admitted fabrication which cannot, by any stretch of patriotic ingenuity, be represented as anything else. As soon as Mary was safely executed, the French Ambassador was apologised to and invited to treat the whole matter as a joke.

† For a fuller account of the matter and, in particular, the effects in Paris where a Requiem Mass was said for Mary on March 12, see *Paris is Worth a Mass* pp. 75–81.

when he refused, lit an immense fire in front of the Embassy. The city remained *en fête*, with dancing, feasting and general merry-making in the streets, for a week when, as a symbolical climax, the grandiose state funeral of Sir Philip Sidney, the Protestant hero, brought it to an end.

Early in the morning of Thursday, February 16 St Paul's Cathedral was crowded by the thousands of citizens who had managed to find standing-room. Outside, the streets from the Tower to the cathedral were lined by the waiting crowd of men, women and children at road level, at the windows, on the house-tops. Marlowe, with Tom Watson and some of their literary friends, including Kyd, had taken up a position in the church-yard near the spot usually occupied by the stall of their pub-lisher-bookseller acquaintance, Edward Blount, who had commissioned a series of tributes which he hoped would make a best-selling anthology.

At the head of the procession of seven hundred mourners were thirty-two aged gownsmen, one for each year of Sidney's age. They were followed by the officers and sergeants of his Foot and the officers, corporals and trumpeters of his Horse. After them came his personal household, preceded by a standard em-broidered with the Cross of St George and the Sidney crest of a porcupine collared and chained between three lions' heads crowned. The sixty gentlemen and yeomen, walking in pairs, his physician and his surgeon and his steward who constituted the Household were followed by twelve knights who were kins-men and friends and included Sir Francis Drake.

Then, announcing as it were the most solemn and personal part of the pageant, marched the bearer of a banner displaying Sir Philip's arms, followed by his two favourite horses, ridden by small pages, one trailing a broken lance, the other carrying a battle-axe reversed. Another standard-bearer preceded the five heralds in long gowns and mourning hoods, bearing the sym-bols of Sidney's knighthood—Portcullis the spurs, Blue Mantle the gauntlets, Rouge Dragon the helmet, Richmond the shield and Somerset the tabard, with Clarencieux King-at-Arms bringing up the rear. The coffin, covered by a black velvet pall, was borne on poles by fourteen yeomen and at each corner a banner was carried by cousins or relations by marriage—two Sidneys, a Pakenham and Edmund Walsingham.

Behind the coffin, walking alone, was Robert, Sir Philip's brother and heir, who was with him at Zutphen and whose grief had been so uncontrollable that the dying man had been unable to endure it and Robert, during the last three days of Philip's life, had had to be kept from his bedside.

The last part of the procession consisted of six mounted nobles who had served in the Low Countries, led by the Earl of Leicester, followed by his stepson, the nineteen-year-old Earl of Essex, who, it was rumoured, was in the process of displacing Sir Walter Raleigh in the Queen's affections and to whom Sidney had left his sword. *

After them rode seven representatives of the Netherlands followed by the Lord Mayor of London, with his sword-bearer, aldermen, recorder and sheriffs. Behind them a hundred and twenty of the Company of Grocers walked in pairs, followed by some three hundred London citizens trained to bear arms, in ranks of three, carrying their weapons reversed.

When the last of the procession had passed through the great west door of the cathedral Marlowe would have left had not the density of the crowd made it impossible. He had appreciated the splendour of the spectacle, but it had nothing in the world to do with the Sidney he admired and regretted never having met—Sidney the great poet and defender of poetry; and he had been behind the scenes at least enough to understand and dislike the propaganda purpose of the show. Also his personal queries had been answered. The absence of Robert Poley from the Household group of mourners was evidence that Sir Francis Walsingham did not yet consider it prudent to release him from his imprisonment. Tom Walsingham, whom Kit had hoped against hope to see even though protocol gave him no official place, was nowhere to be seen and his elder brother Edmund, his face half-hidden in a mourning hood, left no impression apart from a long nose and a drooping moustache.

At last the firing of double volleys announced that the service was over and the coffin had been lowered into its grave in the

---

* Essex subsequently married Sidney's widow.

choir aisle and the crowd began to disperse. Marlowe made his way back to Tom Watson's lodgings, where he was to stay the night. Before returning to Cambridge, he had another appointment to keep.

A few days before he had left for London, an unexpected visitor had called at his rooms in Corpus Christi. He was a powerfully built man in his middle thirties. His swarthy complexion appeared the darker on account of the blackness of his hair and beard. His large eyes suggested a certain candour which was immediately contradicted by the twist of his thin lips. His blunt-fingered hands were almost as hairy as an ape's and his short nails were dirty. Incongruously he was dressed in the height of fashion in a green doublet slashed with rich purple silk.

'You are Master Christopher Marlowe?' He made it sound a statement rather than a question.

'I am. And you?'

'Nicholas Skeres.'

'We have not met before?'

'No. Though you might have seen me when I last saw you.'

'Where was that?'

'At the *Grapes* in London the night you let the traitor Babington slip through your fingers, Master "Thornborough".' Skeres gave a satirical emphasis to the name. 'I was drinking by the door when Babington went out.'

'You were posted there?'

'No. Though it is true that we both serve the same master.'

'I have no master.'

'If you can say that', said Skeres, sitting down and starting to clean his nails with his dagger-point, 'the University must have spoilt your wits. There's a Latin tag for it, no doubt, but I'm no scholar. In English I might say "who sups with the devil needs a long spoon". Not that Sir Francis is the devil—do not misunderstand me—but he has a long arm and if you think you'll ever be out of reach of it you're an addle-pate.'

Marlowe thought it not worth while explaining that, as he understood it, the terms of his 'service' made it occasional and voluntary and that now that Poley was in the Tower it was, for all practical purposes, at an end.

'Sir Francis wishes to see you,' Skeres continued. 'He is at Barn Elms where you are to wait on him when Sir Philip Sidney's funeral is over.'

'Where is Barn Elms?'

'It is his country estate on the river, near Richmond. You must surely know it?'*

'No. I have seen him only at Seething Lane,' said Marlowe, adding with an appearance of *insouciance* he was very far from feeling: 'What if I should find it inconvenient to go?'

'Then I fear I should have to come and fetch you.' He tested the sharpness of his dagger-blade on his thumb. 'Unless, of course, Sir Francis decided on other measures. You have heard that poor young Craven is dead?'

'No, I have not even heard of Craven.'

'He was a student at Oxford, very much in your position, who was beginning to show signs of—shall we call it—ingratitude.'

When, two days after Sidney's funeral, Marlowe presented himself at Barn Elms he was welcomed by John Scudamore who laughingly called him 'Thornborough' and assured him that their incompetence in the matter of Babington's temporary escape had been forgiven and that, as an earnest of pardon, Walsingham was employing Marlowe once more on a confidential mission, this time to the Low Countries.

Though Scudamore believed what he said, this did not in fact represent the case. Walsingham was sending Marlowe with some reluctance merely because he had no one else available to send. The person who should have gone was Robert Poley, but in view of the situation brought about by the execution of the Queen of Scots Walsingham considered that to release Poley from the Tower at that moment would be the height of unwisdom and would invite hostile and dangerous speculation on the part of the French Ambassador. Poley himself agreed with this and, writing from the Tower, suggested that if the matter could not wait till the time was propitious to free him, Marlowe was safe to use, as long as all he was asked to do was to deliver a letter.

He was not yet, Poley advised, fit for any difficult task.

* Now the club house of the Ranelagh Club.

Fortunately, Walsingham decided, a simple arrangement would suffice. He would write a letter which could be answered by an oral 'Yes' or 'No'.

There had arisen in the Council a Peace Party which was prepared to make terms with the Duke of Parma in the Netherlands even at this moment when preparations for the Armada were almost completed. Burleigh himself headed it, with old Sir John Crofts, a pensioner of Spain, as an unfaltering advocate and supported, on the whole, by the Queen who never had any wish for war if it could be avoided and who at that moment, with France alienated and its aid uncertain, was avid for peace. The leaders of the War Party were Walsingham, motivated by his religion, and Leicester who hoped to be made officially Governor of the Netherlands—a post which the Peace Party intended as part of the necessary compromise to offer to the Duke of Parma. The tactics of the War Party were to persuade the Queen to allow Drake to make a raid on Spain itself. His piratical attacks on the Spanish treasure-fleet could be—and were—diplomatically explained away by Elizabeth's official disowning of them; but an attack on Cadiz, for example, would be tantamount to a declaration of war from which there could be no withdrawal. Drake himself, the son of a puritanical lay-preacher, was as fanatical a Protestant as Walsingham himself and was able without hypocrisy to see his lucrative privateering expeditions as part of a Holy War against the Romish Antichrist. When Walsingham suggested to him that he might recruit a company for a raid on the Spanish coast, he was able to report: 'I assure your Honour that no time hath been lost. We are all in loving agreement to stand for our gracious Queen and our country against Antichrist and his members.'

The Peace Party, however, managed to sway Elizabeth who, after giving Drake nine interviews in one day, refused to see him at all for several weeks.

In this rapidly shifting situation, part of the key lay in the Netherlands and much could be deduced from considering the fierceness or the slackness of Parma's attack. As long as Sidney was alive, Walsingham could rely on him for exact information on this point, for Sidney, fervent Protestant, close friend of Drake, nephew of Leicester, son-in-law of Walsingham, belonged emphatically to the War Party and, in his private letters to his father-in-law, gave it the information it needed. But now, with, Sidney dead, the only person who could tell Walsingham what he needed to know was Jan Wychgerde, a respectable corn-merchant of the Netherlands, a broker for Baltic wheat who catered for the Spanish army finding them not only Baltic wheat for biscuit but supplying butter and cheese and salt fish. On the side he occasionally handled consignments of English cloth for the Rhine towns. He spoke Spanish and Flemish fluently, was *persona grata* with the Duke of Parma. He was also one of the toughest and the cleverest of Walsingham's spies.

The question which Walsingham wanted him to answer was whether Parma's present siege of Ostend, which was defended by an English garrison, was intentionally languid and under-taken mainly as a cover for the secret peace negotiations or whether it was merely a feint to cover a projected attack else-where which would lead to an intensification of the war in the Low Countries. If it were the former, then the need to persuade the Queen to allow Drake's raid was peremptory. *

Marlowe, ushered into Walsingham's presence, could hardly believe the change in him which pain and anxiety had wrought since their previous meeting eighteen months ago. Even then Marlowe had not been afraid of him; now he was pitying. The essential kindness of his nature transformed him into a strong young man tending an invalid. He searched the grey, lined

---

* The story of the peace negotiations is complicated, but the theory that they were merely a deep-laid plot by Philip of Spain to give himself more time for building the Armada is too *simpliste* a solution. Philip (for economic if for no other reasons) was genuinely in favour of peace until the autumn of this year, 1587, at which point he instructed Parma that the invasion of England was to go ahead without fail and that no peace was to be made on any terms. Parma himself (who was Philip's nephew) was, in the words of one historian, 'the chief architect of modern Belgium' whose primary loyalty was less to Spain than to the Netherlands of which his mother and his grandfather had been the rulers. Because the attack by the Armada in the summer of 1588 has made the peace negotiations of the first part of 1587 seem irrelevant, it does not follow that they were, at the time, of no importance.

As regards Marlowe's possible part in them, Professor C. F. Tucker Brooke in his *Life of Marlowe* (1930) places it in the June of 1587 and connects it with Parma's plan that month for an armistice. Professor John Bakeless in *The Tragicall History of Christopher Marlowe* (1942) thinks that Marlowe may 'at the very least have been a special messenger carrying secret dispatches of importance'. It seems to me that, considering all the circumstances, the June date is unlikely and that the matter was too complicated and important for 'secret dispatches of importance' to be entrusted to a comparatively untried man still at the University. On the other hand, a simple letter, which would mean nothing if it fell into enemy hands and which needed only an oral answer, would fit the situation.

shrunken face for some hint of his cousinage to the beloved Tom and, once he had allowed the thought of the relationship to dominate his mind, something of affection seemed to spill over.

Walsingham, on his part, found Marlowe quietly intelligent and wondered whether Poley had undervalued him. The young man listened attentively, repeated faultlessly his instructions and asked only one question which, as it referred to Wychgerde's appearance, was relevant enough.

'Above all,' said the Secretary, 'remember that speed is of prime importance. If by any mischance you are hindered in your return, find someone—it does not greatly matter who; I leave it to your judgment—to bring me the answer "Yes" or "No", whichever it is.'

'I understand, Sir Francis. May I—may I ask a small favour?'

'If you are back within ten days you shall have double whatever Poley usually allows you.'

'I appreciate your generosity, sir, but my request is not about money,' said Marlowe and proceeded to explain that he did not wish to take Holy Orders, for which purpose he had been given his scholarship to Cambridge.

The timing of his request was perhaps not appropriate, but it was for this, after all, that Kit had allowed Tom Watson to introduce him to the Secretary in the first place and he felt that the matter must be broached now or never.

'You may rest assured, Master Marlowe,' said Walsingham, 'that as long as you serve the Queen faithfully, Her Majesty's Council will see that you can choose your career. Should you have any trouble at Cambridge when you return, we will see to it.'

Trouble at Cambridge brewed fast enough in Marlowe's absence. It was precipitated by the absence itself. By the University regulations, no scholar could be absent for more than a month during the year and then only by leave of the authorities. This rule Marlowe had consistently broken, though not more, perhaps, than any other normal undergraduate. But on this occasion he had made off without asking permission or even notifying anyone. The irritation of the Master of Corpus Christi, Thomas Norgate, had been rising steadily because of

Marlowe's repeated refusal to 'get a title'—that is to say, to find a vicar prepared to welcome his services as a curate as soon as he left the University. It was beginning to look as if he had secretly no intention of taking Holy Orders. This Norgate found particularly suspicious in the present circumstances.

The number of converts to Catholicism in Cambridge was causing some alarm. As recently as the January of that year a preacher at the University Church, Great St Mary's, had uttered the warning that members of the University were spying for Spain and indicated that the usual practice of converts was to go abroad just before they were due to receive their Cambridge degree and to enrol in the English College in Rome or in Rheims.

Norgate, himself a strict Protestant, began to make inquiries about Marlowe from the senior of the absentee's room-mates, Thomas Lewgar, a dull and reliable youth, son of the vicar of Wymondham. Lewgar, who was the principal butt of Marlowe's wit, arguments and blasphemies, felt compelled regretfully but in honesty to report that Marlowe was, to put it at its lowest, very unsound in his beliefs, that he occasionally entertained strange company, that he had—in Lewgar's opinion based on certain indiscretions in Marlowe's conversation—visited Rheims during one of his absences, and that he might well be a secret Catholic, as he had more than once upheld Catholicism as a better religion than Protestantism and had asserted that all Protestants were fools.

Consequently when Marlowe returned from his mission, having brought Walsingham information that caused him to put such pressure on the Queen that she allowed Drake to sail against Spain,* Kit found that the University authorities had taken the almost unprecedented step of ignoring his *Supplicat* and had refused to give him the M.A. to which he was entitled.

*

---

* She did so on April 1 and Drake, lest she should change her mind, embarked immediately and so did not receive her urgent countermand of April 9 categorically forbidding him 'to enter forcibly into any of the King of Spain's ports or havens, or to offer violence to any of his towns or shipping within harbours, or to do any act of hostility upon the land'. Drake's raid on Cadiz on this occasion is known in history-books as 'singeing the King of Spain's beard'.

The sequel was entirely unprecedented. On June 29, Norgate received a letter from the Privy Council, informing him that 'whereas it was reported that Christopher Marlowe was determined to have gone beyond the seas to Rheims there to remain, their Lordships think it good to certify that he had no such intention and that in all his actions he has behaved himself orderly and discreetly, whereby he has done Her Majesty good service and deserves to be rewarded for his faithful dealing. Their Lordships request that the rumour thereof shall be allayed by all possible means and that he shall be furthered in the degree he is to take this coming Commencement; because it is not Her Majesty's pleasure that anyone employed as he has been in matters touching the benefit of his country should be defamed by those who are ignorant in the affairs he went about'.

Next week, at Commencement on July 4, Marlowe walked proudly in procession, suitably apparelled as Master of Arts of Cambridge University. His first ambition was achieved and he was ready to go out in the world to make further conquests.

Mercifully he could not know that he had less than six years of life left to him.

BOOK III

December 1587 to May 1593:

'The Muses' Darling'

11. Changing Prospects

A week before the Privy Council had taken upon itself to signify the Queen's pleasure in the matter of a degree for Christopher Marlowe, of whose existence she was unaware, Elizabeth herself, in opposition to the Council, had personally expressed her pleasure in the young Robert Devereux, Earl of Essex, by making him Master of Horse. He was her cousin, Leicester's stepson, Burleigh's ward. The centre of the Court was, thus, his natural place and he brought to it not only a handsome presence and a personality which could sway crowds as well as individuals, but some of the oldest blood in England. His ancestry could be traced back, in the female line, directly to King Edward III, and through that line he was descended from most of the great mediaeval families who had intermarried with the Royal House. Beside him, most of Elizabeth's Court, the *nouveau riche* peerage of Henry VIII like Leicester, the Cecils, Walsingham and other creations of the Great Pillage were *parvenus* indeed. He might be the poorest earl in England, but he was among the most certain aristocrats.

This circumstance was of relevance to his dealings with Raleigh, the obscure Devon gentleman. Their relative status was immediately understood by both of them. Moreover, the nineteen-year-old Essex spoke to the Queen, as if by right, in tones that the thirty-five-year-old Favourite would, for all his *panache* and pride of place, never dare to use. And in their first clash that summer the situation was perfectly defined.

Throughout the spring days the Queen had had 'nobody near her but my Lord of Essex; and at night my Lord is at cards, or one game or another, with her till the birds sing in the morning' but Raleigh remained the official Favourite. It was when the

Court went on the Summer Progress that the antagonism became defined and unconcealed. At the Earl of Warwick's mansion one of the guests was Essex's older sister, Dorothy, who had been one of the Queen's Ladies-in-Waiting until she had been disgraced and banished from Court for making a clandestine marriage of a peculiar kind. She and her lover, accompanied by an accommodating Clerk in Holy Orders, broke into a church and managed to complete the marriage-ceremony only minutes before angry relatives galloped into the church porch in vain pursuit.

Dorothy had now persuaded her friend, the Countess of Warwick, to invite her to stay with her at a time when the Queen was expected on the Progress. Essex assumed that he was now in a strong enough position for the Queen, for his sake, to pardon his sister and restore her to Court. He had reckoned without Raleigh who, choosing an appropriate moment, drew Elizabeth's attention to the flagrant act of disobedience, with the result that the Queen peremptorily ordered Dorothy to be closely confined to her room.

Essex flew into a temper and accused the Queen of acting as she had 'only to please that knave Raleigh for whose sake I saw she would both grieve me and my love and disgrace me in the eye of the world'.

Elizabeth immediately defended Raleigh 'and it seemed'—so Essex recorded it—'that she would not endure anything to be spoken against him; and taking hold of one word "Disdain", she said "there was no such cause why I should disdain him"'.

This only further incensed Essex who, deliberately raising his voice so that Raleigh on duty the other side of the door as Captain of the Guard could hear, described as offensively as he could 'what Raleigh had been and what he was'; asked 'What comfort can I have to give myself over to a mistress that is in awe of such a man!' and told her: 'I have no joy to be in any place, but am loath to be near about you, when I know my affection so much thrown down and such a wretch as Raleigh highly esteemed of you.'

Elizabeth, as angry as Essex, turned from defence to attack and, after some scorching remarks about Essex's sister and his mother (whom as Leicester's present wife she in any case detested), refused to continue the conversation.

Essex rushed from the room, sent his sister from the house under an escort of Devereux retainers and himself rode off to

Margate to take ship for the Low Countries and the war,
saying that a good death was better than a disquiet life. He was,
however, overtaken by one of the Queen's couriers before he
embarked, brought back and reconciled to Elizabeth. But she
still would hear nothing against Raleigh and made every effort
to drive Essex into friendship with him—'which rather', as
Essex remarked, 'shall drive me to many other extremities'.

Officially Raleigh could not have heard the conversation
which Essex had taken care he could not miss, and thus he was
prevented from answering it by a challenge to a duel. But he
made a contemptuous answer in words to the words that had
over-topped the rest. On a scrap of paper he wrote:

> If Cynthia be a Queen, a princess and supreme,
> Keep these among the rest, or say it was a dream.
> For those that like, expound; and those that loathe,
>   express
> Meanings according as their minds move more or less.
> For writing 'what thou art' or showing 'what thou were'
> Adds to the one 'Disdain', to th' other but 'Despair'.*
> Thy mind of neither needs; in both seeing it exceeds.

Such allusive riddling verses were one of the Court fashions.
Raleigh had become adept at composing them when periods of
guard-duty confined his active body. He had even written one
which could be read either across or downwards, beginning:

Your face	your tongue	your wit
So fair	so sweet	so sharp
First bent	then drew	so hit
Mine eye	mine ear	my heart
Mine eye	mine ear	my heart
To like	to learn	to love
Your face	your tongue	your wit
Doth tend	doth teach	doth move

and so on for six patterned, intricate verses.

* Until M. C. Bradbrook in *The School of Night* (1936) pointed out that the verse
was obviously related to this situation, it was considered a detached and incompre-
hensible riddle. Its full meaning is far from clear, though it appears to be addressed
indirectly to the Queen and, recalling the phrases of Essex's tirade, asserts his own
disdain of the new Favourite and his own despair at the favour shown to him.

Raleigh's talent for impromptu versifying was the next facet of his extraordinary personality that Marlowe was to discover.

On Marlowe's visit to Walsingham to ask him to intervene in the matter of his degree, he had had the good fortune to meet Tom and to have been given, as it were, an 'official' introduction to him by the head of the house. Sir Francis was sending Tom to discuss with his brother Edmund some family matters mainly connected with Sidney's still undischarged debts and on the way back to London, Tom suggested to Kit that next day he should accompany him to Scadbury.

'But I can't intrude into your family affairs,' said Marlowe, 'and your brother certainly would not welcome me.' He did not add that, from his glimpse of Edmund in the funeral procession, he would equally not welcome seeing the master of Scadbury.

'There's no need for you to see him,' said Tom. 'The business will not take us long and you can explore the woods while I'm with Edmund. Then I'll meet you by the trysting-tree and show you my secret hiding-places.'

So, on a perfect June day under a white-flecked sky, Marlowe wandered solitary in the woods of the Walsingham estate. The oaks and the great beeches, the elms that bordered the drive and the thickets of bramble and the woodland ferns and flowers, the silence tempered only by the faint stirring of leaves and the distant sound of a flock of sheep and the insistent bird-calls transported him to the Arcadia of the ancients. For these many years now the classic poets had made him free of it, yet the actuality of this sudden and unexpected isolation gave him a fresh vision. It was as if he saw a wood for the first time. He even understood a passage from Pliny at which he had been inclined to laugh: 'There is a little hill named Carne not far from Rome, clad and beautiful with a goodly grove and tuft of beech trees, so even and round in the head as if they were kept cut with garden-shears. In it there was one especial fair tree above the rest on which Fabienus Crispus cast an extraordinary liking, in so much as he was wont not only to take his repose and lie under it and to sprinkle it with wine but on occasions to embrace and kiss it.'

The trysting-tree which Tom had shown him before he went into the house and which he had appointed as their rendezvous was also a great beech, whose smooth green-grey trunk supported a wide-spreading mass of graceful branches of shining light-green leaves. On it many lovers had cut their initials and when a distant clock struck the hour of meeting and Tom had still not rejoined him, Marlowe started to carve an elegant 'T.W.' on the bark with his dagger. Absorbed in this, he did not hear his love's approach and was unaware of his presence until Tom's arms encircled him, holding him prisoner.

'Forgive me for being so long, Kit,' he said as he released him, 'but Edmund was in one of his talkative moods and I owe it to Uncle Francis to make him see reason.'

'And did you?'

'I think so. A little, at least. Enough to let me forget it and give all the day to you.'

Marlowe insisted on finishing the flourish on the 'W' and Tom Walsingham, not to be outdone, carved the initials 'C.M.' on the other side of the trunk. *

When their marks were duly made, Tom took Kit on what might have been described as a sentimental journey through his childhood. With the egoism of love he assumed that his private memorial-places would be of equal interest to Kit—the thicket so near the drive that, when hiding in it, he could hear the conversation of passers-by on their way to the house; the elm tree by which he would stand when his father was awaited for dinner so that he could test his speed by trying to race the horse; the oak blasted by lightning with what was left of its stricken branches resembling the jagged wings of a dragon, so that he always thought of the aperture through which, when he was very small, he used to crawl into its hollow trunk as 'the Dragon's Mouth'; the corner of a coppice where he had once found a young blackbird with only half an upper beak and a white tail-feather which, possibly because its handicap had isolated it from its fellows, had allowed him eventually to feed it with ham-fat he collected from the kitchen; the treacherous bank of the water-lilied lake where he had been rescued from drowning by Frizer. . . .

'Is that why you dote on the man?' asked Kit.

Tom, surprised and a trifle irritated, retorted: 'I should have

---

* The 'C.M.' is still easily distinguishable, if a little moss-edged, on the great beech at Scadbury. The 'W' is somewhat higher up at the rear of the trunk.

thought it would be truer to say that he dotes on me. Do you grudge me his attention?'

Marlowe was quick to cover his mistake by protestations of his own affection.

Tom acknowledged it with: 'When Edmund dies and all this is my home again, you must come and live with me here. You shall have the best rooms in the south wing.'

'I should find that too grand, but you could give me one of those cottages over there.'

To commemorate the day, Kit wrote for Tom some fashionable 'Arcadian' verses; and on his next visit to Raleigh to demonstrate proudly that he was now so proficient in tobacco smoking that he could inhale without coughing, he submitted them to Sir Walter's judgment.

Having glanced through them, Raleigh said: 'These, my kind Kit, merit an unkind answer. Allow me to supply it. Let me have the first stanza.'

Somewhat self-consciously, Marlowe recited it:

> Come live with me and be my love
> And we will all the pleasures prove
> That valleys, groves or hills and fields,
> Woods or steepy mountain yields.

Raleigh replied:

> If all the world and love were young
> And truth in every shepherd's tongue,
> These pretty pleasures might me move
> To live with thee and be thy love.

Marlowe continued:

> And we will sit upon the rocks
> Seeing the shepherds feed their flocks
> By shallow rivers to whose falls
> Melodious birds sing madrigals.

Raleigh refilled his pipe. As he knocked out the ash, he said: 'So you still refuse to consider how time changes matter? Very well, then. Let my verse memorialise it.' And he declaimed:

Time drives the flocks from field to fold
When rivers rage and rocks grow cold,
And Philomel becometh dumb
And Age complains of cares to come,

And fading flowers in every field
To winter floods their treasures yield.
A honeyed tongue, a heart of gall,
Is Fancy's spring, but Sorrow's fall.

Marlowe followed with:

And I will make thee beds of roses
And a thousand fragrant posies,
A cap of flowers and a kirtle
Embroider'd all with leaves of myrtle,

A gown made of the finest wool
Which from our pretty lambs we pull,
Fair-linéd slippers from the cold,
With buckles of the purest gold.

'I cannot see', said Raleigh, 'where you are going to find the gold unless your Arcadia is set in my Virginia. However—

Thy gowns, thy shoes, thy beds of roses,
Thy cap, thy kirtle and thy posies,
Soon break, soon wither, soon forgotten,
In folly ripe, in reason rotten.

Does your catalogue continue?'
'It does,' said Marlowe grimly, 'though I fear it returns to your colony:

A belt of straw and ivy buds,
With coral clasps and amber studs;
And if these pleasures may thee move
Come, live with me and be my love!'

'No,' said Raleigh, 'and I'll content myself with your rhymes:

Thy belt of straw and ivy buds,
Thy coral clasps and amber studs,
All these in me no means can move
To come to thee and be thy love!

And now, if I remember, you have but one more stanza of supplication.'

'And I admit,' confessed Marlowe, 'not a strong one:

> The Shepherd swains shall dance and sing
> For thy delight each May-morning!
> If these delights thy mind may move
> To live with me and be my love.'

'Weak indeed,' said Raleigh,

> But could youth last and love still breed,*
> Had joys no date, nor age no need
> Then these delights my mind might move
> To live with thee and be thy love.

You must do better than that, Kit, if you want to persuade your nymph or swain or whatever the fair unknown may be to consider you as a Shepherd.† Indeed if you cannot, you should consider being a parson after all.'

Marlowe did not resent Raleigh's criticism. He was himself too well aware of the triteness of his verses and his only deep annoyance was that Tom Walsingham had called them 'wonderful'. It was so disillusioning a judgment on Tom. As for himself, he did not consider they reflected on his ability as a poet. Everyone had the right to an occasional *jeu d'esprit*. And he was by no means dissatisfied with the lines he had written to express his perceptions on that memorable day when diverse manifestations of beauty—Tom's body, the magnificence of nature, the remembered cadences of the classics—had combined to enslave him. Nor had any poet among his contemporaries—not Spenser, not Watson, not even Sidney, not, certainly, Raleigh—expressed so well the ultimate sadness of the artist who knows that the task laid on him, the communication of beauty, is doomed to eternal failure:

> What is beauty, saith my sufferings, then?
> If all the pens that ever poets held
> Had fed the feeling of their masters' thoughts,
> And every sweetness that inspir'd their hearts,
> Their minds and muses on admiréd themes;

---

* That is, keep continuing.

† 'Shepherd' in this terminology meant 'poet', as in the title given to Spenser, as Raleigh's protégé, 'The Shepherd of the Ocean'.

If all the heavenly quintessence distill'd
From their immortal flowers of poesy,
Wherein, as in a mirror, we perceive
The highest reaches of a human wit;
If these had made one poem's period,
And all combin'd in beauty's worthiness,
Yet should there hover in their restless heads
One thought, one grace, one wonder at the least,
Which into words no virtue can digest.

During the July and August of 1587, Marlowe had little thought for anything but writing *Tamburlaine the Great*. Philip Henslowe's new theatre was in process of construction by Peter Street, 'citizen and carpenter of London', to whom he had given the contract 'for the erecting, building and setting-up of a new house and stage for a playhouse in and upon a certain plot or parcel of ground appointed out for that purpose', the rose-garden on the South Bank, between the bull-ring and the bear-pit. Edward Alleyn was indefatigable in offering advice on every detail of what he saw as the scene of his future triumphs and, when given the opportunity, instructing Marlowe in such technical tricks of his trade as heightening the effect of the hero's entrance by delaying it. The result of the one was that *The Rose* differed from the existing theatres by the addition of a 'turret'—a top storey to the stage—which could be made, if necessary, an integral part of the action. The result of the second was that Marlowe's first scene, showing the deposition of the *fainéant* King of Persia, Mycetes, by his brother, Cosroe, had such force that, despite its references to Tamburlaine, the audience might well suppose that the play was to be about the Persians and Marlowe insisted that a short Prologue should state the main subject unequivocally:

From jigging veins of rhyming mother-wits
And such conceits as clownage keeps in pay,
We'll lead you to the stately tent of war,
Where you shall hear the Scythian Tamburlaine
Threatening the world with high astounding terms
And scourging kingdoms with his conquering sword.
View but his picture in this tragic glass,
And then applaud his fortunes as you please.

141

Marlowe's room was on the first floor of a small house in Bishopsgate Street facing the pillory at the corner of Hog Lane, a road which ran eastward between a 'fair hedgerow of elms' to the three windmills in Finsbury Fields. At the back were the ruins of St Mary's Hospital—'the Spital'—which had been pillaged at the Reformation and which, during the last few years, had been gradually built over. The whole district, which included *The Theatre* and *The Curtain* on the north side, was being gradually developed by speculators, so that a citizen could complain how 'the pleasant fields, very commodious for the citizens therein to walk, shoot and otherwise to recreate and refresh their dulled spirits in the sweet and wholesome air, is now made a continual building throughout of garden houses and small cottages; and the fields on either side be turned into garden-plots, bowling alleys and such like'.

On occasion Marlowe would leave Norton Folgate to visit Raleigh in his palace, Durham House, once the town-house of the Bishops of Durham which was alienated from the see at the Reformation and, as a royal residence, had been assigned to Elizabeth when she was Princess.* Here, in the little turret-study overlooking the Thames 'which had a prospect as pleasant as any in the world and which not only refreshed the eyesight, but cheered the spirits and enlarged an ingenious man's thought', Raleigh, Hariot, the young Earl of Northumberland—he was Marlowe's age—whose abstruse learning and passion for occult knowledge made him known as 'the Wizard Earl', Marlowe himself, Raleigh's half-brother, Adrian Gilbert, who occasionally acted as laboratory assistant to Philip Sidney's sister, Mary Countess of Pembroke ('a great chemist' who presided over a literary-scientific salon in her mansion at Wilton) and other inquiring minds met to discuss every aspect of the universe.

In the writing of *Tamburlaine*, Marlowe's main problem was to understand the character of the ruthless Scythian. His imagination might luxuriate in portraying and even embroidering the Eastern conqueror's cruelties. He could continue his technique of accumulating horrors as he had done in his invented passage on the sack of Troy in *Dido*; but in this much more ambitious play he needed a deeper understanding of a nature which his

* It occupied the site of what is now Adelphi Terrace.

Machiavellianism could admire but which his essential kindness
—or softness—would never allow him to imitate. And here,
Kit decided, Raleigh could be of service to him.

In outward things, the comparison was obviously useful; the
rise of an obscure Devon gentleman to be the most powerful
figure at the English Court paralleled in its way the metamorphosis of a Scythian shepherd into the Emperor of the East; the
suit of silver armour which Raleigh had made for himself as
Captain of the Guard in which he delighted to appear recalled
Tamburlaine 'array'd in golden armour like the sun'; Raleigh
as a choleric man, displaying the effects of a temperament in
which choler was the dominant 'humour', could be used as a
model in that respect for Tamburlaine and Marlowe was able
to epitomise one of the discussions in the turret-study:

> Nature that fram'd us of four elements
> Warring within our breasts for regiment
> Doth teach us all to have aspiring minds:
> Our souls, whose faculties can comprehend
> The wondrous architecture of the world
> And measure every wand'ring planet's course,
> Still climbing after knowledge infinite,
> And always moving as the restless spheres,
> Will us to wear ourselves and never rest,
> Until we reach the ripest fruit of all,
> That perfect bliss and sole felicity,
> The sweet fruition of an earthly crown.

But the question which Marlowe wanted Raleigh to answer
concerned something deeper than these superficialities. What
kind of nature was it that was indifferent to the amount of
murder and massacre it was necessary to indulge in to attain—
or to retain—the crown? What was the effect on oneself of
giving orders for a massacre or for killing the defenceless in
cold blood?

One afternoon Marlowe summoned up courage to put the
matter directly to Raleigh. Sir Walter's part in the Irish massacre six years earlier was common enough knowledge. It had
excited sufficient horror in Europe for official steps to be taken
to exonerate Queen Elizabeth from any suspicion of condonation.
Raleigh, however, had never attempted to exculpate himself

and regarded the matter as one of the conventional, if regrettable, incidents of warfare.

'The garrison was called on to surrender', he said, in answer to Marlowe, 'and, had they done so at once, terms would have been agreed. But they were expecting reinforcements and they refused. When they found that no succour arrived, they beat a parley and hung out the white flag and cried *Misericordia! Misericordia!* But it was too late. We insisted on absolute surrender and they yielded themselves absolutely, only asking for mercy.'

'Which you did not show,' said Marlowe.

'No,' said Raleigh. 'In the circumstances it was not considered expedient.'

'And though women came and on their knees begged for their lives, you ordered them to be slaughtered?'

'Yes,' said Raleigh. 'An act of terror may sometimes shorten war.'

' "Accurs'd be he who first invented war," ' said Marlowe, quoting one of the lines he had given to Mycetes in his play.

'A most admirable sentiment, my dear Kit, but since war has been invented, it must be played according to the rules. That alone makes it tolerable. Had the defenders of Smerwick been promised their lives and I had broken my pledged word to them, I should be too contemptible to face myself. But it was not so.'

'Yet you can face yourself if you order a massacre of women?'

'The order was not mine but the Lord Deputy's; but that is of no consequence for I should have made the same decision. I have told you, it was for terror and for an example, so that others might accept terms when they were offered. It was a common part of warfare. But you, my dear Kit, are quite ignorant of war; so let me instruct you that when you have hazarded your own life a hundred or more times and seen death grinning at you on your enemy's swordpoint, when you know that if you do not kill you will be killed, you see things differently from the scribbler and the parson. Indeed, I'll give you another stanza to our poem:

> When shepherds' sighs cause wars to cease,
> And trumpets are but pipes of peace,
> And eagles emulate the dove,
> And swords are plough-shares, I'm your love.'

So it came about that when Marlowe's play reached one of its climactic points and Tamburlaine summoned Damascus to surrender, one of his captains said:

> Your tents of white now pitch'd before the gates
> And gentle flags of amity displayed,
> I doubt not but the Governor will yield
> Offering Damascus to your majesty,

to draw from Tamburlaine the answer:

> So shall he have his life and all the rest;
> But if he stay until the bloody flag
> Be once advanc'd on my vermilion tent,
> He dies, and those who kept us out so long;
> And when they see me march in black array,
> Were in that city all the world contain'd
> Not one should scape, but perish by our swords.

And when the white had been replaced by scarlet and the scarlet by black, a deputation of virgins came to plead for mercy, and Tamburlaine 'all in black and very melancholy' answered them:

> Alas, poor fools, must you be first to feel
> The sworn destruction of Damascus?
> They knew my custom; could they not as well
> Sent ye out when first my milk-white flags,
> Through which sweet Mercy threw her gentle beams,
> As now when fury and incensèd hate
> Flings slaughtering terror from my coal-black tents,
> And tells for truth submission comes too late?
> Virgins, in vain you labour to prevent
> That which mine honour swears shall be perform'd.
> Behold my sword! What see you at that point?

'Nothing but steel and fatal fear, my lord,' the leader of the women answered.

Tamburlaine replied:

> Your fearful minds are thick and misty, then,
> For there sits Death; there sits imperious Death,
> Keeping his circuit by the slicing edge.
> But I am pleas'd you shall not see him there;
> He now is seated on my horsemen's spears
> And on their points his fleshless body feeds.

He turned to his most trusted follower:

> Techelles, straight go charge a few of them
> To charge these dames and show my servant Death
> Sitting in scarlet on their arméd spears.

And when the play was performed at *The Rose*, the new 'turret' was used to point the sequel. When Tamburlaine asked

> What, have your horsemen shown the virgins death?

Techelles, indicating the inert bodies decorating 'the walls', answered

> They have, my lord, and on Damascus's walls
> Have hoisted up their slaughtered carcasses!

The first performance of the play by the Lord Admiral's Players at *The Rose* with Edward Alleyn in the lead was a prodigious success. Henslowe's experiment of building his theatre on the South Bank, which was traditionally dedicated to the coarser amusements, proved to be a master-stroke. *The Rose*, lying between the amphitheatres where bulls were killed and bears were baited for the delight of the London mobs, was directly in the path of a trail of blood. Though there was enough actual blood spilt in the stage battles—pigs' blood in bladders which spouted when the actors' swords and daggers pricked them—*The Rose* added the sophisticated pleasure of contemplating the effect of intended savagery and degradation and pain. *Tamburlaine* was a pageant of outrageous cruelty, decorated by a splendour of words, so that the audience were given an excuse for their excited blood-lust by their pretensions to an appreciation of poetry.

The spectacle of the defeated Emperor of the Turks, Bajazeth, used as a footstool by Tamburlaine and kept in an iron cage to be fed by his wife on scraps from the conqueror's table, until the shame and degradation of it forced him to beat out his brains on the cage, was only the last of the horrors to precede the massacre of the women. Incongruously—but theatrically effective—this was followed by the soliloquy on Beauty in which Kit had incorporated his lines to Tom Walsingham and connected them with Tamburlaine's love for Zenocrate.

The success of the play was such that a sequel was immediately called for and Marlowe hastily threw together a series of scenes continuing the chronicle until Tamburlaine himself fell mortally ill, and had perforce to consider his end:

> What daring god torments my body thus
> And seeks to conquer mighty Tamburlaine?
> Shall sickness prove me now to be a man,
> That have been term'd 'the Terror of the World'?
> Techelles and the rest, come, take your swords,
> And threaten him whose hand afflicts my soul;
> Come, let us march against the powers of heaven
> And set black streamers in the firmament
> To signify the slaughter of the gods.
> Come, let us charge our spears and pierce his breast
> Whose shoulders bear the axis of the world
> That, if I perish, Heaven and Earth may fade.
> See where my slave, the ugly monster Death,
> Shaking and quivering, pale and wan with fear,
> Stands aiming at me with his murdering dart,
> Who flies away at every glance I give,
> But, when I look away, comes stealing on!
> Villain, away, and hie thee to the field!
> I and mine army come to load thy barque
> With souls of thousand mangled carcasses.

Unable to stand, he turned to his physician to ask:

> Tell me, what think you of my sickness now?

to be treated to a display of factual erudition which, whether it concerned the nature of the planets or the names of jewels, philosophical categories or geographical features, was Marlowe's somewhat pompous reminder to the audience of his learning as M.A. (Cantab), and was to become a hall-mark of his style. The Physician replied:

> I view'd your urine and the hypostasis,
> Thick and obscure, doth make your danger great:
> Your veins are full of accidental heat
> Whereby the moisture of your blood is dried;
> The humidum and calor, which some hold
> Is not a parcel of the elements
> But of a substance more divine and pure,

Is almost clean extinguishéd and spent;
Which, being the cause of life, imports your death;
Your artiers, which alongst the veins convey
The lively spirits which the heart engenders,
Are parch'd and void of spirit, that the soul
Wanting those organons by which it moves
Cannot endure, by argument of art.

In writing *Tamburlaine: Part II*, Marlowe was faced by two main problems—how, having used up most of his historical material, he was to continue the story and how, after the Bajazeth scenes, he was to overtop their theatricality. The first he solved by attaching to the slender thread of Tamburlaine's determination to conquer Babylon a series of episodes culled from other sources—the battle of Varna between the Turks and the Hungarians which took place long after Tamburlaine's death but which offered Marlowe an excellent occasion to indulge his atheistic preferences in portraying Christian perfidy and setting Mahomet against Christ; an entire scene from Ariosto's *Orlando Furioso*; a detailed disquisition on the technique of siege-warfare taken from *The Treatise of Fortification* which Paul Ive, who was his senior at Corpus Christi and, like him, now in Walsingham's service, had just dedicated to their employer; a recital of Tamburlaine's conquests in Africa based on the recent atlas made by the German geographer, Abraham Ortels—Ortelius's *Theatrum Orbis Terrarum*—which Kit had pored over in the Corpus Christi library* in his Cambridge days and which he now studied at Durham House; memories of classical parallels from his translation of Lucan.

The second problem was solved by a spectacle out-Bajazething Bajazeth. 'Enter Tamburlaine, drawn in his chariot by the Kings of Trebizon and Soria, with bits in their mouths, reins in his left hand, and in his right hand a whip with which he scourgeth them.' Tamburlaine's opening words:

Holla, ye pamper'd jades of Asia!
What, can ye draw but twenty miles a day?

provoked such applause as had never yet been heard in any theatre and not only enjoyed more popular fame than anything

* Ethel Seaton in *Marlowe's Map* (1924) pointed out that 'without a single exception every non-classical name appears in the *Theatrum*'.

else Marlowe wrote but became a catchword, in and out of theatrical circles, for the next sixty years. *

The success of *Tamburlaine II* was—almost inevitably since it was a much inferior play—even greater than that of *Tamburlaine I*; and Philip Henslowe, certain that it would be much needed in revivals, stored in the prop.-room of *The Rose* 'Tamberlaine's bridle' to take its place with 'Tamberlaine's coat with copper lace and Tamberlaine's breeches of crimson velvet'.

The most spectacular episode, however, was undesigned. The 'turret' was again used but this time not for the display of the corpses of women but for the more exciting shooting to death of the Governor of Babylon.

On 16 November 1587 a young man visiting London wrote to his father: 'The Lord Admiral's Players have a device in their play to tie one of their fellows to a post and to shoot him to death. Having borrowed their callyvers, one of the players' hand swerved, his piece being charged with bullet, missed the fellow he aimed at and killed a child and a woman great with child forthwith and hurt another man in the head very sore.'

The Rose had received what builders have immemorially considered a necessity for 'luck'—a libation of human blood.

---

* The most famous reference is by Shakespeare (who mercilessly 'sent up' Marlowe at every opportunity: see Postscript: *Marlowe and Shakespeare*) in Pistol's

> These be good humours indeed! Shall pack-horses
> And hollow pamper'd jades of Asia
> Which cannot go but thirty miles a day
> Compare with Caesars and with Cannibals?

Pistol himself is a satire on Alleyn in a Marlovian rôle.

12. The Ominous Year

Tamburlaine gave Marlowe an assured place in the literary and theatrical world in which he now lived and moved. Inevitably he excited envy and he found his fellow-writers reacting to him according to their natures. Thomas Kyd managed to conceal his bitterness by effusive congratulations to which Marlowe replied by reiterating his own admiration of *The Spanish Tragedy* and emphasising that, whatever might be the opinion of the groundlings, he still regarded Kyd as his master. Kyd seized the opportunity to suggest that it might be profitable to them both to collaborate and even to share lodgings. Marlowe approved the principle but declined to set a date.

Tom Watson, who quite properly regarded Kit as his protégé and was genuinely delighted at his success, also offered his help. As the most experienced patter-writer in the theatre, whose 'daily practice' was to 'devise twenty fictions and knaveries in a play', Watson considered that Marlowe's main weakness was the lack of a sense of humour and he would have been gratified if his 'merry jests' which now decorated a variety of 'balductum plays' were to be used exclusively by his young friend. Watson had no jealousy because he considered himself, as the most popular poet of the day, above the battle. He was now living a mere half-mile away from Marlowe in the great house in St Helen's, Bishopsgate, belonging to the Cornwallis family, acting as classical tutor to John Cornwallis, translating a poem, *The Rape of Helen*, from Greek into Latin, to be dedicated to the 'wizard' Earl of Northumberland, Raleigh's friend, and luxuriating in his local celebrity as the 'Wise Man of St Helen's'.

If the attitudes of Kyd and Watson might have been expected, that of Robert Greene was a considerable surprise. Marlowe had known Greene slightly at Cambridge, where he had taken a delayed M.A. at Clare in Marlowe's fourth year and fallen foul of Gabriel Harvey who, with donnish disapproval, noted 'his fond disguising of a Master of Arts with ruffianly hair, unseemly apparel and more unseemly behaviour; his vainglorious bearing; his monstrous swearing; his impious profanity with sacred texts; his other blasphemous and scandalous raving'. In his heart, Greene would not have disagreed, as he himself admitted that the company he kept at Cambridge—'wags as lewd as myself'—instructed him how 'to furnish myself with coin, which I procured by cunning sleights from my father and my friends, and my mother pampered me for so long and secretly helped me to the oil of angels that I grew prone to all mischief'.

He used the parental money for travel in Italy and Spain, where he 'saw and practised such villainy as is abominable to declare'. Back in London 'young yet in years though old in wickedness, I began to resolve that there was nothing bad that was profitable; whereupon I grew so rooted in all mischief that I had as great a delight in wickedness as sundry hath in godliness and as much felicity I took in villainy as others had in honesty'. He married 'a gentleman's daughter of good account' but deserted her after he had 'spent up the marriage money obtained by her'.

At thirty Robert Greene, with his extravagantly long hair, his flaming red beard 'like the spire of a steeple whereon a man might hang a jewel, it was so sharp and pendent', his 'duck's-turd-green cloak' and 'greasy silk stockings', was a familiar figure in alehouses where he was welcomed for his 'inordinate spending' until landlords discovered that there was far more chalked up on his score than he had either the ability or the intention to pay. He lived with a professional prostitute, Em Ball, by whom he had a son whom he ironically named 'Fortunatus'. The other member of the family was the lady's brother, known as 'Cutting' Ball who (till he was hanged) acted as her 'bully' and his bodyguard.

However unsatisfactory Greene's life, his writing was successful enough. He was a born journalist with an intuitive perception of what the public wanted. His novels were best-sellers. He was equally adept at love-romances and slightly fictionised tales of the underworld of London. His satirical pamphlets were snapped up as soon as they were advertised. Moreover, he was a very quick writer. 'In a night and a day he could yerk up a pamphlet as well as in seven years and glad was that printer who might be so blest as to pay him dear for the very dregs of his wit.'

Greene had not so far attempted a play. He considered that as a University man it was beneath his dignity to write for the common stage. Also, he disliked actors. But the success of *Tamburlaine* bred second thoughts and Marlowe was gratified to notice that he diligently attended every performance of the play that Henslowe put on. Marlowe's attitude, however, changed considerably when the reason for Greene's interest became apparent. As a result of his intensive study, Greene constructed an Oriental conquest-play punctuated by perpetual slaughter in exact imitation of *Tamburlaine* which he called *Alphonsus King of Aragon* and in which the scenes, the plot, the versification and the general style were as close an approximation to Marlowe's as he could manage.* Fortunately, when it was put on at one of the inn-yards still used by companies of players, it was a total and unredeemed failure, so that Greene was able to declare flamboyantly that it was only intended as a burlesque of 'Shake-scene', as he appropriately nicknamed Ned Alleyn, and Marlowe could tacitly accept the implied apology.

Far different from the professional approbation of Thomas Watson, the concealed envy of Thomas Kyd or the implied flattery of Robert Greene was the critical outspokenness of Thomas Nashe. This was in part due to Nashe's age. He was not quite twenty-one—three years younger than Marlowe who had been his friend at Cambridge—and had been sent down from St John's for circulating witty scurrilities. Marlowe and he had been sufficiently close for Kit to show him his play on Dido and, *mirabile dictu*, to accept certain emendations and alterations. Nashe's own poetry, in the main abrasively satirical, was approved by Marlowe and the equality of their friendship and their mutual admiration made it possible for Kit to accept with equanimity the younger man's remark that *Tamburlaine* showed

---

* Bakeless in his *Tragicall History of Christopher Marlowe* gives a comparative table which amply justifies his judgment that 'a clearer case of borrowing it would be hard to find'.

him 'trying to outbrave better pens with the swelling bombast of a bragging blank verse and the spacious volubility of a drumming decasyllabon'.

'Kind Kit' and the 'biting young Juvenal' were further drawn to each other by their shared love and knowledge of the classics, by their hatred of clerical hypocrisy (Nashe's father was an indigent country parson) and by their detestation of the Harvey brothers at Cambridge, Gabriel, the egregious don, and Richard, who was reading Divinity as a student, but who found Aristotle beyond his understanding and—according to Marlowe—was 'an ass, good for nothing but to preach in the Iron Age'. His main interest was in weather predictions by aid of the stars, which led Nashe to nickname him Adam Foulweather, Student of Ass-tronomy.

By a strange coincidence, Richard Harvey's first cure of souls was the parish of Chislehurst, in which lay Edmund Walsingham's manor of Scadbury, and there as the year 1587 was drawing to an end he spent his extensive leisure composing an almanack for 1588 entitled *A discoursive Problem concerning Prophecies, how far they are to be valued or credited, devised especially in abatement of the terrible Threatenings and Menaces peremptorily denounced against the Kingdoms and States of the World this present famous Year 1588 supposed the Great-wonderful and Fatal Year of our Age.*

The pamphlet opened by quoting the prophecy of John Muller, the great fifteenth-century mathematician who had provided Columbus with astronomical tables and who was known as Regiomontanus. Plotting the heavens-to-come, Regiomontanus had discovered that the year 1588 would have an eclipse of the sun in February and two total eclipses of the moon, one in March and one in August, while in March the planets Mars, Jupiter and Saturn would be in ominous conjunction in the Moon's own house.

Post mille exactos a partu virginis annos
Ex post quingentos rursus ab orbe datos
Octavagesimus octavus mirabilis annus
Ingruet et secum tristitia satis trahet.
Si non hoc anno totus malus occidet orbis,
Si non in totum terra fretumque ruant,

153

Cuncta tamen mundi sursum ibunt atque decrescent
Imperia et luctus undique grandis erit.*

Successors of Regiomontanus during the next century confirmed his interpretation and from one end of Europe to another
the prophecies were interpreted and discussed in fear and apprehension. In Catholic countries where, officially, attempts to
forecast the future were considered as impious, popular almanacks circulated despite official prohibition while in Protestant Amsterdam the enterprising printers of them made a
fortune. In England, the matter needed particularly careful
handling, since the more disastrous of the eclipses of the moon
came at the beginning of the Queen's ruling sign, Virgo, and
just twelve days before her birthday, so that the Privy Council
thought it wise to give the Stationers' Company a reminder that
to prophesy the sovereign's death, even by inference, was high
treason.

Apprehension was intensified by a discovery in the ruins of
Glastonbury Abbey. A mysterious earth-tremor disclosed a
marble slab, hidden for centuries beneath the crypt, on which
were carved the eight lines of Regiomontanus's prophecy. *Post
mille exactos a partu virginis annos.* This was taken to prove that
the lines were not the invention of the fifteenth-century German
astronomer, but the warning of Merlin himself that the empire
of Uther Pendragon, of which Queen Elizabeth was the last
representative, was doomed to perish.

The discovery was considered of sufficient importance for a
Catholic correspondent to inform Father Allen at Douai, who
duly forwarded a fair copy of his letter to the Vatican. Against
the words foretelling the dwindling of empires the Pope's
secretary noted, in Italian: 'No indication of which empires or
how many.'

That was, in practical terms, the vital question. Would the
Spanish Armada, which could no longer be delayed, result in
damage to England, to Germany and the Low Countries, to
France—or to Spain? The most obvious application was to

---

* A thousand years after the Virgin Birth and five hundred more allowed the
world, the wonderful eighty-eighth year begins and brings in its train enough
misery. If, this year, total catastrophe does not destroy the world, if land and sea do
not collapse in total ruin, nevertheless the whole world will suffer upheavals and
empires will shrink and everywhere there will be great lamentation.

Spain, but King Philip refused to take any notice of such super-
stitious nonsense, even though many of his courtiers thought
that the prediction of the terrible weather alone might have
caused second thoughts about the wisdom of launching a vast
amphibian operation. As for England, she could not avoid attack
if Spain decided on it, but she was hardly an 'empire' in the
Spanish sense. The possibility that Merlin was speaking of 'the
empire of Uther Pendragon' was thus not to be countenanced
and Richard Harvey in his almanack was careful to follow the
lead of Lord Henry Howard who, four years earlier, had written
A Defensative against the Poison of Supposed Prophecies. Richard
Harvey challenged the accepted interpretation of Regiomontanus, impugning on the one hand the accuracy of the astrological facts and readings and, on the other, insisting that many
equally—or almost equally—ominous conjunctions of planets in
the past had caused alarms which the actual events had not
justified.

In the circumstances, Marlowe found the subject for his next
play virtually chosen for him and, in his mind, confirmed by the
strange discovery at Glastonbury. For Marlowe was of Merlin's
race. The modern spelling of the family name was merely a
variant of it and in every official college entry at Cambridge he
had seen to it that it was spelt 'Marlin'.* His affectation had
survived in the memory of his contemporaries at the University
and Robin Greene had perpetuated it by an unkind reference to
'mad and scoffing poets bred of Merlin's race that set the end of
scholarism in an English blank-verse'. And yet, in view of the
matters so avidly discussed in the turret-study of Durham
House, was it merely an affectation? Raleigh and Hariot and the
Wizard Earl would have said that it approximated more nearly
to a boast and a badge.

The great Merlin apart, however, it was clear that the popular
interest of the moment lay in astrology and everything connected with it. On the Continent it had crystallised round Johann

---

* Though the chaotic nature of Elizabethan spelling (which has no less than sixty-
eight known variants for 'Raleigh') made it on occasion 'Malin' or 'Marlyn'. The
Elizabethan 'e' was pronounced as 'a', as the custom survives in such words as
'clerk'.

Muller's—'Regiomontanus's'—successor as the leading astrolo-
ger of Germany, Dr Johann Faust, who in the fifteen-thirties was
credited with having made a pact with the Devil and having been
duly carried off to Hell. In 1587 there was published in Frank-
furt *A History of Dr Johann Faust, the widely-noised conjuror
and Master of the Black Art* which was immediately reprinted
twice and went into three more editions during 'the ominous
year' following.* It became internationally known, was soon
embellished and embroidered with memories of mediaeval tales
of magicians and, in England, was popularised by *The Ballad of
the Life and Death of Dr Faustus, the Great Conjuror.*

No subject could have better suited Marlowe. It satisfied his
primary consideration—a leading part for Alleyn which should
be as compelling as Tamburlaine. 'The stalking steps of his
great personage' (as a Cambridge undergraduate described
'Shake-scene's' performance), his magnificent voice and his
increasing histrionic power could be utilised to the full in a part
demanding the casting of spells, the conjuration of devils and
the agonised terror which accompanied his final realisation of
damnation. And, as a play concerned with the power of knowledge, it would allow the actor to subtilise effects which he had
used more broadly in delineating the power of soldierly might.

From his own point of view, Marlowe welcomed the opportunity to write of the things he actually knew from experience
rather than those for which he had to rely on his reading or his
imagination. The arguments of scholars at a university were
easier to exhibit with verisimilitude than the exchanges between
Eastern potentates in Persepolis. He was more at home with
theology than with warfare. Another fortunate circumstance
was that the story of a magician demanded a series of conjuring
scenes in the comic manner of which Tom Watson was the
acknowledged master. His proffered help would now be in-
valuable. Marlowe decided that, all things considered, *Dr
Faustus* should not take him more than a month to write.

---

* Because there is no record of an English translation before 1592, Dr Boas in his
Christopher Marlowe (1940) assumed that Marlowe could not have known it and
drew the conclusion that, in consequence, he could not have written *Dr Faustus* till
the last year of his life. The overwhelming circumstantial evidence to the contrary
and the consensus of critical opinion since 1831 that it was written in 1588 are now
set aside by 'Eng. Lit.' followers of Dr Boas's academic quibble, which rests on a
belief in the infallibility of bibliography.

The one disappointment was that he was unable to consult Raleigh, whom the Queen had ordered, as a member of the Council of War, to make a special study of fortifications. Sir Walter drew up a list of places particularly open to invasion, and, in the course of his inspection of the coast, went as far north as King's Lynn to advise in person the Norfolk authorities. After a general supervision, Raleigh left London (after six years Elizabeth had found she could bear his absence with equanimity and transferred to Essex the prohibition to leave her side) and, as Lord Warden of the Stanneries, Lieutenant of the County of Cornwall and Vice-Admiral of Devon and Cornwall, he rode down to his own territory to consult with the local magnates at Exeter plans 'for the drawing together of 2,000 foot and 200 horse'. He personally superintended the training of the levies and, in addition, showed interest and curiosity in the strange faerie rites and dances which were ritually performed on the beaches by the country-folk as a protection against possible invaders. Considering the year, they did not seem altogether incongruous.

The prophecies of doom, at least as far as Spain was concerned, began to appear apposite enough. In February the Marquis of Santa Cruz, the greatest sailor of the age, veteran of Lepanto, 'the light of war, the father of his troops, that valiant and unconquered leader' who had from the beginning been in charge of preparations for the Armada, died suddenly. In his place King Philip appointed the Duke of Medina Sidonia, who had no illusions about his total unsuitability and did his best to refuse the honour by pleading with the King that he 'had no experience of the sea or of war' and that, were he made Admiral, he foresaw nothing but disaster. But the King insisted and in April Medina Sidonia went aboard his flag-ship at Lisbon in weather 'as unfavourable as if it were December'. It remained so for a month, during which time the storms in the Atlantic, as fierce as the astrologers had predicted, kept the fleet bottled up in the harbour on the Tagus.

During the enforced weeks of waiting Medina Sidonia had a detailed inventory of the fleet drawn up as a confidential report to the King. By some mischance it was published while the Armada was still in the Tagus. Two weeks later translations appeared in Rome, Paris, Cologne and Delft. Amsterdam, as in the astrological almanacks, catered for both Catholics and Protestants and for the latter added to the lists of stores and equipment whatever whips and pincers, chains and gridirons, racks and thumbscrews, would be appreciated by that public. The more enterprising publishers kept the type standing so that it could be used again whenever rumour suggested that a new pamphlet on the Armada might be profitable. One of them added a ship carrying a cargo of halters for the hanging of Protestants and another filled with faggots for burning them.

On May 28 the weather had moderated sufficiently for the Armada to put to sea, but it worsened again almost immediately and the fleet took a fortnight to reach Finisterre, 160 sea-miles away. In the meantime the food and water were in such a state that revictualling was essential and, on June 19, Medina Sidonia had to put into Corunna to carry out that operation.

On Midsummer Eve, celebrated from the far pre-Christian centuries as the greatest and most powerful of the witch-festivals, there came howling out of the Atlantic the worst tempest of that abominable season. Even in the shelter of the harbour, one ship tore loose from its moorings and a pinnace dragged its anchor and collided with a galleon. The ships still cruising off-shore were driven before the storm into the open sea. Next day Medina Sidonia wrote to the King, reporting the storm. He explained that it had scattered the fleet and that he feared that the news would soon be known in England and that English ships aided by the Huguenot pirates of La Rochelle would hunt down the distressed vessels which had not been able to make some sheltering port. The weather, he said, was still wintry; there was much sickness among the soldiers and sailors; supplies were so short that there was no possibility of continuing the voyage until the ships had been repaired and reprovisioned and reinforcements collected. The rebels in Flanders would take great heart at the news of this mishap to the fleet and Medina Sidonia even went so far as to predict that Parma would be unable to muster the required invasion force even if the Armada reached the Channel. In the circumstances, the reluctant Admiral ventured to suggest to the King that the Great Enterprise should be considered to have miscarried and that His Majesty should seek to make peace on honourable terms. An additional reason for this was that, according to the information he had collected, the Armada would have to engage a far superior force.

Such, indeed, was the opinion of Europe, summed up by the Venetian Ambassador: 'It is commonly thought that, in spite of all preparations Spain will not attack England because the King knows full well how much the English fleet is to be feared, not only for its numbers, but also because the English have the reputation of being the best sailors in the world and great fighters at sea.' Such, also, was the actuality. The English fleet had an overwhelming preponderance of gun-power; they had not only more ships, but their vessels were altogether superior in sailing qualities; their crews were better; and their tactics were of the new school, which allowed the enemy no chance to grapple and board.* And as the secret peace negotiations with Parma were still proceeding, there was no reason except his own obstinacy why Philip should not have taken his Admiral's advice. Instead, he instructed him to proceed and at the same time deprived him of the one chance of success by peremptorily ordering him on no account to attempt to land on the English coast until he had covered Parma's landing from the Netherlands.

Consequently, although he might easily and safely have landed ten or fifteen thousand troops in the wide anchorage of Tor Bay, with its convenient beaches and coves, sheltered from all westerly and southerly winds—and was, indeed, urged to do so by his captains—Medina Sidonia, to the astonishment of Howard of Effingham, the English Admiral, and Sir Francis Drake, his Vice-Admiral, sailed stolidly on towards the Straits of Dover. Howard and Drake, naturally presuming that, having ignored the Devon ports, the Spanish objective was the Isle of Wight (repeating French invasion-tactics of forty years earlier), followed the Armada up-Channel, fighting occasional skirmishes but not, in spite of three Spanish losses, damaging or breaking the majestic formation.

But neither at Portland nor at the Solent did Medina Sidonia turn aside to the English coast and, on the evening of Saturday, July 27,† a week after the Armada had been sighted and engaged

---

* Cf. Sir John Neale's great *Queen Elizabeth* p. 297. The point is important, because the popular English legend of the event obscures it.

† Spanish historians, who use the Gregorian calendar introduced on 4 October 1582, date this as August 6. England retained the 'Old Style' until 1752, whereas

off Plymouth, he anchored in the open off Calais. He immediately sent a messenger to Parma, who was at Bruges, announcing his arrival and asking when the Duke would be ready to cross to England. Parma wrote that he was delighted by the safe arrival of the Armada and promised that in six days everything would be ready for the sortie across the Narrow Seas.

Howard dropped anchor less than a mile behind the Spanish fleet and so throughout the Sunday it remained—the entire naval force of England, one hundred and fifty sail, all the Queen's galleons, as many more armed merchantmen and private men-of-war and a hundred smaller craft, 'the Grand Fleet in fact if not in name'. All that was needed now was to force the Armada away from the Calais Roads and bring it to an engagement in the open sea. During the night, with the wind blowing and the tide running in the right direction, the English stuffed eight merchantmen with all the tar barrels available, with the guns loaded and shotted to go off as the flames reached the priming, and sent them, like blazing volcanoes, into the Spanish fleet. Fire, that terror of 'wooden walls', produced the panic required to disrupt the disciplined formation which, so far, nothing had been able to break. Most of the captains cut their cables to escape at any cost and, crashing and bumping against each other in the darkness, ran before the wind, a disorderly mob of ships driven by a rising gale out through the straits into the North Sea to find destruction in the swirling tides of the rocky Hebrides.

On the medal struck to commemorate the great victory, the Queen was scrupulous to describe the cause of it. The winds of God blew and they were scattered.

Nor did the pamphleteers fail to remind their readers that it was, after all, the ominous year. 'It was foretold that the year

the 'New Style' was adopted almost immediately by the Catholic countries, France, Italy and Spain. In dealing with events which involve England and the Continent, this occasionally leads to some confusion. Garrett Mattingley in his authoritative *The Defeat of the Spanish Armada* uses the New Style throughout; Sir John Neale in his equally authoritative *Queen Elizabeth* uses the Old Style. Thus the latter writes 'on the evening of the twenty-seventh [July] the Armada came to anchor off Calais' while the former dates it 'the evening of August 6'. Both are speaking of the same day. Translation from O.S. to N.S. is done easily enough by adding ten days (or from N.S. to O.S. by subtracting ten days). Though I agree with Garrett Mattingley that the New Style 'corresponds to the actual season and ten days do make a difference to how much daylight there is', I have kept to the Old Style to avoid confusion.

one thousand five hundred and eighty-eight', began one pamphlet, 'would be the *Climacteral* year of the world, which is in some measure accomplished in the glorious and never-to-be-forgotten deliverance vouchsafed by God to us in England by the fatal overthrow of the Spanish Navy.'

On September 8, the morrow of Queen Elizabeth's fifty-fifth birthday, a great service of thanksgiving was held in St Paul's, with a special sermon preached from Paul's Cross. Two deaths the previous week robbed it of its savour for her. Leicester, her continuing love, despite every rival and vicissitude, for thirty-two years and who, as 'Lieutenant and General of the Queen's Armies and Companies',* had ridden by her side when she reviewed her troops at Tilbury, died almost incidentally on his way back from taking the waters at Buxton—a needed refreshment after his unresting efforts to mobilise the land forces. 'They have put me to more travail', he had written to Walsingham as the Armada came up the Channel, 'than ever I was in my life.'

The other death was that of Richard Tarlton, the Queen's jester and the leading comic actor of the day. He had been introduced to her years ago by Leicester, who discovered him as a young swineherd on his estate and who thought that his quick wit, combined with his squint and his flat nose, would provide her with passing amusement. Their subsequent association, however, had assumed a permanence and reached a depth of understanding that justified the judgment that 'when the Queen was out of good humour, he could *un-dumpish* her at his pleasure. Her highest favourites would, in some cases, go to Tarlton before they would go to the Queen and he was their usher to prepare their advantageous access unto her. In a word, he told the Queen more of her faults than most of her chaplains and cured her melancholy better than all of her physicians.'

Tarlton died on September 1 at the house of Em Ball, Robin Greene's disreputable mistress, and his last act was to write to Sir Francis Walsingham imploring his aid against 'a sly fellow fuller of law than of virtue' who would try to get his estate away

---

* She wanted to make him Lieutenant-General of England and Ireland in the event of anything happening to her, but refrained because such a step would raise the delicate question of the Succession.

from the actor's mother and son—'a silly old widow of fourscore years of age and a poor infant of the age of six years'. Tarlton reminded Walsingham that the boy, Philip, was Sir Philip Sidney's godson and bore his name.* Sir Francis, as mindful as ever even in so small a matter of his son-in-law's posthumous honour, saw to it that a successful Chancery action was immediately brought against the 'sly fellow'.

Tarlton's death, besides spreading gloom not only at Court but over the theatrical quarter—Em Ball's house was in Holywell, a stone's throw from *The Curtain*—affected the whole theatrical situation. The Queen's Men, of whom he was the pivot and the star and the most certain attraction at Burbage's *The Theatre*, began rapidly to decline and to lose their hold on London. The premier company, in fact if not in name, was henceforth to be the Admiral's. Indirectly the defeat of the Armada contributed to it, for inevitably something of the nation's gratitude to Lord Howard spilled over on to his Players. And the 'astrological' topicality of their new play, *Dr Faustus*, as well as the popularity of Edward Alleyn, now acknowledged as England's leading actor, in the main part, drew the crowds across the river to *The Rose*.

Marlowe had been careful to introduce many pertinent allusions and such lines as Faustus's announcement that with magical spirits at his command:

> I'll have them fly to India for gold,
> Ransack the ocean for orient pearl
> And search all corners of the new-found world;
> I'll levy soldiers with the coin they bring
> And chase the Prince of Parma from our† land,

won patriotic applause. Even more popular was the anti-Papal scene, which was in essence Tom Watson's where Faustus and Mephistophilis assumed the appearance of Cardinals to wreck the Pope's ruling in a conclave and subsequently attended a banquet where Faustus, granted the gift of invisibility by Mephistophilis, snatched away the Pope's food and drink just as he was about to taste them and drove him away from the

---

* That King Philip of Spain was Sidney's godfather and Sidney, Philip Tarlton's, provides a neat epitome of this closely-knit society.
† Faustus as a citizen of the Empire naturally refers to the Netherlands as 'our'.

feast with belabouring blows. When some Friars entered to exorcise this unquiet spirit presumably 'a ghost crept out of Purgatory', 'Mephistophilis and Faustus'—so the stage direction ran—'beat the Friars and fling fireworks among them and so exeunt.'

This scene achieved a lasting fame. Not only was Alleyn's change into ecclesiastical dress at the conclave mentioned by other writers as a well-known fact:

> The Gull gets on a surplice,
>   With a cross upon his breast,
> Like Alleyn playing Faustus—
>   In that manner he was dressed,

but a visitor to the play epitomised it: 'There a man may behold shaggy-haired devils run roaring over the stage with squibs in their mouths while drummers make thunder in the Tiring House and the twelve-penny hirelings in their Heavens.'

From first to last, the 'tragical history' tended to become a comic spectacle and the farcical scene introducing the Seven Deadly Sins, which Marlowe and Watson had introduced as a tribute to the dying Tarlton (who had written for the Queen's Players a highly successful play of that name to exhibit his own genius as a comedian), hugely pleased the groundlings who were quite incapable of appreciating either Marlowe's poetry or his theology.*

And yet in *Doctor Faustus* Marlowe reached heights he was never to touch again. His theological understanding enabled him to clothe catechetical accuracy in memorable words. When Faustus questions Mephistophilis why he is out of hell, the emissary of Lucifer replies:

> Why, this is Hell nor am I out of it.
> Think'st thou that I, who saw the face of God
> And tasted the eternal joys of Heaven,

---

* The deterioration continued through the years, until Pope could write:

> All sudden Gorgons hiss and Dragons glare
> And ten-horn'd fiends and giants rush to war.
> Hell rises, Heaven descends, and dance on earth,
> Gods, imps and monsters, music, rage and mirth,
> A fire, a jug, a bottle and a ball,
> Till one wide conflagration covers all.

Am not tormented with ten thousand hells
In being depriv'd of everlasting bliss?
Hell hath no limits, nor is circumscribed
In one self place; for where we are is Hell: *
And, to conclude, when all the world dissolves
And every creature shall be purified,
All places shall be Hell that are not Heaven.

And when the hour strikes for the inescapable judgment,
Alleyn was given a speech to match his unforgettable acting:

Stand still, you ever-moving spheres of Heaven
That time may cease and midnight never come;
Fair Nature's eye, rise, rise again and make
Perpetual day; or let this hour be but
A year, a month, a week, a natural day
That Faustus may repent and save his soul!
'O lente, lente, currite, noctis equi!'†
The stars move still, time runs, the clock will strike,
The devil will come and Faustus must be damn'd.
O, I'll leap up to God!—Who pulls me down?—
See where Christ's blood streams in the firmament!
One drop would save my soul, half a drop. Ah, Christ—
Rend not my heart for naming of my Christ,
I yet will call on him—O, spare me, Lucifer!
Where is it now? 'Tis gone; and see where God
Stretcheth out His arm and bends His ireful brows!
Mountains and hills, come, come and fall on me
And hide me from the heavy wrath of God!

---

* A passage which might classify Marlowe as the first 'existentialist' inspiring
Kierkegaard (The crowd is untruth) to Sartre (Hell is other people).
† O, slowly, slowly run, ye horses of the night. This line from Ovid's *Amores* I.
xiii, which Marlowe had already translated,

> Hold in thy rosy horses that they move not
> Ere thou rise!

and entitled the elegy 'To the Dawn, not to hasten' haunted him and he was to
return to it in his last poem *Hero and Leander* in the form,

> And now she wished this night were never done
> And sighed to think upon th'approaching sun
> For much it griev'd her that the bright day-light
> Should know the pleasure of this blessed night.

And the invocation to Helen of Troy:

> Was this the face that launch'd a thousand ships
> And burnt the topless towers of Ilium?
> Sweet Helen, make me immortal with a kiss—
> Her lips suck forth my soul: see where it flees—
> Come, Helen, come, give me my soul again.
> Here will I dwell, for heaven is in these lips,
> And all is dross that is not Helena.
> I will be Paris, and for love of thee,
> Instead of Troy shall Wittenberg be sacked;
> And I will combat with weak Menelaus,
> And wear thy colours on my pluméd crest;
> Yes, I will wound Achilles in the heel,
> And then return to Helen for a kiss.
> O, thou art fairer than the evening air
> Clad in the beauty of a thousand stars;
> Brighter art thou than flaming Jupiter
> When he appear'd to hapless Semele;
> More lovely than the monarch of the sky
> In wanton Arethusa's azured arms;
> And none but thou shalt be my paramour!

exhibited his passion for the classics at its best, because at its simplest and pruned of the plethora of recondite references which too often advertised his learning at the expense of his poetry.

And, in spite of the farce and the fireworks, the propaganda and the topicalities, the power of the play lay in its basic theme. How much of his knowledge of spells and high magic gleaned from the 'forbidden' knowledge Marlowe studied with Raleigh, Northumberland and Hariot—especially Hariot—was incorporated in the play it was difficult to tell.* Kit made no secret of Hariot's knowledge and one of his remarks aimed at irritating the conventionally-minded Kyd was that Moses was a mere conjurer and that 'Hariot could do better than he'. But there was

---

* The obvious comparison is with Shakespeare's *Macbeth*. As everyone acquainted with the theatre knows, this has been a permanently 'unlucky' play from its first production until today and to quote from it in a dressing-room at any time is a major *bêtise*. The reason is supposed to be that somewhere in the witch scenes— no one agrees exactly where, though experiments have been made—Shakespeare introduced a real spell.

no doubt about the effect. Strange stories of apparitions at some of the performances began to circulate in the city and though they may have originated in Alleyn's or Henslowe's mind as an effective kind of advertisement, they assumed a different guise when Alleyn took the company on a provincial tour. It was at Exeter 'as a certain number of devils kept every one his circle there and as Faustus was busy with his magical invocations, on a sudden were all dashed, every one hearkening other in the ear, for they were all persuaded that *there was one devil too many among them*; and so, after a little pause, they desired the people to pardon them, they could go no further with this matter. The people also understanding the thing as it was, every man hastened to be first out of doors. The players, spending the night in reading and in prayer (contrary to their custom) got them out of the town next morning.' As for Alleyn himself, 'the apparition of the Devil so worked on his fancy that he made a vow' to perform some work of Christian charity in reparation. *

While *The Rose* prospered under the formidable Henslowe–Alleyn management with Marlowe as its playwright, James Burbage in the original houses in Shoreditch was faring less well and the death of Tarlton worsened his situation. A year or two previously when an apprentice lay sleeping in the fields between *The Theatre* and *The Curtain*, a young actor-dancer intent on demonstrating the lightness of his toe performed a dance on the sleeper's belly. Thus rudely awakened, the apprentice hit the actor and they fell to serious fighting, encouraged by at least five hundred who took opposing sides when the actor described apprentices as the scum of the earth. Heads were broken and arrests made. Next day the apprentices tried to liberate the prisoners and started another riot at the door of *The Theatre*, whereupon the Chief Justice, who was hearing the case, sent two Aldermen to the Privy Council to request that *The Theatre* and *The Curtain* might be pulled down. The Privy Council agreed and the Recorder of London, delighted that at last he had a mandate to destroy the phenomenon so hated by the clergy and the civic authorities, informed Burbage, who appealed for help

* In fulfilment of it, as soon as he had made his fortune, he founded and endowed Dulwich College.

166

to Tarlton whose protests to the Queen soon caused the Council's order to be countermanded.

In the more recent troubles, however, Tarlton, even if he had been alive, could have been of little assistance to his friend, whose Theatre he had so often graced with his genius. Burbage's brother-in-law, Brayne the grocer who had contributed capital to *The Theatre* and made, on that account, pretensions to owning it, had died, leaving his widow to carry on the financial feud. She armed herself with a court order, collected some male assistants from the soap-factory which was one of her late husband's ventures, and descended on *The Theatre* determined to install her own 'gatherer' to collect the pennies of the audiences.

Her sister-in-law, Ellen Burbage, was the first to see the little procession advancing on *The Theatre* and told them to leave at once or her son would break all their heads. James Burbage put his head out of the window and, calling Mrs Brayne a 'murdering whore', reinforced his wife's threat. Accompanied by his sons, Cuthbert and Richard, he arrived on the scene armed with broomsticks. When Richard began to belabour the legs of the would-be 'gatherer', the soap-maker flourished the court order and said that Mrs Brayne was within her legal rights. The only result was that Richard, as the injured man later deposed, 'scornfully and playfully played with this deponent's nose'.

When the first actors arrived to dress and make-up for the afternoon performance, young Richard was still laughing and making passes in the air with his broomstick.

The ominous year had not left France unscathed. In the summer the Duke of Guise had driven the King from Paris and at the end of the year the King in revenge had had him assassinated by a gang of hired bravoes. After kicking the dead face of the champion of Catholicism, the last Valois had announced: 'At last I am King of France: the King of Paris is dead.'*

Marlowe decided that at last his long-projected play on Guise might be written and he started 1589 by roughing-out a dying speech for the hero:

> I will not ask forgiveness of the king.
> O that I have not power to stay my life

* The story of this year is told in detail in *Paris is Worth a Mass*.

167

Nor immortality to be revenged!
To die by peasants, what a grief is this!
Ah, Sixtus, be revenged upon the king!
Philip and Parma, I am slain for you!
Pope, excommunicate! Philip, depose
The wicked branch of wicked Valois's line!
Vive la messe! perish the Huguenots!
Thus Caesar did go forth and thus he died.

13. *Theatre Business*

With the defeat of the Armada the English Government's fear of a Catholic rising somewhat abated and the threat to the stability of the Established Church moved to the extreme Protestant wing of it—the Brownists who, in the opinion of Sir Walter Raleigh, numbered in all about twenty thousand. Wonderful as was England's 'late deliverance out of the hands of the Spaniards', it must not be taken to mean, they said, that God condoned 'the wicked ecclesiastical constitution' of the Church of England and they moved to do battle against it.

To a learned 1400-page tome written in defence of the Anglican system, they replied by a lively Tract written by 'Martin Marprelate'. 'There are many', the writer claimed, 'who dislike my doings. I have my faults, I know, for I am a man. But my course is lawful. I saw the cause of Christ's government and of the Bishops' anti-Christian dealing to be hidden. Most men could not be gotten to read anything in defence of the one and against the other. I bethought me therefore of a way they might be drawn to do both—by perceiving the humour of men in these times and so to be given to mirth. The Lord being the author of both mirth and gravity, is it not lawful for the truth to use either of these ways?'

Martin's humour played most freely about Whitgift of Canterbury, Aylmer of London and Cooper of Winchester, the three leading prelates to be marred. All England soon knew that Aylmer had sold the timber off the church estates to enrich himself. In a Tract entitled by the street cry: *Have you any work for the cooper?*, the unfortunate matrimonial affairs of Cooper, whose wife was not only a termagant who threw his writings into the fire but was of so profligate a character that Dr Day, a

Canon of Christ Church, had to be bound in £100 not to go near her, became public property. All instances of Whitgift's persecution of the Puritans were put on record and lost nothing in the telling. The threat to reveal something worse about some leading ecclesiastic in the next number unless he mended his ways gave the Tracts something of the fascination of a serial.

Martin's purpose was to demonstrate that the Anglican bishops in general ought not to be maintained by the authority of the magistrate in any Christian commonwealth. And he proposed that if they would encourage good preaching, make only fit and godly persons preachers, punish nobody for refusing to wear Popish garments or omitting Popish corruptions from the Prayer Book, he on his side would promise 'never to make any more of your knavery known unto the world'.

The popularity of the Tracts was immense. The Court read them, the politicians read them, the professors read them. Even the Queen, who had no high opinion of her bishops, secured copies and tempered her public indignation with private laughter, but officially the Archbishop of Canterbury was bidden 'to use all privy means, by force of your Ecclesiastical Commission or otherwise to search out the authors thereof and their complices and the printers and the secret dispensers of the same'.

The printers were John Penry and another Brownist using their 'Pilgrim Press' which evaded discovery by moving from place to place under cover of darkness—itself a considerable feat in view of the cumbrous nature of the press, with its heavy boxes of type and the vigilance of the pursuivants on all the roads. Yet Penry managed to take it secretly from Kingston-on-Thames to Fawsley in Northamptonshire, then to Coventry, then to Hazely in Warwickshire, where the press was at last seized—though not the printer—just after the issue of *More Work for the Cooper* in the July of 1589. Penry set a seventh and last Tract on another press before retiring to the safety of Calvinist Scotland. *

The Government were at their wits' end for a countermeasure. They licensed an official answer: '*An Admonition to the*

* Many believed that Penry was the author as well as the printer of the Tracts, but the identity of 'Martin Marprelate' remains a leading literary and historical mystery. 'Criticism has not solved the problem of the Tracts' authorship, but it has established them as prose satires of quite extraordinary genius and established their claim to a permanent place among English classics.'

People of England; wherein are answered, not only the slan-
derous untruths uttered by Martin the Libeller, but also many
other crimes by some of his brood, objected against all Bishops
generally and the chief of the Clergy purposely to deface and
discredit the present state of the Church.'

Learned as it was, however, there was a general feeling that
it did not quite answer the situation if only because 'the People
of England' were unlikely to read it. ''Twas thought therefore
the best way was to answer a fool according to his folly and
combat these pamphleteers with their own weapon. They were
served in this manner by one Tom Nashe who had a genius for
satire, a lively turn and spirit for the encounter.' The idea of
using pamphlets and the stage in an anti-Martin campaign
originated with the secretary of the Archbishop of Canterbury
who, approving it, instructed John Lyly that attacks on Martin
would be welcomed by the authorities.

John Lyly, private secretary to the Earl of Oxford and the
writer of elegant classical-pastoral pieces, acted as the master of
Paul's Boys, a private company of players, composed of the
choir-boys of St Paul's with the addition of others drawn from
the Chapel Royal and the private chapel of the Earl of Oxford,
which presented plays in a little playhouse constructed in an
old building of the dissolved Dominican priory at Blackfriars.
Lyly was responsible for both the musical and the theatrical
training of the Paul's Boys—'Vicemaster of Paul's and Fool-
master of the Theatre,' Gabriel Harvey called him—and
occasionally wrote for them pieces to act at Court.

Lyly and Nashe went to work with a will. *Pap with a Hatchet*,
An Almond for a Parrot, *A Whip for an Ape* and *A Mirror for the
Martinists* appeared in quick succession and on the stages of
Blackfriars and *The Theatre* might be seen hastily concocted
plays, such as *The May Game of Martinism* and *Martin's Month's
Mind* in which an allegorical figure of Divinity entered, 'with a
scratched face, holding of her heart as if she was sick, because
Martin would have forced her; but, missing of his purpose, he
left the print of his nails upon her cheeks, and poisoned her with
a vomit, which he administered to her to make her cast up her
dignities and promotions'. In another scurrility, Martin was
brought on dressed as a monstrous ape, wearing a cock's comb,
with a wolf's belly and cat's claws. He was whipped and made

to wince and then 'wormed and lanced to let the blood and evil humours out of him'.

The general tenor of these plays, however, ensured that, however popular they might be, they missed their mark. Many of those who enjoyed the bawdy horseplay began to look more than a little askance at it when it was rumoured that the Archbishop of Canterbury was behind it; and one of Burleigh's nephews, Francis Bacon, who was M.P. for Liverpool, spoke for many when he expressed the hope 'that my Lords of the clergy have non-intelligence with this interlibelling, but do altogether disallow that their credit should be thus defended'. Quite aware that they did nothing of the sort, he admonished them by writing: 'To turn religion into a comedy or satire, to intermix Scripture and scurrility sometimes in one sentence, is a thing far from the devout reverence of a Christian and scant beseeming the honest regard of a sober man.'

The Archbishop, to do him justice, had soon realised his mistake and as soon as he had certain news that Penry's press had been captured and that, in consequence, the Tracts were at an end he made haste to lay the intractable spirits he had so imprudently called up to counter them. An order was made that, because 'the players take it upon themselves to handle in their plays certain matters of Divinity unfit to be suffered', no play was henceforth to be presented until it had been submitted to a committee of three consisting of 'a fit person well learned in Divinity' appointed by the Archbishop, 'a sufficient person learned and of judgment' to be nominated by the Lord Mayor, and the Master of the Revels himself as the third. The Privy Council then enacted that 'the players (whose servants so ever they be) forbear to present any comedy or tragedy other than such as they three shall have seen and allowed'. The penalty for disobedience was that actors contravening the new censorship 'shall be not only severely punished but made incapable of the exercise of their profession for ever hereafter'.

The order was promulgated early in November 1589, six weeks after Marlowe had been released on bail from Newgate where he had spent a period of uncomfortable imprisonment and where Tom Watson was still languishing.

*

Marlowe's weeks in prison were quite unconnected with the 'Martinist' uproar in the theatre, though they were in a sense the consequence of theatrical conditions. He had taken no part in the controversy because he had no sympathy with either side. If he detested the narrow bigotry of the Brownists as heartily as did Nashe, he was equally, if not more, antipathetic to the Anglican Establishment of which he had refused to become a part and whose essential doctrines he persistently contradicted and ridiculed in conversation. Indeed at the moment he was particularly incensed against the bishops, for the year had opened with the burning of Francis Kett.

Kett had been Marlowe's tutor in his first year at Corpus Christi and he had first opened his mind to the possibility of subjecting the Bible to ordinary criticism. Kett held that Christ was 'not God but a good man who suffered once for his own sins and would suffer again for the sins of the world and be made God after the second resurrection'. It was an eccentric interpretation and Kett, musing on it, went to lengths of speculation which aroused doubts about his sanity. He opined that Christ was 'now personally in Judaea' with His Apostles 'gathering of His Church' and the faithful must go to Jerusalem to meet Him there and be fed on angels' food. For this opinion he was sentenced to be burnt alive. He went to his death, clothed in sackcloth, 'leaping and dancing' and, in the fire itself, 'above twenty times together clapping his hands, he cried nothing but "Blessed be God" '.

Kett was described as 'a devil incarnate' by the Establishment, but Marlowe, if deploring his old tutor's excesses, found in his essential theism an echo of his own beliefs and preferred him to the Archbishop of Canterbury who burnt him as part of his anti-Marprelate activities. Kett's fate alone would have prevented Marlowe from assisting the Archbishop in his theatrical propaganda.

The reason for Marlowe's trouble with the law which landed him in prison was distinctly more mundane. It could be traced back to the conversation which had taken place in *the Unicorn* on the day Tom Watson had first taken him there after his original interview with Sir Francis Walsingham. He himself indeed had no part in it, but he still remembered clearly how Tom Watson had warned John Alleyn, the landlord, against paying what might be interpreted as blackmail, however small the actual sum, to two professional brawlers, William Bradley and George Orwell, to ensure that they did not wreck his trade. That was four years ago, but little had altered except the circumstances of John Alleyn. William Bradley still brawled and borrowed, but John Alleyn had shared in the fast-rising fame and fortune of his elder brother and at the beginning of 1589 he got rid of the *Unicorn* and became the manager of the Admiral's Players and part-sharer with Edward of 'playing apparels, play-books, instruments and other commodities'. He now needed all the money he could lay his hands on and among other debtors whom he dunned was William Bradley who, by this time, owed him £14.* For a year Bradley had been promising to pay and had actually been bound before a magistrate to do so.

Losing patience, John Alleyn asked his lawyer, Hugh Swift, to call on Bradley to threaten a suit in the Court of Common Pleas if the money was not forthcoming. Hugh Swift was Tom Watson's brother-in-law, with a reputation for energy rather than honesty (he had endeavoured to help his young brother to marry an heiress by inducing the lady to sign what she thought was a receipt but was actually a promise to wed) and Watson was involved in his doings, partly from interest, partly from curiosity. He did not exactly claim credit for warning John Alleyn against Bradley in the first place, but he entered the family and theatrical feud as if it were his own affair.

Hugh Swift, calling on Bradley at his father's inn, *The Bishop's Head* in Holborn, was attacked by the bravo, George Orwell, who, with a succession of unpleasant oaths, threatened to kill him if he did not drop the matter. Swift thereupon went straight to a magistrate in the Queen's Bench to petition 'securities of the Peace against George Orwell, being in fear of death'.

The application was granted, but, once he had returned home, Tom Watson and John Alleyn suggested that in the meantime they might make the matter more secure by giving William Bradley, now deprived of his bravo, a lesson which would induce him immediately to pay the fourteen pounds. The three

---

* In the currency of the time. It is impossible to give exact equivalents, but some idea may be gained from the fact that, in a year when the cost of living had risen steeply, it was considered scandalous profiteering to charge threepence for a pound of beef. The sum of £14 was worth suing for.

set out for *The Bishop's Head* but news of their intention—the feud having become something of a *cause célèbre* in the taverns—reached him before they did and William Bradley rushed to the courts and, in his turn, obtained from a magistrate securities of the Peace against Hugh Swift and John Alleyn and Thomas Watson 'being in fear of death' from them.*

Marlowe could not have avoided becoming entangled in the case even had he wished it. His professional association with Edward Alleyn and his personal friendship with Tom Watson ensured that. But he wanted no part of the physical brawling and he had refused to assist in the intended castigation of William Bradley. Nevertheless, when shortly after two o'clock in the afternoon of Thursday, September 18 he set out to pay a visit to Burbage just up the road, he found William Bradley waiting for him with his sword drawn.

'Where is that murdering whorson Tom Watson?' Bradley yelled. 'Or is he afraid to meet me man to man?'

'I know nothing of his doings,' Marlowe answered in a tone intended to be pacificatory.

In fact, he knew quite well. Tom Watson was still in the house, where they had been discussing Kit's new play. Marlowe himself was more anxious than ever to complete *Guise*, for now history itself had given a final shape to the tragedy. The murdered Duke had been avenged. The Catholics of France, led by his brother, had risen against his royal murderer and King Henri III had in his turn been assassinated by a dedicated young Dominican friar. When, at the beginning of August, the news of it had arrived in England, Marlowe immediately pointed out to Edward Alleyn that the play could now be finished and presented. Events had shaped a perfect tragic plot. But Alleyn and Henslowe still hesitated. Although their former objections no longer held and, as Marlowe was quick to point out, the new King of France, Henry of Navarre, was a Protestant, Henslowe, in view of the impending legislation concerning censorship in the theatre, had no wish to risk a brush with the law to which a contemporary political play might too easily lead. Marlowe,

---

* Both are recorded on the same leaf of the Queen's Bench Controlment Rolls for the Michaelmas Term of 1589 and the aggressors in each case commanded to appear at Westminster Hall on November 25. The applications must therefore have followed hard on each other's heels.

unconvinced and angry, was, on Tom Watson's suggestion, at this moment on his way to offer the idea to Burbage.

The sudden appearance of Bradley lurking outside the door threw him off his balance. The brawler was obviously drunk, but not too drunk to be dangerous. Marlowe's first instinct had been to shout a warning to Watson, but Bradley's question had stopped that. So he had professed ignorance as nonchalantly as he could.

'Never mind where the bastard is skulking,' said Bradley. 'I'll accept you as his substitute.'

A crowd had already gathered at the corner of Hog Lane and people were running across the fields to watch the fight and cheer on the combatants as the fancy took them. Marlowe was not unpopular and the bully was hated, but whatever outcome sympathy might have desired it was realism that dictated the betting. It was ten to one on Bradley, but one old man shouted: 'Come on, Master Kit! Give him the Tamburlaine touch!'

Cold with fear, Marlowe drew his sword and lunged at Bradley, only to be parried with contemptuous ease. He wondered how long he could last and whether his opponent would kill him or be content with merely wounding him. Raleigh's words came back to him—'when you know that if you do not kill you will be killed you see things differently from the scribbler'—and he found that Raleigh was in one respect wrong. It was as a 'scribbler' that Kit hoped that, if he were badly wounded, it would not be in his right arm or wrist.

Help came unexpectedly. The shouts of the crowd brought Tom Watson to the window to discover the meaning of it. When he saw Marlowe and Bradley engaged, he knew that, even though he was bound over to keep the peace, he must go to his friend's rescue. As soon as he emerged from the house, Bradley called to him: 'So you've come at last!' and, leaving Marlowe, went over to him, sword and dagger poised. Watson, waving Marlowe away, engaged and, in the words of the official report issued next day, 'instantly William Bradley made assault upon Thomas Watson and then and there wounded, struck and ill-treated him with sword and dagger of iron and steel so that he despaired of his life; wherefore Thomas Watson with his sword of iron and steel (of a value of three shillings and fourpence) did defend himself and fled from Bradley for the saving of his life as far as a certain ditch beyond which Thomas Watson could not flee without peril of his life. William Bradley, continuing his attack, had closely followed Thomas Watson, upon which Watson, for the saving of his life, struck Bradley with his sword, giving him a mortal wound on the right side of his chest near the breast, six inches in depth and one in breadth, from which mortal wound William Bradley instantly died.'

By this time the tailor, Stephen Wyld, who was constable of the precinct, had come upon the scene, accompanied by his assistants to quell a breach of the peace. But the matter was now one of murder. Wyld charged Watson and Marlowe to stay and abide the course of law. Though they immediately protested that they had acted only in self-defence, they made no effort to resist arrest and accompanied the constable—who was their friend and neighbour—to the nearest Justice of the Peace, Sir Owen Hopton, the Lieutenant of the Tower, whose private house was in Norton Folgate, barely ten minutes' walk away. Sir Owen issued a warrant 'on suspicion of murder' committing them to Newgate to await the findings of the Coroner's jury and that night Marlowe and Watson found themselves manacled in the terror-striking gloom of the prison's 'Limbo'.

14. Prison

The 'Limbo' at Newgate was the hold above the gateway to the prison, entered by a hatch above it which made many prisoners imagine it was below ground. It was 'a dark opace wild room', lacking a window and lit by a single candle set on a black stone, known as 'The Black Dog of Newgate', against which a desperate prisoner had once dashed out his brains. The legend ran that an alchemist imprisoned there for 'his charms and devilish witchcrafts' three centuries ago at the time of the prosecutions associated with the famous Franciscan 'wizards', Friar Bacon and Friar Bungay, had 'maugre his Devils, Furies, sprites and goblins been by the famished prisoners eaten up'. Thereupon he haunted them in the shape of a hound, though the changing of the dog into a stone was left unexplained.

In an attempt to keep their spirits up—or, rather, each other's—the two prisoners made a jest of it, suggesting that they should spend their enforced leisure by inventing a suitable metamorphosis which they could insert into *Doctor Faustus* when they were released. It was a brave pretence, but the atmosphere soon chilled to ice 'the froth of witty Tom Watson's jests'.

The visit to 'Limbo' was merely the conventional treatment initially meted out to all prionsers in order to terrify them. Next morning the gaoler would come to demand his 'garnish'—the bribe in return for which he would strike off the prisoner's legbolts and give him his choice of lodging in the Master's or the common side according to the weight of his purse. On the Master's side the felon would have reasonable conditions and access to a vaulted cellar known as 'the Boozing Ken' where he could talk and drink to the limit of his means. The alternatives were the overcrowded Middle Ward and the underground, rat-infested Stone Hold where fever and starvation might well kill him before he came to trial.

Marlowe and Watson naturally chose the Master's side. As the Coroner's jury found that William Bradley had been killed in self-defence, they could count on their acquittal and release at the next Sessions at the beginning of December. Indeed Marlowe, as the lesser offender—if an offender at all—could be released on bail immediately if he could find the required surety.

The obvious surety was Raleigh, but Raleigh unfortunately was in Ireland. As soon as the peril from the Armada was past, he had gone to develop the vast Irish estates the Queen had granted him. The gossips, who interpreted all political moves in the light of the Favouriteship, reported that 'My Lord of Essex hath chased Mr Raleigh from the Court and confined him to Ireland.' It was, however, not true. Sir Walter was ordering his property. He rebuilt Lismore Castle, made experiments in mining, drained bogs, planted trees, studied crops and plants—and introduced the potato. More importantly he made the acquaintance of his neighbour at Kilcolman Castle, Edmund Spenser, who was writing an epic of England *The Faerie Queene* which inspired Raleigh to devote himself seriously to poetry and begin the first of the twelve books of his own epic love-poem to the Queen, *The Ocean's Love to Cynthia*.

With Raleigh's support unobtainable, Marlowe's mind turned immediately to Robert Poley. Though the last thing he wanted was to become again entangled in 'the Service', he saw no reason why his past contributions should not be acknowledged by present assistance. He remembered how at their first meeting Poley had explained to him that the most valuable agents had to spend profitable periods in gaol and he assumed that Poley himself was turning to good account his spell of incarceration in the Tower. But Marlowe's imprisonment in Newgate, so patently for a simple disturbance of the public peace, with no religious or political overtones, could do no good to anyone.

Poley had, as a matter of fact, been released from the Tower immediately the danger from the Armada was past. He was too valuable to be wasted when there was no point in continuing the farce that he was a Catholic plotter with Babington, and Walsingham needed him for special service in Denmark and

Scotland. Mary Queen of Scots's son, now King James VI of Scotland, had just come of age and was to marry the fifteen-year-old Anne, daughter of the King of Denmark.

In spite of the young King of Scots's protestations of affection to Queen Elizabeth and loyalty to the English alliance, Walsingham distrusted him and, through his spies, already knew that he was involved with the Catholic nobility of Scotland in their plan to make available to Spain two ports near the English border from which an invasion of England could be launched. Walsingham considered it imperative to have accurate information about the undercurrents in Denmark where representatives of the various powers would gather for the wedding festivities. As soon as Poley was released Walsingham sent him first to Oslo and then to Berwick, where he now was.

Marlowe, unaware of these developments, asked a gaoler, to whom he gave what he hoped was a suitable 'consideration', to carry a letter to a Robert Poley who was a prisoner in the Tower, The man, genuinely surprised, informed him that Robert Poley was not in the Tower, but here in Newgate and that he could be met any day in the 'Boozing Ken'. But when 'Poley' was pointed out to him Marlowe knew even from a glance at his back that the wispy little man with the long neck and the dropping shoulders was not the ebullient spy-master. It transpired that his name was indeed the same, but he was a coiner, imprisoned for counterfeiting, and Kit was soon fascinated by his conversation, which seldom left the subject of money in one of its aspects. His eyes lit up at the mere mention of gold. He expatiated on the power of it in the tones of a lover hymning the beauty of his mistress. He opined that it was the greatest power in the world and that every other kind of power was a mere adjunct to it. When he explained how to mix metals to simulate gold and silver and how, with the help of 'a cunning stamp-maker, to coin French crowns, pistolets and English shillings', it was less like an expert workman passing on a practical recipe than an initiate interpreting a cabbalistic mystery.

The necessity of money (especially at this moment) and the proper husbandry of it Marlowe understood, though his treatment of it and his manner of life, as that of his companions, ensured that he and they were perpetually in debt, were it

£65,000 like Raleigh or a comparatively trifling sum like Nashe and Greene and Kyd. Indeed they would all have been prepared to argue that debt was a necessary specific against the idolatrous worship of Mammon and that to be a spendthrift was far better, by any moral scale, than to be a miser.

This improbable meeting with a dedicated miser had the effect of determining Marlowe's next play. He would complete his trilogy on power and its effects; to the power of the sword and the power of knowledge he would add the power of gold. The actual figure who should incarnate that power and stand beside Tamburlaine and Faustus in Alleyn's repertoire he had not yet chosen. The refusal of *Guise* was a warning against too instant a topicality, the success of *Doctor Faustus* a reminder of its advantages.

After discussing the matter with Watson, he chose a European rogue who had died only ten years earlier and linked him with the siege of Malta by the Turks which had been watched with a breathless interest by all Europe and produced a plethora of pamphlets and newsbooks, printed and reprinted in all languages, including English. At the same time, Marlowe determined to allow himself considerable latitude in his treatment of his Machiavellian hero-villain and did not, as he had in his two previous plays, use his real name. The protagonist of *The Rich Jew of Malta* was named merely 'Barabas'. *

The prototype was a sinister Portuguese Jew who, nine years before Marlowe was born, headed the emigration of five hundred of his co-religionists to Constantinople, *en route*, so he said, to establish a new Jewish state in Palestine on the shores of the Sea of Galilee. He changed his name from Juan Miques to Joseph Nassi and became the favourite and confidential adviser of the Sultan, Selim the Sot, who made him Duke of Naxos and the Cyclades. Nassi's main object was to procure for himself Cyprus as a Jewish colony and he kept in readiness a crown and a royal banner inscribed *Josephus Rex Cypri*. As Duke of Naxos he coined his own money as *Josephus Nassi Dei Gratia Dux Pelagi*. He was a relentless enemy of the Christian powers and

---

* Unfortunately—and misleadingly—the title which Marlowe gave it and under which it was first published is popularly contracted to *The Jew of Malta*, partly, one supposes, to balance it with *The Merchant of Venice*, whose Shylock owes much to Barabas. (Bárabás incidentally is the pronunciation demanded by the scansion.)

urged the Sultan to break faith with Venice and seize the island of Cyprus. Both the attack on Cyprus and the attack on Malta were attempts to gain a Mohammedan base in the Mediterranean from which to attack the fleets of Christendom. At the same time Nassi's enormous wealth made him able to deal directly in financial and political matters with Venice, Poland and the Netherlands, as well as with the Emperor and with the French throne—he lent Catherine de Medici 150,000 ducats—until he was unmasked as the enemy of both.

Marlowe, sketching in the character, did so with precision and gave Barabas, contemplating his successful career, the reflections:

> These are the blessings promis'd to the Jews,
> And herein was old Abraham's happiness!
> What more may Heaven do for earthly man
> Than thus to pour out plenty to their laps?
> Who hateth me but for my happiness?
> Or who is honour'd now but for his wealth?
> Rather had I, a Jew, be hated thus
> Than pitied in a Christian poverty;
> For I can see no fruits in all their Faith
> But malice, falsehood and excessive pride,
> Which methinks fits not their profession.
> Haply some hapless man hath conscience
> And for his conscience lives in beggary.
> They say we are a scatter'd nation.
> I cannot tell, but we have scrambled up
> More wealth by far than those who brag of faith.
> There's Kiriam Jairim, the great Jew of Greece,
> Obed in Bairseth, Nones in Portugal,
> Myself in Malta, some in Italy,
> Many in France and wealthy every one;
> Ay, wealthier far than any Christian!
> I must confess we come not to be kings;
> That's not our fault: alas, our number's few!
> And crowns come either by succession,
> Or urg'd by force; and nothing violent,
> Oft have I heard tell, can be permanent.
> Give us a peaceful rule; make Christians kings,
> That thirst so much for principality.

And for the opening of the play he had 'Barabas discovered in his counting house, with heaps of gold before him' discarding the silver with

> Fie, what a trouble 'tis to count this trash!
> Well fare the Arabians, who so richly pay
> The things they traffic for with wedge of gold,
> Whereof a man may easily in a day
> Tell that which may maintain him all his life.
> The needy groom that never finger'd groat
> Would make a miracle of thus much coin;
> But he whose steel-barr'd coffers are cramm'd full
> And all his life-time hath been tired,
> Wearying his fingers' ends with telling it,
> Would in his age be loath to labour so,
> And for a pound to sweat himself to death.
> Give me the merchants of the Indian mines
> That trade in metal of the purest mould;
> The wealthy Moor, that in the eastern rocks
> Without control can pick his riches up
> And in his house heap pearl like pebble stones,
> Receives them free and sells them by the weight!
> Bags of fiery opals, sapphires, amethysts,
> Jacinths, hard topaz, grass-green emeralds,
> Beauteous rubies, sparkling diamonds,
> And seld-seen costly stones of so great price,
> As one of them indifferently rated,
> And of a carat of this quantity,
> May serve in peril of calamity
> To ransom great kings from captivity
> —This is the ware wherein consists my wealth!
> And thus, methinks, should men of judgment frame
> Their means of traffic from the vulgar trade
> And, as their wealth increaseth, so enclose
> Infinite riches in a little room.

When Marlowe tried the effect of these lines on the coiner by reciting them slowly to him, he was gratified to observe the miser's tense appreciation.

The gold and jewels of imagination, however, had to give way to the practical necessity of finding sureties for £40 which would enable Marlowe to leave Newgate on bail. With both Raleigh and Poley out of the country, he did not know where to turn and he was almost in despair when, like an answer to prayer—could he have brought himself to indulge in such a practice—a visitor arrived. It was Tom Walsingham.

Marlowe was overjoyed to see him for his own sake, for in the last year they had seldom met; Tom had been increasingly used by Sir Francis on foreign missions, while Kit had immersed himself in the world of the theatre. And when Tom announced that he had now been commissioned by 'Uncle Francis' to discover the exact circumstances of the arrest and to arrange bail, Marlowe had an additional sense of relief.

This, however, was quickly dispelled by another, more complex emotion, part anger, part jealousy. Tom should have come on his own account not as what amounted to an official emissary from 'the Service'. Yet, in whatever character he had come, his presence immediately reduced Kit to the state of helpless enslavement which had characterised his first sight of him. But it was now even more binding. Their meetings in the interim, with their passion and fulfilment, had given a new dimension to desire. Now as their hands touched Kit found himself trembling a little in his effort to feign a casual indifference before the curious eyes of the other prisoners in the 'Boozing Ken' and to control himself till they were alone . . . But they would not be alone. He was a prisoner. When Tom left he could not go with him. And with this stab of actuality, Marlowe suffered jealousy such as he had never known.

The relationship between them had not been one which had allowed possessiveness on either side. They revelled in the moment, accepting their absences from each other as their natural condition. Neither demanded fidelity. Had they been able to leave Newgate together that afternoon, it was unlikely that they would have met again for some time nor would either have been unduly curious about the actions of the other. But the mere fact that Kit could not be with Tom even if he wished, made him inordinately desire it and immediately bred in him a possessive jealousy which demanded an accounting of all actions in absence.

It would have been unreasonable to have expected Tom to divine this, but it was unfortunate that the other news he had to bring was delivered in such a way as to inflame the sudden wound. Edmund Walsingham was mortally ill. He could not last more than a few weeks. Before Christmas, as far as his physicians could foresee, he would be dead and Tom would inherit Scadbury.

'How certain?' asked Marlowe. 'I do not trust physicians.'

'Certain enough for Ingram to put *The Angel* at Basingstoke up for sale, as we'll need it no longer.'

'What will Frizer do?'

'Be my majordomo at Scadbury, of course. He'll order the place to perfection. And you'll be there, too.'

'If Ingram allows it.'

The sneering inflection on the Christian name roused Tom's usual irritation at Kit's attitude to the servant, but it also signalled to him the extent of the hurt he had thoughtlessly inflicted.

'You know that you are the only one who *must* be at Scadbury with me,' he said.

Marlowe was silent.

'Do you not?'

Marlowe nodded.

'For ever and ever,' said Tom Walsingham.

Nevertheless Tom did not return to visit Newgate to report on his success with the sureties. He arranged for them expeditiously enough—Richard Kitchen, a Puritan lawyer of Clifford's Inn, and Humphrey Rowland, a horner, whose horn-handles for knives were of an excellence to gain him admission to the Cutlers' Company, both of whom were accustomed to act as sureties (for a 'consideration') when 'the Service' needed it. But, having put things in train, Tom decided that his proper place was at Scadbury at Edmund's death-bed and he left another to break the news of release to the prisoner. It was natural enough, but he could have made a happier choice than Nicholas Skeres.

Marlowe found Skeres's presence at Newgate even less welcome than had been his visit to Cambridge even though he now brought promise of release. In the interval the spy had grown in self-confidence and he had added a heavy facetiousness to his natural lack of charm.

'My poor friend,' he said tut-tutting, 'it grieves me to find you fallen into such company.'

'As *you* know', said Marlowe, 'I have had to endure worse outside.'

'Fortunately', said Skeres, ignoring the insult, 'our good Sir Francis has arranged for your release.' And he gave Marlowe the details of the procedure to be followed.

'On Wednesday you will be out on bail. I have arranged for you to see Master Poley at his house on Thursday.'

'But I was told Master Poley was abroad.'

'He came back on Saturday and is anxious to see you at once.'

'Why?'

'I am not so far in his confidence, but I should suppose it is something to do with Scotland.'

15. *A Meeting in Scotland*

Marlowe's meeting with Robert Poley took place at 'The Garden', his house hear the Bishop's Gate. It was in the well-stocked garden which gave the house its name that Marlowe had last seen him just over three years ago when Poley had entertained several of those—including himself as 'Thornborough'—connected in some way with the 'Babington Plot'. The profusion of roses that had graced that August seemed in memory the more prodigal by comparison with the few falling blooms of this October. The identity of place intolerably recalled the image of Babington in thrall to his 'dearest Robin' who was only too soon to reveal himself *'omnium bipedum nequissimus'*—of all two-footed creatures the wickedest.

Marlowe's own part in the betrayal of Babington to death, small and in practice a failure though it was, he had memorialised for himself in *Tamburlaine*:

> I know, sir, what it is to kill a man:
> It made remorse of conscience in me.

Yet, inexplicably, his attitude to Poley, once they were again face to face, was unaffected. Poley, by making no effort to exert his usual charm, in fact exercised more. The unspoken assumption was that they were now old friends between whom there was no need of pretence and that Marlowe, as an acknowledged star of the theatrical firmament, was a man of the world in his own right to be consulted rather than instructed. The flattery was the greater in that Poley had no interest whatever in the theatre and never attended a play—'I find life more amusing'—and yet he knew and acknowledged the position Marlowe had attained in it. Instead of telling him he had a service he wished from him, he inquired whether Marlowe could spare enough time from his theatrical activities to accompany him on a short visit to Scotland.

'Scotland? Why Scotland?'

Poley explained how the centre of Catholic intrigue had shifted for the moment to Edinburgh. The Catholic Earls of Huntly, Errol and Angus had, with the secret connivance of the young King James, asked Philip of Spain for 30,000 of Parma's troops in the Netherlands to be landed in Scotland to join with the 15,000 men whom the Scottish Catholics would raise for the invasion of England.

'Sir Francis has entrusted me with the discovery of this plot,' Poley explained, 'but I need your help in it.'

'How?'

'Only that you should be acquainted with our man in Edinburgh so that, if I am elsewhere, you may be able to take my place—as you did with much credit while I was in the Tower. Sir Francis has great faith in you after your handling of the last matter.'

'It was nothing but a message.'

'This may not be even that. All you are asked to do is to know the man to whom you might have to go if I am away in the Low Countries.'

'Who is he?'

'His name is William Fowler. A Scot. Your own age. Writes poetry—though not as good as yours. His father Sir Thomas helped the late Queen of Scots in money-affairs. We've been using young Will in the French Embassy. You will like him, I think.'

'When do I meet him?'

'As soon as possible. There will be no need to stay in Scotland more than a day or two. You must be back to answer to your bail on December 3. For me, it would be best if I were in Denmark by mid-November—that's when the King of Scots is being married to Princess Anne.'

'I thought he was already married to her.'

'By proxy only. He'll be in Oslo in person—his own shambling, dribbling, drunken person—in November. Can you manage to start for Edinburgh on Monday or Tuesday?'

Marlowe nodded.

'Then I'll engage a passage from Deptford and you can meet me there. At old Mistress Bull's house. D'you know it?'

'No. But I'll find it.'

'It's near the church. Anyone will direct you.'

On leaving Poley, Marlowe went back to Newgate, not this time as a prisoner but as a visitor to see Tom Watson, who had not managed to procure bail.

The action was a combination of kindness and business. Kit had experienced enough of Newgate to know the value of a visitor and he also wished to encourage Watson to continue thinking of situations to be used for the play on Barabas. Discussing it had relieved the tedium of recent days and now that Watson was alone he would need the distraction even more. As soon as he returned from Scotland, Marlowe would finish it and even before he went he promised to discuss it with Alleyn and Henslowe so that production should not be too long delayed.

Watson was disproportionately grateful. He was unable to dispel a feeling of guilt that ultimately he was responsible for Marlowe's imprisonment. To help in the new play was, besides being profitable, to make a token restitution. He promised to provide breath-taking gags and spectacles for the groundlings, though at the moment the only thing he could think of was the construction of a gallery upon the stage which would collapse at the cutting of a cord 'so that it doth sink into a deep pit past recovery' and precipitate Barabas, as 'the biter bit', screaming into a boiling cauldron. As a stage effect this would rival the shooting of the women in *Tamburlaine* or the appearance of the devils to claim the soul of the wizard in *Doctor Faustus*. Marlowe approved it and went immediately to consult Henslowe and Alleyn about the practical possibilities. They were enthusiastic and 'a cauldron for the Jew' was duly added to the prop-room which already held 'a dragon in *Faustus*' and 'Tamberlaine's bridle'.

But the theatre that October was in a state of confusion and uncertainty, arising partly from the impending censorship which was to come into effect at any moment and partly from the disorganisation of the companies due to the virtual collapse of the Queen's Men on Tarlton's death and the suppression of

189

Paul's Boys. The Admiral's decided to transfer temporarily to *The Theatre* and took a six months' lease from Burbage. Lord Strange's Men, a new company patronised by the son and heir of the Earl of Derby, took over *The Rose* and found Kyd and Greene only too willing to serve as its playwrights. Alleyn, though retaining his personal status as a servant of the Admiral, was prepared to act with 'Strange's', and, having cemented his partnership with Henslowe by marrying Henslowe's step-daughter, the 'sweet mouse', Joan Woodward, was engaged in forming what was in fact, if not in name, his own company.

Though Alleyn was sufficiently enthusiastic to make Marlowe a preliminary payment for *The Rich Jew of Malta* on the outline and the scraps that were completed and Henslowe half-promised to stage the Guise play at *The Rose* if the workings of the censor-ship did not prevent it, Marlowe was oppressed with a feeling of distrust. One effect of the days in Newgate had been to make him see his chosen world and friends with a cynical clarity. It was as if the Machiavellianism which he so magnificently endorsed on the great scale had suddenly revealed itself in all its petty dishonesty with himself as the victim instead of the exponent. This sensation was increased by the discovery that during his imprisonment, Greene had offered to Burbage the play that, in the manner of his unsuccessful imitation of *Tamburlaine*, he had written quickly and secretly to take advan-tage of the tide of popularity of *Doctor Faustus*—the story of the English necromancers, *Friar Bacon and Friar Bungay*. Finally, Raleigh had returned from his Irish 'exile' bringing with him Edmund Spenser, whom he was extolling as the greatest living English poet and, introducing him to the Queen, pleaded with her to recognise and pension him. Try as he might, Marlowe could not rid himself of an unworthy resentment. But there was no time at the moment to brood. He could sort matters out when he returned from Edinburgh.

The visit to Scotland was, as far as its admitted object was con-cerned, of no particular interest. Fowler, a loquacious and self-important young man, Marlowe found anything but sympathetic and could see no reason for the insistence on a personal intro-duction. Poley could just as well have given him his name and whereabouts for use in a crisis. Yet, by chance, Edinburgh provided a meeting of considerable importance. Three days after Marlowe and Poley arrived, John Penry, having seen the last Marprelate Tract safely printed from his hiding-place at Newcastle-on-Tyne, crossed the Border to take refuge in the Scottish capital as the guest of the dominant Kirk. Though Marlowe and Poley, as pretended Catholics, attached themselves to the Huntly circle, and Penry, as a Puritan refugee, was under the protection of the ruling Presbyterians, Edinburgh society was so small and interwoven that a meeting was inevitable, especially in the crowded succession of celebrations, parties and discussions which inevitably preceded the departure of the King of Scots for Oslo on October 12.

That the two should meet at all—Penry, suspected of being the much-wanted 'Martin Marprelate',* and Marlowe, the leading English playwright and secret Government spy—was the strangest of chances with unpredictable developments. Yet the circumstances were such that it seemed the most natural thing in the world—the chance meeting of two Cambridge contemporaries whose paths had diverged. Their greeting, each half doubtful of the other, was the conventional formula for such recognition.

'Penry . . . Peterhouse?'

'Marlowe . . . Corpus?'

'Of course.'

They were the same age; they had both read theology; they had taken their B.A. the same year; they had both come to some extent under the influence of the visionary, Francis Kett, whom that year the Archbishop of Canterbury had had burnt at Ipswich; both in their earlier carefree days had drunk together at *The Eagle* and *The Cardinal's Hat*.†

In those days Penry (who was a cradle Catholic) had not yet been converted to extreme Puritanism nor had Marlowe hardened into militant atheism. When they now emerged from their reminiscences into the present, they became wary of each other and remained on the plane of theological generalities which followed naturally from their mention of Francis Kett's fate.

* The Queen and the Archbishop of Canterbury had written to the King of Scots asking him to arrest Penry and to hand him over to them.
† This famous hostelry was on the site of what is now the Pitt Press.

'He was fortunate', said Penry, 'in that he could so testify to the truth that was in him.'

'Do you never fear', asked Marlowe, 'that you might go the same way to death?'

Penry shrugged. 'In this cause of God's, I am not afraid of death. If I perish I perish.' His eyes became glazed, his features tightened, his voice grated: 'If my blood were an ocean sea and every drop a life, I would give them all, by the help of the Lord, for the maintenance of His true religion.'

'But have you not still work to do?' asked Marlowe, argument quietened by the searing sincerity.

'If I might live upon this earth the days of Methuselah twice told and that in no less felicity than Peter, James and John on the Mount of Transfiguration; and after this life might be sure of the Kingdom of Heaven, yet to gain all this I dare not keep silent in bearing witness to the faith of Jesus Christ.'

Marlowe found himself at a loss for words. This kind of faith could not be answered by his usual quip to the orthodox that religion had been invented 'in order to keep men in awe' and that as an atheist he considered his duty was to teach them 'not to be afraid of bugbears and hobgoblins'. Still less could he oppose to Penry's intense mystical devotion to the person of Christ his own critical interpretation, agreeable to his particular temperament, that 'St John was bed-fellow to Christ and lay always in his bosom and that he used him in the manner of the sinners of Sodom'. The power of Penry's belief, mistaken or not, dwarfed Marlowe's negations, whose intellectual brightness seemed a mere shadow against the sun of the Puritan's certainty.

Yet, in one respect, Marlowe's own honesty coincided with Penry's. From opposite sides, their contempt and hatred converged on the accommodating compromises of the Church of England as by law established and as administered by the persecuting Archbishop Whitgift. And one thing Marlowe resolved. He would not allow himself to be used in any way by the authorities to injure Penry. Also he found himself unaccountably pleased that he had taken no part in the stage-warfare against Martin.

16. Questions of Patronage

Marlowe was back in London just before the return of the latest Virginia expedition which, under the command of Captain John White and with Thomas Hariot as navigator, had set out in August to make contact with the original settlers on Roanoke. They put in at Southampton on 8 November 1589, having failed in their quest because the colonists had moved to another island sixty miles from Roanoke; but they brought back an Indian chief who, after having been duly baptised at Bideford, was exhibited to the Court, as well as, for the further enlightenment of possible investors in the New World, eighteen superb water-colours Captain White had done of the natives and their customs.

Raleigh's interest in the return was personal only, not financial. He had spent £40,000 on trying to build the colony and had at last realised that 'it would require a prince's purse' to complete what he had begun. He surrendered his patent for Virginia to a company of businessmen and henceforth devoted himself to building more privateers which, by plundering the Spanish treasure fleet, would give him the coveted profit which his effort to found an overseas empire for England denied him.

Marlowe was delighted that the return of Hariot ensured the resumption of the turret meetings and discussions which he found like a fresh wind cleansing the atmosphere fouled by the crude rivalries of the theatre and the mean deceptions of political intrigue. Now, after his meeting with Penry, he tended to initiate discussions on Biblical criticism, mainly to reassure himself that the Bible in general and the book of Genesis in particular were unworthy of credence. The 'little school of atheism' decided that 'the Indians and many authors of antiquity certainly wrote over 16,000 years ago, whereas Adam was said to have lived within 6,000 years'. Moses, they opined, made the Jews wander in the wilderness for forty years before they came to the Promised Land (which journey could have been done in less than a year) in order that 'those who were privy to most of his subtleties' might die on the journey and so 'an everlasting suspicion might remain in the hearts of the people'. It was an easy matter for Moses who was brought up by the Egyptians and instructed in their occult arts 'to deceive the Jews, being a rude and gross people'. That Moses was an initiate and adept and so could perform 'magic' no one need dispute, but Hariot, who combined a knowledge of ancient lore with modern scientific observation, could have done much better than Moses!

Marlowe found the New Testament as suspect as the Old. For one thing, as he pointed out truly enough, it was written in execrable Greek. This was not surprising as the Apostles 'were fishermen and low-born fellows of neither wit nor worth' and that even Paul, who was certainly intelligent enough, 'was a timorous fellow in bidding a man to be subject to magistrates against his own conscience'.

It was this question of personal integrity that haunted Marlowe during the three weeks of waiting for his formal discharge. Suppose the jury at the Old Bailey on December 3 for some reason did not concur with the verdict of the Coroner's jury and that he and Tom Watson were not freed on the grounds of self-defence? He had no doubt that, even so, Poley would by some means or other manage to procure a pardon for him, but the implications of this were disturbing. Because of his use to the Establishment in hunting down those, either Catholic or Puritan, who put conscience before conformity, he would be protected. Yet was not their cause—the right to practise their own beliefs —fundamentally his own? That both Catholic and Puritan would have found his atheism totally repellent and, had they the power, would have treated him even worse than the Government treated them was irrelevant. Raleigh epitomised it for him in a scornful outburst against allowing personal beliefs to be judged by a jury of ordinary men 'who are like dogs that bark at those they know not'.

Marlowe's dilemma of buying his freedom by continuing to serve men whom he not only despised but who were implicitly his own enemies was for the moment resolved by his complete discharge from Newgate on December 3. Thomas Watson also was found to have acted in self-defence in the killing of William Bradley and recommended for the Queen's official pardon, which he received on 12 February 1590. Together they rapidly completed *The Rich Jew of Malta* which Henslowe and Alleyn 'tried out' at the inn, *The Cross Keys*, in Gracechurch Street, early in March when both *The Theatre* and *The Rose* were obediently closed for Lent. It was an immediate success.

By this time Marlowe was spending most of his time at Scadbury. Edmund Walsingham had died in November and Tom had immediately asked Kit to come to him. Their greeting, after the strain of the interview in Newgate, was one of such genuine and unconcealed affection that Ingram Frizer, resplendent in his new clothes as majordomo, experienced a deadlier pang of jealousy than usual.

'As I promised you,' said Tom, 'the best rooms in the south wing are yours.'

'And as I told *you*,' said Kit, 'they are too grand for me.'

'But the little cottage you wanted is occupied. Besides, I want you near me. You are *my* laureate now.'

'A poor one. You should have—'

'I do not envy Raleigh, Kit. Though he should envy me.'

Tom's quick tact was a measure of the change his inheritance of Scadbury had wrought in him. Marlowe remembered Poley's judgment the day when they had first met in the Secretary's house that Tom had nothing 'but gives himself all the airs in the world'. But now that Tom had everything—an acknowledged status as head of one of the leading families of Kent, a valuable estate and a sufficient income—he gave himself no airs at all. He was the reverse of one come suddenly into riches without the necessary training in responsibility. He was rather one who was at last able to act as he had always assumed he should have acted.

Perceiving the change, Marlowe at once signalled that he understood it by suggesting that Tom should extend his patronage to artists by purchasing the water-colours of Virginia which White and Hariot had recently brought home.

'How good they would look', he said, 'on the staircase in the south wing!'

'They shall be there, Kit, to welcome you when you come to take possession.' *

The one drawback to Scadbury, as far as Marlowe was concerned, was the presence of Ingram Frizer, but he tried to accept that their mutual detestation would inevitably increase with proximity and to find some way to lessen it. To Tom he explained that he would still have to spend long spells in London to be near his work in the theatre.

A new theatrical company was forming under the patronage of the Earl of Pembroke whose seat, as President of Wales and Warden of the Marches was at Ludlow, but whose residence was at Wilton in Wiltshire. It would have been more accurate to have called the new group of actors 'the Countess of Pembroke's Company', for it was she, the elderly Earl's third wife whom he had married when she was sixteen, who had turned Wilton into a centre of the arts and sciences so that it was 'like a college, there were so many learned and ingenious persons'. The young Countess, 'a beautiful lady of excellent wit, with a sharp-oval face and hair of a reddish-yellow', was the adored sister of Sir Philip Sidney. To her 'my dear Lady and Sister, principal ornament to the family of Sidneys' he had dedicated his *Arcadia* and after his death she considered it her duty to continue his patronage of poetry and to try to raise the stage to the level of his ideals as he had expressed them in his *Defence of Poesie*. The Countess considered that the contemporary French dramatist, Robert Garnier, with his historical plays written in a classical Senecan manner, pointed to the style to 'chase away gross barbarism'. She herself translated into English Garnier's tragedy on Mark Antony and encouraged the poet Samuel Daniel, who was tutor to her ten-year-old son, to write a companion piece on Cleopatra. Her own work she had published in a fine edition, but the obvious necessity was an acting company.

---

* When Scadbury Manor was demolished in 1727, these eighteen pictures were hanging on 'the John White staircase'. They eventually passed to the British Museum where they may now be seen in the Print Room (Add. MSS 5270).

Her husband had no objection. His name and position could ensure at least one and possibly two appearances of his players at Court at Christmas and, if there were no theatres subsequently available, they could always play the circuit Rye, Bath, Bewdley, Shrewsbury and Ludlow, where they could stay for the summer, returning home by way of York, Leicester, Coventry and Ipswich for a late autumn season in London.

The Countess of Pembroke's activities and interests naturally overlapped those of the Raleigh 'school'—Sir Walter's half-brother, Adrian Gilbert, actually worked with her in her alchemical laboratory—and Marlowe, when the matter was broached to him, was willing enough to provide a new play for the new company. Alleyn was fully occupied with Barabas and when the receipts for *The Rich Jew of Malta* started to fall he and Henslowe had *The Guise* to fall back on.

The Guise had made him interested in writing a history-play which should find its dramatic effects in the history itself instead of using it as a lightly-sketched background for the continuous rhodomontades of a leading actor. And in his reading of Raphael Holinshed's *Chronicles* of English history, of which a new and revised edition had recently been published, he found a subject which appealed to him. The life and reign of King Edward II had not hitherto been dramatised, and Marlowe found points of similarity in that unfortunate king's temperament, his actions and his fate with those of the French King Henri III whose assassination occupied the last act of *The Guise*.

On a short visit to Scadbury, when he ascertained that the reissued Holinshed was in the library there, he informed Tom that he intended to work on his new play in his new home.

'Then my laureate is not deserting me?'

'Never,' said Kit. 'And when I've done the play, I'll write you a poem on Hero and Leander. Meanwhile here are a few poor verses as an earnest of it.' And he handed Tom a dozen lines he had hastily written:

> Ne'er shall thy shepherd leave this moated park
> Until together thou and I embark
> And sail from hence to Greece, to lovely Greece:
> I'll be thy Jason, thou my golden fleece.
> Where painted carpets o'er the meads are hurl'd

And Bacchus' vineyards overspread the world,
Where woods and forests go in goodly green
I'll be Adonis, thou shalt be love's Queen.
The meads, the orchards and the primrose lanes
Instead of sedge and reed bear sugar-canes.
Thou in those groves, by Dis above,
Shalt live with me and be my love.

But in the play he would not need to make use of the changed
sex by which so many poets hid their love for boys under the
more respectable appearance of girls. The lovers of whom he
would write were King Edward and his favourite, Piers
Gaveston, and in order to justify an affection which was well
enough understood though seldom openly approved, he put in
the mouth of an elder statesman the apologia:

The mightiest kings have had their minions;
Great Alexander loved Hephaestion,
The conquering Hercules for Hylas wept,
And for Patroclus stern Achilles droop'd.
And not kings only, but the wisest men;
The Roman Tully loved Octavius,
Grave Socrates wild Alcibiades.

The opening of the play gave Kit scope to fuse his own
feelings with his art. Gaveston, summoned to Edward's side by
the message:

My father is deceas'd. Come, Gaveston,
And share the kingdom with thy dearest friend,

exclaims:

Sweet prince, I come! these, these thy amorous lines
Might have enforced me to have swum from France,
And like Leander gasped upon the sand,
So thou wouldst smile and take me in thine arms.
The sight of London to my exiled eyes
Is as Elysium to a new-come soul:
Not that I love the city or the men,
But that it harbours him I hold so dear,—
The King upon whose bosom let me lie,
And with the world be still at enmity.

Music and poetry is his delight,
Therefore I'll have Italian masques by night,
Sweet speeches, comedies and pleasing shows;
And in the day when he shall walk abroad,
Like sylvan nymphs my pages shall be clad;
My men, like satyrs grazing on the lawns,
Shall with their goat-feet dance an antic hay.
Sometime a lovely boy in Dian's shape,
With hair that gilds the water as it glides,
Crownets of pearl about his naked arms,
And in his sportful hands an olive-tree
To hide those parts which men delight to see,
Shall bathe him in a spring.

Later in the play, when the barons in revolt force the King to
banish the Favourite, Edward, in mourning garments, laments:

He's gone, and for his absence thus I mourn:
Did never sorrow go so near my heart
As doth the want of my sweet Gaveston;
And could my crown's revenue bring him back,
I'd freely give it to his enemies
And think I'd gained to buy so dear a friend.
My heart is as an anvil unto sorrow,
Which beats upon it like the Cyclops' hammers
And with the noise turns up my giddy brain,
And makes me frantic for my Gaveston.
Ah had some bloodless Fury ris'n from Hell
And with my kingly sceptre struck me dead
When I was forced to leave my Gaveston!

And on their meeting after the exile Edward confesses:

Thy absence made me droop and pine away;
For as the lovers of fair Danae,
When she was locked up in a brazen tower,
Desired her more and waxed outrageous,
So did it sure with me,

to be answered by Gaveston's

Sweet lord and king, your speech preventeth mine
Yet have I words left to express my joy:

> The shepherd, nipt with biting winter's rage,
> Frolics not more to see the painted spring
> Than I do to behold your majesty.

The personal application of the play seemed natural enough for Kit to indulge in a gibe at Frizer with his airs induced by his new status. To 'learn to court it like a gentleman',

> 'Tis not a black coat and a little band,
> A velvet-cap'd cloak, fac'd before with serge,
> And smelling of a nosegay all the day,
> Or making low-legs to a nobleman,
> Or looking downward with your eyelids close
> And saying 'Truly, an't may please Your Honour'
> Can get you any favour with great man:
> You must be proud, bold, pleasant, resolute,
> And now and then stab as occasion serves.

For the main plot of *Edward II*, however, Marlowe followed his source, although he had wrenched the story completely out of Holinshed's perspective by focusing attention on Gaveston who was murdered in the fifth year of Edward's twenty-year reign,* whereas to Holinshed the key was in the horror of the King's imprisonment and death.

'They lodged the miserable prisoner in a chamber over a foul, filthy dungeon, full of dead carrion, trusting so to make an end of him with the abominable stench thereof,' the chronicler had written, 'but he, bearing it out strongly, as a man of tough nature continued still in life. Whereupon when they saw that such practices would not serve their turn, they came suddenly one night into the chamber where he lay asleep and with heavy *featherbeds* or a *table* (as some write) being cast upon him, they kept him down and withal put into his fundament a horn and through the same they thrust up into his body a *hot spit*, the

---

* Dr Boas in his *Christopher Marlowe* comments: 'Why did Marlowe choose the comparatively unattractive reign of Edward II? The reason is, I believe, to be mainly found in the relation between the King and Gaveston, which he brings to the forefront of the play. Homosexual affection, without emphasis on its more depraved aspects, had a special attraction for Marlowe. Jove and Ganymede in *Dido*, Henry III and his "minions" in *The Massacre*, Neptune and Leander in *Hero and Leander*, are all akin, though drawn to a slighter scale, to Edward and Gaveston.'

which passing up into his entrails and being rolled to and fro burnt the same.'

Paradoxically it was this typically 'Marlovian' horror, dwarfing the ending of his three previous plays, which Marlowe, to please the Pembrokes, would be expected to put in Senecan narrative, to be reported, not exhibited. Yet, when it came to the point, he could not so falsify his own style and he compromised only to the extent of making the murderers call for a red-hot spit, a table and a feather-bed, but giving as a stage direction: 'King Edward is murdered by holding him down on the bed with the table and jumping on it.' That the Countess of Pembroke could safely read. The actors would know what to do.

For the rest Marlowe experienced the excitement of writing in a new vein and experimenting with a variety of characters * as well as elaborating the character of the King, introspective in adversity

> But what are kings when regiment is gone
> But perfect shadows in a sunshine day?

He had just finished the play when Sir Francis Walsingham died after a long and painful illness of the bladder. The Secretary was buried in St Paul's Cathedral as he had requested, but secretly at midnight lest his creditors should inflict the final insult of seizing his body. A Spanish agent sent the news immediately to King Philip with the comment that his death was the cause of great sorrow. Philip scribbled in the margin: 'There, yes. But it is good news here!'

Whichever view was adopted, no one denied that, with the passing of Mr Secretary, an epoch was ended.

* The enforced change in Marlowe's style is remarkable. *Tamburlaine* with 2361 lines has 392 speeches; *Edward II* with 2670 lines has 952 speeches.

17. *Historical Retrospect*

Not long before Sir Francis Walsingham died, the Earl of Essex became his son-in-law by secretly marrying Frances, Sir Philip Sidney's widow. Sidney had left 'to my beloved and much honoured Lord, the Earl of Essex, my best sword'. The bequest was made in a codicil a few hours before his death and it was supposed that he had also at that moment privately commended his wife and his friend, who were both at his bedside, to each other. There seemed, in view of Essex's life-long indifference to the lady, no other explanation; though if it chimed in well enough with the romantic idea of brothers-in-arms caring for each other's widows, it had a strong touch of realism in that it enabled Essex to take the dead Sidney's place as the white hope of the extreme Protestant party led by Walsingham. Equally realistically, news of the marriage was kept from the Queen* until Frances's pregnancy was too obvious to be concealed. Elizabeth, as was expected, was furious. She roared and raged and slapped Essex's face in public, so that he immediately disowned his wife and sent her back to her mother's house. But the royal anger was surprisingly short-lived and in a few weeks he was back in favour.

The more lasting result was in the effect of the episode on Raleigh who, though his principle that anything Essex could do he could do better was well enough in general, might have had the wisdom not to apply it in this particular. Sir Walter, in due course, also married secretly. In his case Elizabeth's jealous anger was so overwhelming that she sent him to the Tower for indefinite imprisonment 'during the Queen's pleasure'.

---

* And, incidentally, from posterity. No one knows when or where the marriage took place.

Marlowe was inevitably affected by these events. The death of Sir Francis Walsingham without a son to inherit meant that Tom Walsingham's status both in the family and in the affairs of Kent was considerably increased.* His standing in 'the Service', however, was diminished. The new spymaster-in-chief was, pending the appointment of a new Secretary, Sir Thomas Heneage, a friend of Sir Francis Walsingham and as firm in his extreme Protestantism. Heneage could be relied on to continue the existing policy and to retain the services of Poley and men of similar experience, but he was not disposed to patronise those like Tom Walsingham who had been employed occasionally for personal reasons. The change, Marlowe reflected hopefully, might affect him.

After finishing *Edward II* and finding it appreciated by his new patron who duly had it 'played by Pembroke's men', Marlowe stayed for a time in London, superintending the printing of *Tamburlaine* by Richard Jones 'at the sign of the Rose and Crown near Holborn Bridge' and fraternising with other stationers of his acquaintance, especially Edward Blount and Thomas Thorpe, in St Paul's Churchyard; discussing things scientific and occult with Thomas Hariot and politics with Matthew Royden (whom Poley had like himself introduced to the Scottish situation); inducing Richard Cholmley, who was also in 'the Service', to become a professing atheist; and encouraging Thomas Watson, who since his release from Newgate had not been in the happiest of circumstances, to write a memorial eclogue to the memory of Sir Francis Walsingham. Such a poem, Marlowe suggested, if dedicated to Tom Walsingham who was now in a position of patronage, might mend his fortunes and refurbish his reputation.

Watson agreed and, in Latin hexameters, wrote a pastoral elegy entitled *Meliboeus* as a dialogue between himself, as

* He was not, however, knighted till 1597 at earliest, four years after Marlowe's death, and either at the end of 1598 or the beginning of 1599 he married a Norfolk lady, Etheldreda Shelton. Unfortunately most books on Marlowe refer to 'the poet's influential patron, Sir Thomas Walsingham' from the start and assume that there was a 'Lady Walsingham' at Scadbury during Marlowe's stay there. It has even been suggested that when Marlowe, early in 1593, announced his intention of going to Scotland he was going north on 'business connected with Lady Walsingham'. This simple point may assist the reader in evaluating the judgment and understanding of those who make such an elementary mistake about Marlowe's circumstances.

Corydon, and Tom Walsingham, as Tityrus, who was the principal mourner for Sir Francis Walsingham, the dead shepherd, Meliboeus. One reason for consolation, the writer suggested, was that Meliboeus was now free to join the dead Astrophil (Sir Philip Sidney). The introduction of Sidney, natural though it was, was slightly overstressed because the patron Watson would have preferred was Sidney's sister, but Marlowe's apparent certainty of Tom Walsingham's munificence—which, from gossip and his own observation, Watson was aware that Marlowe could ensure—made him follow Kit's advice and earmark his next poem for the Countess.

As far as Marlowe's next work was concerned, he was prepared to follow the Countess's advice and provide another English historical play, this time on that civil war between York and Lancaster which was eventually to be known as the Wars of the Roses.* For a moment Marlowe thought of enlisting a collaborator, but Kyd was writing for the company of Lord Strange, a curious withdrawn character whom certain Catholics at home and abroad regarded as the rightful heir to the English throne and who piously insisted on his actors and playwrights starting each day with corporate prayer; and Greene had found the theatre less to his taste than he had expected when he started his smooth plagiarisms of Marlowe and he was now devoting himself to highly successful pamphlets on criminal aspects of London life which, rapidly reprinting, provided him with the wherewithal to consistently over-drink himself.

Kit found, much to his surprise, that both the morose, envious Kyd and the ebullient, rip-roaring Greene were genuinely shocked by his atheism and refused to argue it with him. Their change of attitude to him—if, indeed, it was a change and not merely Time's development of inherent differences—as well as the unpredictable state of the theatre under the combined attacks of the Government, the Puritans and the Archbishop of Canterbury, all of whom would be only too pleased to suppress it altogether, made Marlowe decide to return to Scadbury. For his new play all he needed was his Holinshed and his imagination.

There was another factor in favour of writing *The Contention between the two famous houses of York and Lancaster* in Kent, for an important part of it would be devoted to the Kentish rebel-

* The name was given them by Sir Walter Scott.

lion under Jack Cade which almost unseated King Henry VI.
At Sevenoaks a detachment of the royal forces had been cut to
pieces. The manor of Scadbury itself had been overrun by the
pillaging rebels on their way to London. Cade was eventually
killed in a Kentish garden by Alexander Iden who was knighted
for that service and whose grandchildren were neighbours whom
the Walsinghams visited. In the writing of these 'Cade' scenes,
Marlowe was able to pay a tribute to the lovely county which
was now, by residence as well as birth, doubly his:

> Kent, in the Commentaries Caesar writ,
> Is termed the civilist place of all this isle.
> Sweet is the country, because full of riches;
> The people active, valiant, liberal, wise.

And he could call on his own feelings at the moment by giving
Iden, walking in the garden, the soliloquy,

> Lord, who would live turmoiléd in the court
> And may enjoy such quiet walks as these?
> This small inheritance my father left me
> Contenteth me and worth a monarchy.
> I seek not to wax great by others' waning,
> And gather wealth I care not with what envy.
> Sufficeth what I have maintains my state
> And sends the poor well pleaséd from my gate.

By contrast he was able to indulge his contempt for the acquisitive and unlearned mob and characteristically he made one of the
rioters say, when a nobleman quoted a Latin tag: 'Away with
him! Away with him! He speaks Latin.'

For himself, Marlowe made his quotations from the classics
even more recondite. In *Edward II*, he had troubled to explain
to the groundlings the meaning of the ambiguous message
which secured the King's death:

> *Edwardum occidere nolite timere, bonum est.*
> 'Fear not to kill the King, 'tis good he die.'
> But read it thus, and that's another sense:
> *Edwardum occidere nolite, timere bonum est.*
> 'Kill not the King, 'tis good to fear the worst.'
> Unpointed as it is, thus it shall go:
> *Edwardum occidere nolite timere bonum est.*

But in dealing with a similar ambiguity in *The Contention*, he merely made the reader of it exclaim:

> Why, this is just
> *Aio te, Æacida, Romanos vincere posse!*

a reference to Ennius which only a classical scholar could appreciate—the answer which Phyrrus received from the oracle at Delphi before his war against the Romans: meaning either 'I say that thou, the descendant of Æcus, mayst conquer the Romans', or 'I say that the Romans may conquer thee, descendant of Æcus.' In a similar manner, a line from Virgil was introduced without explanation in a speech to Cardinal Beaufort:

> What, Cardinal, is your priesthood grown peremptory?
> *Tantaene animis celestibus irae?*
> Churchmen so hot? Good uncle, hide such malice!

without any guidance that the second line meant 'Is such resentment found in heavenly minds?' And when York's young son is struck down he cries to his killer in a line from Ovid's *Heroides*,

> *Di faciant laudis summa sit ista tuae*

where the terseness of the Latin is so much more effective than 'May the gods grant that this may be the sum of thy glory!'—he offered no help.* The Pembrokes and those for whom Marlowe was writing would understand it well enough as the classic expression of an unworthy deed. Also it served to point that from this murder of the boy sprang the irreconcilable bitterness of the civil war, for Margaret of Anjou, when York was brought before her as a prisoner,

> Laughed in his face; and when with grief he wept
> The ruthless Queen gave him to dry his cheeks
> A napkin steepéd in the harmless blood.

---

* Since to a non-classical generation like our own this particular myth is not too well known, I may perhaps without discourtesy explain that the line occurs in an imaginary letter written by Phyllis to Demophoon, the son of Theseus, who, returning from the Trojan war, was entertained by her and, after a short affaire, left her. This particular line sums up her bitterness and she prays that among the statues of the great men of Athens, his may have the inscription: 'This is he whose wiles betrayed the hostess that loved him' (*Hic est cujus amans hospita capta dolo est*)—a conquest radically different from the exploits of his famous father in, among other things, killing the Minotaur.

This episode gave Marlowe the opportunity for one of the great pieces of rhetoric which he might have provided for Alleyn. York replies to the Lancastrian Queen:

> She-wolf of France, but worse than wolves of France
> Whose tongue's more poisonous than the adder's tooth!
> How ill-becoming is it in thy sex
> To triumph like an Amazonian trull
> Upon their woes whom Fortune captivates.
> O tiger's heart wrapped in a woman's hide,
> How coulds't thou drain the life-blood of the child
> To bid the father wipe his eyes withal
> And yet be seen to bear a woman's face?
> But you are more inhuman, more inexorable,
> O ten times more than tigers of Hyrcania.
> See, ruthless Queen, a helpless father's tears!
> This cloth dipped in the blood of my sweet boy
> And I with tears do wash the blood away.
> Keep thou this napkin and go boast of this!

and so on for fifty-seven lines of increasing invective. It would, Marlowe thought, be magnificent if 'Shake-scene' could deliver it; he had become so accustomed to writing for and with Alleyn that his absence from *Edward II* had disturbed him; but, with the present chaos in the theatre, it was quite possible that Alleyn might be induced to make an appearance in *The Contention*.

The difficulty was that the play was too long. The variety of characters and the wealth of incident demanded two plays, in which case the death of York, which made so splendid a climax to *The Contention*, would have to be transferred to the second play. With a touch of his old arrogance, Marlowe decided that even though by this rearrangement the scene between Margaret and York would come at the end of the first act which was too early, the impact of it would be strong enough to last throughout the entire play and allow him to call it *The True Tragedy of Richard Duke of York*. At the end it would be to that first murder that the audience's thoughts would turn when York's other sons avenged their brother by killing Margaret's son and it was the 'she-wolf's' turn to cry:

They that stabbed Caesar shed no blood at all,
Did not offend nor were not worthy blame,
If this foul deed were by to equal it!
He was a man; this in respect a child:
And men ne'er spend their fury on a child.
What's worse than murderer that I may name it?
Butchers and villains! Bloody cannibals!
How sweet a plant have you untimely cropped!
You have no children, butchers! If you had
The thought of them would have stirr'd up remorse;
But if you ever chance to have a child
Look in his youth to have him so cut off
As, deathsmen, you have rid this sweet young prince!

The plays at last completed, Marlowe reluctantly left
Scadbury for another visit to London to submit them to the
Pembrokes.

Note:
The Contention and *The True Tragedy* 'as it was sundry times
acted by the Right Honourable the Earl of Pembroke his
servants' were first published in 1594. Both plays, under the
title of *The Whole Contention*, were reissued in 1619 and attributed
to Shakespeare who, by then, had been dead three years, but
whose reputation might be expected to sell the plays. In 1623
the plays, slightly revised and altered, were included in the
First Folio of Shakespeare's plays, with the addition of *Harry the
Sixth* (see next chapter), under the titles of *King Henry VI,
Parts I, II and III.*

It is remotely possible that, at some time, Shakespeare may
have had a hand in revising them and it is probable that his
company acted them after the death of Marlowe and the dis-
bandment of Pembroke's Men. But there is no doubt that they
are not by Shakespeare, nor were they claimed for him in the
published versions in his lifetime.

From the earliest days of Shakespearian criticism the most
perceptive commentators—Malone, Farmer and Chalmers in
the eighteenth century, Hallam, Dyce and Swinburne in the
nineteenth, and Thorndike, Tucker Brooke and John Quincy
Adams in the twentieth—have acknowledged them as Mar-

lowe's; and nearly everyone has admitted that in some way Marlowe 'had a hand in them'. The alternative theory, which is still academic orthodoxy, is that '*The Contention* and *The True Tragedy* are early "Bad Quartos" of *II and III Henry VI*'—which need not be taken seriously.

This matter is further referred to in the *Postscript*.

18. *A Play in a Hurry*

The Contention and *The True Tragedy* were played successfully at *The Theatre* which James Burbage, overborne for the moment by lawsuits, debts and plans for building a new playhouse across the river at Bankside to compete with Henslowe's *The Rose*, had leased to the Admiral's Men. As the Lord Admiral and the Earl of Pembroke were personal friends and colleagues who held the same political views—they had sat together on the tribunal which condemned Mary Queen of Scots to death—there was no difficulty in arranging for Pembroke's Men to play at *The Theatre* on certain days. Moreover, with the companies working so closely together and the dearth of great actors, it proved possible, as Marlowe had hoped it would, for Alleyn to play Richard Duke of York.

The great speech had only one drawback for him. According to the instructions voiced by Queen Margaret, he had to deliver it standing on a little mound, with a paper crown on his head and his arms held by his captors. On this occasion he could not shake the stage with his majestic tread or impress the audience with his ample gestures. He had to rely solely on his voice, his facial expression—and Marlowe's words. Yet, perforce accepting a physical discipline so alien to him, he revealed himself a greater actor than ever.

Meanwhile at *The Rose* plays by Kyd and Greene continued to be performed by Lord Strange's Men till, because they contravened the Lent closing, they were ordered by the Privy Council to refrain from playing at Henslowe's house and permitted to appear only at a diminutive, out-of-the-way house at Newington Butts—and that for only three days a week.

Henslowe faced ruin; but his usual energetic ingenuity did not desert him. He urged Lord Strange to protest to the Privy Council that a tour of the country at that time would be ruinous and might be a means 'to bring us to division and separation by which we shall not only be undone but also unready to serve Her Majesty* when it shall please Her Highness to command us'. They reinforced this somewhat specialised plea by an appearance of consideration for the Thames watermen who did good business by transporting the playgoing public from one bank to the other. 'And for the use of our playhouse on the Bankside, by reason of the passage to and from the same by water, is a great relief to the poor watermen and our dismission thence is to those poor men in a manner an undoing, we petition your good Honours to permit us the use of the playhouse again.'

Henslowe then persuaded the watermen themselves to write to the Lord Admiral that as 'we your poor watermen have had much help and relief for us, our poor wives and children by means of the resort of such people as come unto the playhouse, it may please your good Lordship, for God's sake and in the way of charity to give leave unto Philip Henslowe to have playing in his said house as it hath been accustomed'.

The double plea was successful. The Privy Council notified the Justices of the Peace that 'whereas not long since we did restrain Lord Strange his servants from playing at the Rose and enjoined them to play three days at Newington Butts, now, forasmuch as we are satisfied that by reason of the tediousness of the way, and that of long time plays have not there been used on working-days, and that a number of poor watermen are thereby relieved, you shall permit and suffer them or any others there to exercise themselves as they have done heretofore'.†

Having received permission to reopen his theatre, Henslowe was concerned to have a new play there which should draw the town. Fortunately the perfect subject presented itself—a third play on the reign of Henry VI, dealing with the events which preceded *The Contention*. It could centre on the exploits of the famous Lord Talbot in the war with France—which could provide Alleyn with an ideal part—and, by introducing Joan of

---

* i.e. appear at Court to give special performances.
† Unfortunately neither the petitions nor the Privy Council Order is dated, but as all the circumstances suggest 1591, which is the year also favoured by Sir Edmund Chambers, the great authority on the Elizabethan theatre, I have adopted it here.

Arc, would allow also the introduction of some supernatural beings.

The only remaining problem was time and, after some argument, Marlowe consented to collaborate with Kyd and Greene in the manner usual for hack-writers who were anxious to complete a play quickly for a try-out. The agreed story would be 'plotted' and the various scenes distributed among the writers. The best 'plotter', often used by the Admiral's Men, was Antony Munday, an amusing rogue who was also a valued member of 'the Service' who had penetrated the English College in Rome, as well as an occasional actor and a long-standing apprentice to one of the stationers. Marlowe knew him casually in all his guises and disliked and distrusted him in them all. But he did not dispute his excellence as a 'plotter' and, as one professional to another, accepted his services.

To Marlowe himself were naturally enough allotted the Talbot episodes and Kit insisted on writing in addition the scene in the Temple Garden when the opposing nobles first picked the red rose or the white rose for a badge. Kyd was entrusted with the scenes at the Courts of England and France, culminating in the betrothal of the young Henry VI and Margaret of Anjou; while Greene was given the Joan of Arc—La Pucelle— scenes. Certain areas of course overlapped, particularly those of Marlowe and Greene, and there was much detailed wrangling among the collaborators as well as general discussion.

Altogether it was an unhappy time. They worked in Kyd's rooms, as Marlowe had no *pied-à-terre* in London, and Greene's attendance was erratic. In spite of ample literary earnings, Robin Greene's way of life, his chronic drinking and the demands of his whorish mistress and her swashbuckling brother ensured that he was a permanent pauper sponging on new acquaintances, dupes or admirers, for his temporary lodgings. His detestation of Alleyn had increased as he grew poorer and the actor grew richer. And it was based on principles of a kind as much as on envy. Actors were mere puppets animated by the words of the playwrights. Two years ago, in one of his pamphlets, Greene had rebuked an actor for failing to realise this and had likened him in his pride to 'Æsop's Crow, pranked out with the glory of others' feathers—for of thyself thou canst say nothing'. Yet the actors grew rich while the authors languished in poverty and the worst offenders were those like Alleyn who not only bought plays outright for a pittance but became an unofficial money-lender, advancing small sums when the writers were on the verge of starvation, and setting them, with interest, against payment for their next work.

The situation became more tense because in the preparation of *Harry the Sixth* Alleyn interfered incessantly. He insisted that the turret of *The Rose* should be spectacularly used early in the play instead of being reserved to the end, as it had been in both parts of *Tamburlaine*. Consequently he had a cannon trained on the turret where he, as Talbot, made his first entrance. Here he delivered an eighteen-line speech, narrating the circumstances of his recent imprisonment. It would be dull, as all such narrations tended to be; nor could even Alleyn's genius make it anything else, but the audience could, even so, be kept on tenterhooks by uncertainty as to when the cannon would go off.

Marlowe by now was accustomed to the actor's as opposed to the writer's point of view, but Kyd and Greene inquired derisively how verisimilitude was to be secured for a long speech to be delivered, as it were, in the cannon's mouth on the turret.

'Simplicity itself,' said Alleyn. 'I can give you the very lines pat. I make my usual entrance down-stage and Lord Salisbury greets me with:

> Talbot, my life, my joy, again returned!
> How wert thou handled being prisoner?
> Or by what means gotst thou to be released?
> Discourse, I prithee, on the turret's top!'

Despite the lack of enthusiasm which greeted his effort, Alleyn from that moment interfered even more not only in procuring acting effects but in actually contributing speeches. One of these compared a company of English soldiers to 'deer with heads of steel' and gave Talbot the rallying cry:

> Sell every man his life as dear as mine
> And they shall find dear deer of us, my friends.
> God and Saint George, Talbot and England's right,
> Prosper our colours in this dangerous fight!

All agreed that he would deliver it magnificently and be rewarded with rounds of applause, but Greene was moved to describe him to the others as 'an upstart Crow beautified with our feathers who now thinks he can bombast out blank verse as well as the best of us'. It was an insult that this common actor, even though he might rightly consider himself the greatest 'Shake-scene' in the country, should be in a position to tyrannise over University wits like Greene and Marlowe. What was more, his heart was as flinty as that of any moneylender—any *other* moneylender.

'A tiger's heart wrapped in a player's hide,' said Marlowe, parodying his own line in *The True Tragedy* which Alleyn delivered with such effect.

While Marlowe the dramatist was giving shape to past history, his other profession, concerned with the making of present history, irrupted into it. Poley called on him. Since Sir Francis Walsingham's death, Poley had been continuously engaged either in Berwick or in the Low Countries in acquainting himself with the details of the Spanish attempt at invasion through Scotland. The time was almost ripe and the Scottish Catholic emissaries were on the point of setting out with three blank sheets, signed and sealed by the three leading Catholic earls, which, for safety's sake, were to be filled in with the conditions only when the bearers were safely out of the reach of England.* The English Government had all the details necessary to make an arrest. The only thing still undecided was whether it should be made before they set out from Scotland or when they arrived in the Low Countries.

'I want you to go to Edinburgh to see our friend Fowler,' Poley said.

'When?'

'Tonight if you can; tomorrow if you must.'

'That is quite impossible,' said Marlowe.

'What do you mean?'

'I cannot leave London. The play must be finished.'

'A play?' said Poley incredulously. 'A *play*?'

---

* These are known in history as 'the Spanish Blanks'. Certain Catholic writers at one time contended that the whole affair was a pseudo-plot engineered by the Kirk to discredit the Catholics; but the discovery of various papers in the Simancas MSS put the genuineness beyond question.

'Yes.'

'You presume to put a *play* before your duty to the Queen?'

'Has the Queen ordered me to Edinburgh?'

'Her Majesty knows nothing of it. Why should she? You take your orders from me.'

'I took orders, when I did take them, from Sir Francis. Now he is dead, I am dispensed.'

'You will remember, he entrusted your instruction to me.'

'When I was still at Cambridge and ignorant of the great world. Now I can make my own choice, having discharged my debt of gratitude to Sir Francis by services freely rendered.'

Marlowe spoke slowly, choosing his words. The moment was critical. The memory of the threatening interview with the odious Skeres reinforced his resolve. His determination communicated itself to Poley who summoning his charm said agreeably: 'If it is a matter of such importance to you, Kit, I am sure I can find a substitute for this mission, but I shall not promise not to ask you, one day, of your kindness to give me your aid.'

Marlowe softened immediately: 'Nor on those terms, Robin, should I be likely to excuse myself, as I do now.'

So, for the moment, matters were left, though Marlowe could not escape, any more than the rest of the country, the atmosphere of panic which the Government fostered by letting it be known that 'the malice of the King of Spain has been increased by his loss and shame in 1588 and his resolution is still to invade this kingdom and he is therefore labouring to plant himself in Brittany and has raised factions and conspiracies in Scotland'. Further to impress the matter on the minds of Londoners there was another batch of Catholic executions at Tyburn on 10 December 1591, while on the same day at Holborn a special gallows was erected outside a house near Gray's Inn where Edmund Gennings, a young Jesuit priest, had been discovered saying Mass for the tutor to the young Earl of Southampton. The priest and the tutor were both to be executed outside their door to bring the matter home more vividly to the young lawyers who were showing signs of sympathy to Catholicism.

Marlowe, who refused to attend the spectacle at Tyburn, was impelled to go to Holborn. The detection had been the work of John Florio, an Italian dictionary-maker who was the chief spy planted in the Southampton household and who had occasionally joined the turret-group in their occult discussions. Moreover the whole neighbourhood of Gray's Inn—quite apart from associations with William Bradley—was alive with memories of the past which Marlowe wanted to put into perspective.

When Gennings, drawn to the gallows, was urged to confess his treason, for so the Queen would doubtless pardon him, he said: 'I know not ever to have offended her, but if to say Mass be treason, I confess I have done it and I glory in it.' This reply so enraged the man in charge of the execution that he refused him leave to say any more, but ordered him to be turned off the ladder and the rope immediately cut. Gennings was thus thrown on his feet 'but the hangman tripped up his heels, cut off his members and disembowelled him. In his agony, Gennings began to call on St Gregory to the great astonishment of the hangman who cried out with a loud voice: "God's Wounds, his heart is in my hand and yet Gregory is in his mouth!" ' This episode became the talk of the town but Marlowe returned from the execution as sceptical of eyewitness accounts as Sir Walter Raleigh (who was apt to maintain that six eyewitness accounts of the same event would describe six different events).

Marlowe did not attempt to maintain that the apparent miracle had not happened. All he said was that personally he had heard only a scream of agony which might have been interpreted as anything. What most disturbed him was the fortitude which faith—in his opinion, a foolish and unjustified faith—gave a sufferer. As Penry would have died for his beliefs, which were the exact opposite of Gennings's with no less courage and certainty, the truth of the rival creeds was in no way confirmed by their respective martyrs. He hoped, should it ever come to it, that an atheist would die as bravely for his disbelief.

What had increased was Marlowe's contempt for the Establishment which persecuted both Catholics and Puritans for their beliefs. This manifested itself in his attitude to his collaborators. Kyd's sanctimonious insistence on observing his patron's rule of corporate prayer before beginning work was supported by Greene and when he was early enough to partici-pate in the devotions he was wont to punctuate them with alcoholic sobs. Nor did Alleyn, who headed his letters with 'Emmanuel' (in reply to Henslowe's 'Jesus'), have any objection to the semi-public piety. But Marlowe bitterly refused to have anything to do with it and when he was alone with Kyd (as usually happened) he turned the occasion into one of ribald jesting or of acrimonious debate.

At one such moment Kyd turned on him and demanded a statement of his own belief instead of epigrammatic negations or carping attacks on orthodoxy. In reply Marlowe next day produced a book by a Catholic theologian forty-four years earlier in which the author had summarised the main Arian arguments in order to attack them. 'The whole course of the Gospel', this section began, 'doth show Jesus Christ a man subject to hunger, thirst, weariness and fear; and to believe that a nature subject to these infirmities is God or any part of the Divine Essence is folly.'

Passing the book to Kyd, Marlowe said: 'If you wish to do a service to yourself, to me and to Sir Walter Raleigh, you might copy out these three pages in your so-excellent script.'

'Explain,' said Kyd. 'How would that be of benefit to you, me and Sir Walter Raleigh?'

'To you and Sir Walter because he is anxious to have these passages by him for a lecture he is giving and the book, as you see, is cumbrous. He would undoubtedly reward you handsomely. To me, it would be of benefit because if you do not do it, I shall have to and with my vile calligraphy it will take an age and even then will be displeasing to the reader.'

Kyd, who was by no means averse to gaining the favour of Raleigh and who regularly added to his income by practising his old occupation of noverint by copying letters and documents in his exquisite Italianate script, said that, if he could find time, he would certainly consider it.

Harry the Sixth was finished at last and the date fixed for the first performance at *The Rose* was the afternoon of Friday, 3 March 1592. Henslowe had acknowledged the work of the collaborators by putting on, in the three previous weeks, Greene's *Friar Bacon and Friar Bungay*, Kyd's *The Spanish Tragedy* and Marlowe's *The Rich Jew of Malta*. Their takings were less than 25 shillings a performance, but the first afternoon of *Harry the Sixth*, as Henslowe carefully noted in his diary, brought in £3 16s. 8d.

19. The Plague takes Toll

The success of *Harry the Sixth* continued throughout the 1592 season, during which it was played at *The Rose* every week until Midsummer Eve when the theatre closed. A first whiff of warning of an approaching plague reinforced the enemies of the theatre in their insistence that 'the cause of plagues is sin and the cause of sin is plays; therefore the cause of plagues is plays'. To this Tom Nashe retorted that, on the contrary, plays were a 'rare exercise of virtue'.

'First, for the subject of them (for the most part),' wrote Nashe, 'it is borrowed out of our English Chronicles, wherein our forefathers' valiant acts (that have lain long buried in rusty brass and worm-eaten books) are revived, and they themselves raised from the grave of Oblivion and brought to plead their aged honours in open presence; than which, what can be a sharper reproof to these degenerate, effeminate days of ours? How it would have joyed brave Talbot (the terror of the French) to think that after he had lain two hundred years in his tomb, he should triumph again on the stage and have his bones new embalmed with the tears of ten thousand spectators at least (at several times) who in the tragedian that represents his person, imagine that they behold him fresh bleeding!'

A potent factor in *Harry the Sixth*'s popularity was its sudden topicality. In the civil war in France, Queen Elizabeth refused to give any further aid to the Protestant King in his losing struggle with the Catholic League on the grounds that he had refused to take Rouen when he could easily have done so 'wasting his own people and her treasure to no purpose'. But when she heard that the Duke of Parma's forces were marching to raise the siege of

Rouen, she rapidly changed her mind and ordered 1,600 men to be raised and immediately sent overseas.

In London on March 1 the Lord Mayor issued a proclamation for the impressment of an additional 200 men for the attack on Rouen. On March 3 *Harry the Sixth* opened and Londoners could listen to Alleyn as Talbot proclaiming before Rouen:

> As sure as in this late-betrayéd town
> Great Coeur-de-Lion's heart was buriéd,
> So sure I swear to get the town or die.

Theatrical success, at least, could hardly be avoided.

At the beginning of June, Marlowe visited his family at Canterbury to reassure himself they were not in need. He had returned to Scadbury to spend the rest of the summer and write his poem on *Hero and Leander*. During his absence in London Tom Walsingham, young as he was, had been called to take up the family burden of magistracy in the county in succession to his grandfather, his father and his brother and, in his new capacity, he had received a notification from the Privy Council to inquire into the affairs of Canterbury. The imposed immigration of the seventies had had its inevitable effect and 'the decayed estate of the city and the great number of poor people' had created a crisis. To counteract the massive unemployment, the Council was considering making work by implementing a seventy-five-year-old plan of Henry VIII's reign for 'the making of the river navigable for boats and lighters to pass to the town of Fordwich'. The magistrates of Kent were, therefore, required to meet together expeditiously to consider an estimate for the whole work 'and first to set down a liberal contribution themselves'.

On visiting Canterbury, however, Marlowe found that his family if they could not be said to have prospered had at least held their own and that, as far as they were concerned, charity was neither necessary nor acceptable. For Kit, the most interesting item of news was that his sister, Margaret, had at last, at the age of 25, managed to get her reluctant tailor to the altar, and for once her brother waived his principles to the extent of attending the baptism of the offspring, a boy named John.

*

In London, the immigrant situation was as bad as, and on a more explosive scale than, in Canterbury. The City Fathers complained that 'the numbers of strangers are so much increased within the City and the suburbs that the freemen of the City are supplanted and their living taken from them. The strangers who came hither the better to enjoy the free exercise of their consciences are so extraordinarily favoured that some are grown to great wealth. Some of them convey beyond the seas the commodities of this realm, whereby the prices of divers things are increased and the Queen deceived in her custom.' The Privy Council thereupon ordered a most exhaustive inquisition to be made 'with as much secrecy as may be whereby neither the English artisans and apprentices take any comfort or boldness to contemn the strangers, nor the poor strangers to be made afraid to be hardly used'.

Secrecy, however, was out of the question, and the apprentices, always militant, took comfort sufficiently to riot in favour of a feltmaker in Southwark and to threaten more violence on Midsummer Eve. 'To prevent this mischief', the magistrates ordered, 'a strong and substantial watch sufficient to suppress any tumult is to be kept. Moreover for the avoiding of unlawful assemblies no plays may be used at *The Theatre*, *The Curtain*, *The Rose* or other usual places until the Feast of St Michael.'

On Tuesday, 20 June 1592, *Harry the Sixth* had its last performance before the closure, nor did *The Rose* reopen at Michaelmas for by September the plague was in control and all playhouses were closed indefinitely.

The onset of the plague became a matter of official concern early in August and by September 7 the number of deaths from 'this pernicious and contagious fever, one of those called *Epidemia*, which may be easily perceived by the extreme heat and inflammation which inwardly they do feel that are infected therewith'—as one physician called it—were high enough to justify the authorities putting into effect the statutory regulations to control a major outbreak.

Graves were to be dug at least six feet deep for humans and four feet for dogs, which were to be shot by the Common Huntsman if they were found in the street. The College of

Physicians was to designate a certain number of its members to attend to infected patients only. Every house containing a sick person had to display (under penalty of imprisonment) a large notice 'in a place notorious and plain for them that pass by to see it' bearing the words: 'Lord, have mercy upon us'. From such a house, quarantined for twenty-eight days after a death or twenty after a recovery, only one person was allowed to go out to shop for necessities and that person had to carry 'a red wand of three feet at the least held openly upright in the plainest manner to be seen, without covering any part of it with their cloak or other garment'. All householders possessed of 'a well or pumps' were to sluice their gutters with twenty buckets of water a day (ten before 6 a.m., ten after 8 p.m.) and every street was 'to be made clean by the Scavenger and Raker every day except Sunday'.

With the orders, the Mayor and Aldermen of London issued a list of preventatives and cures which, on September 19, they recommended also to the justices of Kent with the request that the minister of every parish should acquaint all householders with it. Richard Harvey, as Rector of Chislehurst, thus found a new use for his leisure and, abandoning for the moment his astrological predictions and his efforts at pamphleteering in his brother Gabriel's interest against Nashe and Greene, rushed round the parish, not excluding 'the big house' at Scadbury, advising his flock to promote vomiting by taking a mixture of oil of walnuts, celandine juice and powdered radish. 'Let not the party sleep for two hours after,' the instructions said, 'and it is better than any purgative.'

Marlowe when this was reported to him by Tom said that he knew no better recipe for vomiting than hearing one of the Rector's sermons, but in that case it would be quite impossible to keep awake for anything like two hours. Richard Harvey, ever since their Cambridge days, was one of the most enduring of his hates. On the occasions when it was impossible to avoid him Kit took refuge in such innocent badinage as asking his opinion on the relationship between the plagues of Egypt recorded in the Old Testament and the present outbreak in England. Was, for example, the plague of frogs the reason for the official assertion that a sign of the approaching plague was that 'in the beginning of harvest we see great store of little frogs, red toads and mice on the earth abounding extraordinarily'? Had the Rector happened to see any frogs lately? Or, better, toads 'creeping on the earth with long tails'? The Rector, uncertain of Marlowe's purpose in such inquiries, soon learnt to avoid him in his pastoral peregrinations.

When the plague struck, Robin Greene was dying. Reduced to the extremity of pawning his sword, he would pitifully beg 'a penny-pot of Malmsey' in the taverns where he could no longer pay. Nashe, meeting him one day when he himself had a little money, entertained him to 'a banquet of pickled herring' which in his disordered condition brought on his final illness. He collapsed in the street and was succoured by a cordwainer who took him to his home where he was nursed by the cordwainer's wife until he died.

With death imminent, Greene wrote a last pamphlet, *The Repentance of Robert Greene*, in which he addressed his fellow-playwrights. His message for an easily identifiable Marlowe was: 'Wonder not, thou famous gracer of tragedians that Greene, who hath said with thee like the fool in his heart "There is no God", should now give glory to His greatness; for penetrating is His power, His hand lies heavy upon me, He hath spoken unto me with a voice of thunder, and I have felt that He is a God that can punish enemies. Why should thy excellent wit, His gift, be so blinded that thou should give no glory to the Giver? Is it the pestilent Machiavellian policy that thou hast studied? O peevish folly! What are his rules but mere confused mockeries? The broacher of this Diabolical Atheism is dead and in his life never had the felicity he aimed at. Wilt thou, my friend, be his disciple? Look unto me, by him persuaded to this liberty, and thou shalt find it an infernal bondage. I know the least of my demerits merits this miserable death, but wilful striving against known truth exceedeth all the terrors of my soul. Defer not (with me) till this last point of extremity; for little knowest thou how in the end thou shalt be visited!'

Then, after addressing Kyd and Nashe in similarly appropriate terms, he returned bitterly to his attack on actors in general and Alleyn in particular: 'Base-minded men all three of you, if by my misery you be not warned; for unto none of you like me sought those burrs to cleave, those puppets, I mean, that spake from our mouths, those antics garnished in our colours.* Is it not strange that I, to whom they have all been beholding— is it not like that to you to whom they have all been beholding? —shall, were ye in the case as I am now, be at once of them forsaken?

'Yes, trust them not. For there is an upstart crow, beautified with our feathers, that with his *"Tiger's heart wrapped in a player's hide"* suppose he is as well able to bombast out a blank verse as the best of you; and, being an absolute *Johannes fac totum* is in his own conceit the only Shake-scene in a country. O, that I might entreat your rare wits to be employed in more profitable courses; and let those apes imitate your past excellence, but never more acquaint them with your admired inventions.'†

Greene died on September 2 and as soon as the rumour of it reached him, Gabriel Harvey hurried down to his lodgings to make certain that his enemy was no more—that, as he put it, 'the King of the Paper Stage has played his last part and is gone to Tarlton'—and to publish to the world the details of his poor end, recounting with sniggering amusement how 'his sweet hostess, for a tender farewell, crowned him with a garland of bays to show a tenth Muse honoured more being dead than all Nine honoured him alive'.

Marlowe needed no encouragement to cease writing for Henslowe and Alleyn. Until they produced his *Guise* he had no intention of giving them more plays. He would return to poetry and the classics.

This decision was not uninfluenced by his association with the Pembrokes. During the last year or two the Countess had become 'the subject of all verse'. To her Edmund Spenser had dedicated his *The Ruins of Time*, Samuel Daniel his *Delia*, Nicholas Breton his *The Pilgrimage to Paradise*, Barnabe Barnes

* Marlowe and the others were essentially dramatists; Greene was a successful novelist and seems to imply that he took to the stage only at the request of the actors and managers.

† As an artist's protest against the non-creative who make a profit from his imaginative work, Greene's outburst may be thought to anticipate Vincent van Gogh's dying letter to his brother, Theo.

some sonnets, Thomas Morley his *Canzonets*, Abraham Fraunce his *Amyntas' Dale* while Thomas Watson was finishing his poem on the joys of Amyntas, *Amintae Gaudia*, by which he was to seek her patronage. But that autumn, in plague-ridden London, Watson died and it was left to Marlowe to perform the last act of their long and close friendship by supplying the intended dedication: 'To the Most Illustrious Noble Lady, adorned with all gifts of both mind and body, Mary Countess of Pembroke. Delia born of a laurel-crowned race, true sister of Sidney, the bard of Apollo, fostering parent of letters, Muse of the poets of our time and all most happily burgeoning wits, deign to be patron to this posthumous Amyntas as to thine adoptive son, the rather as his dying father had most humbly bequeathed to thee his keeping. And though thy glorious name is spread abroad, yet, crowned as thou art by the songs of many as a starry diadem, scorn not another star upon thy crown. So shall I, whose slender wealth is but the seashore myrtle of Venus and Daphne's ever-green laurel, on the foremost page of every poem invoke thee, as Mistress of the Muses, to my aid.' *

But whatever later poem of his own Marlowe might find it expedient to dedicate to the Countess, *Hero and Leander* was Tom Walsingham's. Kit made him the model for the protagonist:

> Amorous Leander, beautiful and young
> (Whose tragedy divine Musæus sung)
> Dwelt at Abydos; since him dwelt there none
> For whom succeeding times make greater moan.
> His dangling tresses that were never shorn,
> Had they been cut and unto Colchis borne,
> Would have allur'd the venturous youth of Greece
> To hazard more than for the Golden Fleece.
> His body was as straight as Circe's wand:
> Jove might have sipped out nectar from his hand.
> Even as delicious meat is to the taste,
> So was his neck in touching, and surpast

---

* This dedication (which I have shortened) is in Latin and was first printed, with a translation, in 1934 in *Christopher Marlowe in London* by Mark Eccles pp. 165, 166.

The white of Pelops' shoulder: I could tell ye
How smooth his breast was and how white his belly,
And whose immortal fingers did imprint
That heavenly path with many a curious dint
That runs along his back . . .
Some swore he was a maid in man's attire,
For in his looks were all that men desire—
A pleasant-smiling cheek, a speaking eye,
A brow for love to banquet royally.

The impact of this, following as it did the description of the heroine,

> Hero the fair
> Whom young Apollo courted for her hair

with twenty-five lines devoted exclusively to her clothes and no further insistence on her beauty than that her face was so 'lovely-fair' that Cupid would mistake her for his mother, Venus, and 'often-times into her bosom flew', was, so Tom suggested critically, a trifle injudicious.

Kit, reflecting that his new status was making Tom unbearably conventional, retorted not in words but by writing eighty lines describing Neptune's attempted seduction of Leander as he swam the Hellespont. They might appear to some of his readers somewhat irrelevant, but Tom, with the memory of summer swims in the lake, would understand them well enough.

> He watched his arms and as they opened wide
> At every stroke betwixt them he would slide
> And steal a kiss and then run out and dance
> And as he turned cast many a lustful glance
> Upon his breast, his thighs, and every limb
> And up again and close beside him swim
> And talk of love.

He would understand, too:

> It lies not in our power to love or hate,
> For will in us is over-ruled by fate.
> The reason no man knows; let it suffice
> What we behold is censured by our eyes.

Where both deliberate the love is slight.
Whoever loved that loved not at first sight?*

Marlowe was not altogether right when he considered that
Tom's increasing responsibilities had resulted in a corresponding
growth in respectability for there was an area of activity which
the master of Scadbury carefully concealed from his companion—
though less because he thought that Kit would intrinsically
disapprove than because, as it involved Ingram Frizer, he
wished to avoid an increase of tension.

Though Frizer had managed to sell the inn at Basingstoke
which he had bought while Edmund Walsingham was still alive
and Tom's necessities were clamorous, he had not managed to
collect the money. He had asked double what he paid for it—
£240 as against £120—and the buyer had signed the necessary
bond. But he had shown no sign of honouring it and that summer
Frizer took him to court and obtained judgment against him.
His removal to prison for debt, however, was a poor substitute
for the cash and Frizer, who was in need of it, persuaded Tom
Walsingham to raise the money by a temporary return to the
expedients they had used in their poverty-stricken days. They
had been, not to put too fine a point on it, 'conny-catchers'.

Robin Greene, in his pamphlets on criminal London, had
defined the practice: 'The Conny-catchers, apparelled like
honest, civil gentlemen, with smooth faces as if butter would not
melt in their mouths, as soon as they see a plain country fellow
in a coat of home-spun russet say: "There is a conny!" At that
word, out flies the setter and, overtaking the man, begins to
salute him thus: "Sir, God save you, you are welcome to London.
How are all our good friends in the country? I hope they are all
in health." The countryman, seeing a man quite unknown to him

---

* Marlowe wrote only eight hundred lines of *Hero and Leander*. After his death,
George Chapman 'completed' it. In this form it is printed in the Everyman edition
of Marlowe. The editor, the late M. R. Ridley, writes in the introduction that in so
doing he has followed standard practice but he does so reluctantly and finds it hard
to understand 'why anyone should wish to overlay the fire and air of Marlowe with
the laboured scholarship, the ponderous conceits, personifications and philosophiz-
ing of Chapman. The proper place for the completion is in the works of Chapman
and only there.' Personally I am so greatly in agreement with this that I recom-
mend anyone unacquainted with *Hero and Leander* to read it in the reprint of the
first (1598) edition, containing Marlowe's lines only, by Fairfax Hall at the
Stourton Press (1934).

accost him so courteously and being somewhat bemused by the strange salutation, enters into conversation with him.'

Tom Walsingham himself could obviously no longer 'walk up and down Paul's, Fleet Street, Holborn, the Strand and such places with cozening companions to spy out a prey'. This lowly —but always exciting—rôle could be entrusted to Nicholas Skeres who, though he had risen to higher things in 'the Service', had once been an expert 'Setter' and was, indeed, noted as such in a Government report on 'masterless men and cut-purses in and about London'. Skeres, having found a 'country-conny', would at an appropriate moment introduce him to Frizer who, in his turn, would take him to 'a gentleman of good worship', that is to say Tom, to complete the conning. All Tom had to do was to sit impressively in the library at Scadbury.

The pull of the past and the pervasive power of Ingram Frizer in the present were sufficient to make Tom assent on one condition—that the subject was not mentioned to Marlowe.

Frizer and Skeres had little difficulty in finding their prey. A peculiarly gullible youth named Drew Woodleffe, who lived with his widowed mother in Buckinghamshire, was on a visit to London when he fell in with them. Skeres took him to Tower Hill where he pointed out some 'guns and cannon and great iron pieces' and suggested that they might be bought for a comparatively small sum and resold at a great profit. The country boy was impressed, but although he had inherited a small estate he had very little ready money. Could Skeres, perhaps, lend him some? Skeres unfortunately could not, but, happily, he knew someone who could. So Ingram Frizer was brought on the scene and Drew Woodleffe, not altogether understanding the financial intricacies of the transaction, signed a bond to repay him £60 at the end of a month for a £30 loan. Meanwhile, Frizer and Skeres undertook to buy and resell on his behalf the 'great iron pieces'.

Drew Woodleffe was disappointed that nothing was sold (though, as the artillery was official Government property, it was hardly surprising) but he was persuaded that it was only a matter of time. Frizer having in the meantime verified that he did in fact own sufficient property near Aylesbury to act as security for a loan, Woodleffe was taken to Scadbury where he was so impressed by the opulence, charm and courtesy of the

Lord of the Manor that he found himself signing another bond, this time to repay Mr Thomas Walsingham £200 within eight weeks for his gracious loan of £100.*

The interview was carefully arranged to take place during the time when Marlowe was visiting London to congratulate Raleigh on his release from the Tower.

Sir Walter's release was not due to any relenting on the part of the Queen. He was given his liberty for a severely practical reason. His last expedition had captured a treasure-ship, a great Spanish carrack, the *Madre de Dios*, which had proved to be the richest single prize ever taken. Her cargo consisted of pepper and cloves and cinnamon, cochineal, mace, nutmegs and musk. The pepper alone was worth £102,000. But there were also precious stones, pearls, amber and ebony, satins, tapestries and silks. It took ten English ships eventually to carry the fabulous cargo from Dartmouth to London—and by that time a portion of it had disappeared. For when the Great Carrack was towed into Dartmouth, there was an outbreak of looting on a country-wide scale. The West Country went mad for jewels, pearls and amber. One sailor alone was found in possession of 'a chain of orient pearls, two chains of gold, four great pearls of the bigness of a fair pea, four forks of crystal and four spoons of crystal set with gold and stones and two cords of musk'. Other looters had bags of rubies and diamonds. Every man on the road going east 'did smell of prizes'—musk and ambergris—and rushing to meet them were over two thousand merchants and goldsmiths in wild competition to buy what they could as cheaply as they could from the simple sailors. In one such bargain, 1,800 diamonds and 300 rubies went for £130.

Order had somehow to be restored or the treasure, enormous as it was, would, little by little, melt away. To attempt to enforce the law was quite useless. The Queen sent her officers, but they were as powerless as anyone else. Putting the sailors on their oath was 'lost labour and an offence to God'. It was clear

---

* Eventually Drew Woodleffe's mother brought and won an action against Thomas Walsingham for this cozening of her son 'in his then unwary age'. The law's delays were such that it took five years and is thus outside the bounds of this book.

that Raleigh—whose prize after all it was—was the only man who could cope with the situation, especially as the sailors' lawlessness was increased by their indignation on hearing that he was in prison. So, discreetly accompanied by his keeper, Raleigh went.

His success surprised the Government. 'I do vow to you before God,' wrote Sir Robert Cecil (who had just been appointed Secretary in succession to Walsingham) to his father, Burleigh, 'that his credit with the mariners is greater than I thought of.'

Raleigh also wrote to Burleigh: 'Fourscore thousand pounds is more than a man ever presented Her Majesty as yet. If God have sent it for my ransom, I hope Her Majesty will accept it.' But if Raleigh could bargain, so could the Queen. In the end, she got half the entire booty and he got nothing but his freedom.

20. Arrest

By the end of the year, the plague had accounted for the lives of 16,503 Londoners but as it seemed to be abating, the Queen ordered her players to perform as usual for the Christmastide festivities. Henslowe, following the royal example rather than waiting for official permission, consequently reopened *The Rose* at the New Year and on 26 January 1593 Marlowe at last saw the staging of his *Guise*. Again his work was a clamorous success and the takings that Friday afternoon, £3 14*s*., fell only 2*s*. 4*d*. short of the record-breaking first-afternoon of *Harry the Sixth*, which was revived the following Monday. Kit hoped that the next performance of *Guise*, which was fixed for the coming Friday, would over-top it. But on that day, February 2, the theatre was officially closed and so he was cheated of that most important occasion for any dramatist—the second performance.

The latest mortality figures had shown that the plague, far from lessening, was alarmingly on the increase—so greatly, indeed, that the City Fathers decided to devote some of their profits from the Great Carrack (they had invested £6,000 in Raleigh's expedition and had now been allotted £12,000 worth of the spoils) to the building of an up-to-date pest-house.

Conditions in the capital were such that the various knights and burgesses who had to come up from the country to attend the opening of Parliament on February 19 were anxious to get away again as soon as possible and showed a certain amount of sympathy for the Queen's speech in which she told them plainly that 'where heretofore it hath been used that many delighted themselves in long orations, full of verbosity and vain ostentation, more than in speaking things of substance, the time that is precious should not be thus spent and the good hours not be lost in idle speeches'.

What the Queen wanted was money to prepare for the threatened war with Spain by way of Scotland and penal laws of even more severity against Catholics and Puritans. She got both.

There was also the immigrant situation to be dealt with. A Bill was introduced 'against Alien Strangers selling by Retail any Foreign Commodities' which Sir Walter Raleigh defended against 'liberal' attacks: 'You argue that it is against Charity, against Honour and against Profit to expel these Strangers. In my opinion it is not true Charity to relieve them for those who flee hither have forsaken their own King, and Religion is only a pretext for them. As for Honour, it is indeed honourable to use Strangers as we are used among Strangers, but it is baseness in a nation to give liberty to another nation which they refuse to grant to us. In Antwerp we are not allowed to have a single tailor or shoemaker living there; at Milan we cannot have so much as a barber. And as for Profit, they are discharged of subsidies, they pay nothing, yet they eat our profits and supplant our own nation.'

During the debate, reference was made to a similar situation at the beginning of the century. On 1 May 1517—which had become known in history as 'Evil May Day'—the apprentices of London had staged a violent anti-immigrant riot which was quelled only by the personal intervention of the Sheriff, Sir Thomas More. This example—or warning—made little impression on the House of Commons, but it attracted the attention of Lord Strange in the Upper House who, as a Catholic, revered the memory of More as one of the first martyrs of the century. He mentioned the possibility of a topical play to his players.

Strange's Men were the only company of actors left in London, hoping against hope that the plague would diminish at least enough to allow the reopening of one of the houses, even if it were only the despised Newington Butts. Henslowe and Alleyn immediately summoned the team of writers, headed by Kyd and guided again by Antony Munday as 'plotter'. The places of the dead Greene and the absent Marlowe were taken by two young hacks, Dekker and Chettle, and the play thrown together in less than a week. Munday himself made a fair copy which was sent off, accompanied by the statutory fee of seven shillings, to the office of the Master of the Revels, Sir Edmund Tilney, who, at the time of the Marprelate troubles, had had his powers of censorship extended from the Court to the public theatres.

Tilney returned *Sir Thomas More* immediately, refusing a licence until alterations had been made which destroyed the whole point of the play. 'Leave out the insurrection wholly,' he scribbled at the top of the first page, 'and the cause thereof and begin with Sir Thomas More at the Mayor's Sessions, with a good report afterwards of his good service as Sheriff of London upon a mutiny against the Lombards. Only a short report and not otherwise, at your perils!' At various points the word 'strangers' was crossed out and 'Mend this' written in the margin.

A few days later, a series of slogans and placards appeared on the walls of the city, with a particularly inflammatory one on the Dutch Church: 'Doth not the world see that you, the Belgians, or rather drunken drones, and faint-hearted Flemings; and you, fraudulent fathers, Frenchmen, by your cowardly flight from your own natural countries, have abandoned the same into the hands of your enemies and have, by a feigned hypocrisy and counterfeit show of religion planted yourselves here in a most fertile soil under a most gracious and merciful Prince who had been contented, to the great prejudice of her own natural subjects, to suffer you to live here in better case and more freedom than her own people? Be it known to all Flemings and Frenchmen, that it is best for them to depart out of the realm of England between this [April 22] and the ninth of July next. If not, then to take what follows. For there shall be many a sore stripe. Apprentices will rise to the number of 2,336. And all prentices and journeymen will down with Flemings and Strangers.'

Prompted by ambassadorial protests, as well as fears of a rising, the Privy Council held a special meeting to draft instructions for the Lord Mayor and Aldermen: 'There have been of late divers lewd and mutinous libels set up within the City of London. For the discovery of the author and publisher thereof, Her Majesty's pleasure is that extraordinary pains and care be taken in examining such persons as may be in any way suspected. This is to require and authorize you to make search and apprehend every person so to be suspected and for that purpose to enter into all houses and places where any such may be remaining; and, upon their apprehension to make like search in any of the chambers, studies, chests, or other like places for any manners of writings or papers that may give you light for the discovery of the libellers. And after you shall have examined the persons, if you shall find them duly to be suspected and they refuse to confess the truth, you shall put them to the torture in Bridewell and by the extremity thereof, draw them to confess their knowledge of the said libels.'

On May 12, the day after the Privy Council Order was made, Thomas Kyd was arrested and taken to Bridewell.

Meanwhile the other subject of legislation—the measures against the Puritan extremists—had produced its own crop of unrest. On March 1 one of the sect, Roger Rippon, had died in Newgate and his fellow-believers had placed his coffin outside the house of the magistrate who had committed him, Richard Young, with the inscription attached: 'This is the corpse of Roger Rippon, a servant of Christ and Her Majesty's faithful subject, who is the last of the sixteen or seventeen whom that great enemy of God, the Archbishop of Canterbury, has murdered in Newgate for their testimony to Jesus Christ. His blood crieth out for vengeance against the Archbishop and against Mr Richard Young for abusing his power.'

In revenge, as soon as the new legislation had been passed, the Archbishop had had his two other leading co-religionists hanged, which left at liberty among the leaders only John Penry, whom the Archbishop insisted on describing as the much-wanted Martin Marprelate himself.

Penry had left the safety of Edinburgh in the autumn of 1592 and attached himself to the newly-formed 'Brownists' * who met in a school-house off Lombard Street. Here they held their Sunday services in the winter between four and five in the

---

* So called after their founder, Robert Browne. As one of their tenets was that each individual congregation was 'the Church', in accordance with Christ's promise: 'Where two or three are gathered together in my name, there am I in the midst of them,' they eventually became known as 'Congregationalists'.

morning when the London streets were deserted and the chance of detection small. In the summer they would leave the city at dawn to spend the day in the country—the woods at Deptford or the fields and woods of Islington. The services were of the simplest kind—prayers, the reading of the Bible and preaching, followed, on the first Sunday of the month, by an observance of the Lord's Supper.

It was on March 4 that the Archbishop's pursuivants, having discovered that there was to be a meeting in Islington Woods as a memorial for Roger Rippon, prepared to round up the whole assembly. Penry himself (who was using the name 'John Harrison') was arrested before he reached the place of meeting and, with several others, he was detained in the constable's house. But he was not recognised by his captors and 'in the bustle' he managed to escape. That evening the Privy Council had an emergency meeting and a warrant was issued to all 'public officers' ordering them 'by all possible means to arrest John Penry, who gives himself the name of Harrison, and to bring him before Their Lordships'.

Nevertheless Penry managed to retain his liberty by hiding with various co-religionists until March 22 when he ventured to visit Stepney. There, by the merest chance, he was recognised by the Vicar, Anthony Anderson, a bellicose character who prided himself on his skill with his 'two-handed staff' and who, in one of the Marprelate Tracts, had been accused of robbing the poor-box, playing a lewd part in a morris-dance and of getting his housemaid with child. The Vicar immediately raised a hue and cry and Penry was captured and led off to gaol. On April 10, at the Sessions House at Newgate, he was examined by the Archbishop of Canterbury and the persecuting magistrate, Richard Young. He was committed for trial at the King's Bench on May 21.

With the printer of the Marprelate Tracts (or, as the authorities officially pretended to believe, the formidable Martin himself) safely in custody, one fount of the current unrest was cut off. With Kyd in Bridewell, they hoped they had also found the propagandist of the anti-immigrant apprentices. His part in writing *Sir Thomas More* was alone sufficient to suggest his guilt and the fact that Alleyn and the rest of the company had made hurried preparations to go 'on the road' and play in

Cheltenham that very May strengthened the suspicion. The plague, of course, was the excuse for the tour; but as that week the deaths had fallen to only 34, it was unlikely to be the reason for men who had held on doggedly through the worst of it.

But an examination of Kyd's papers revealed nothing to suggest any political activities, and even a taste of the rack could not change his protestations of innocence. Eventually, however, the officers going through the manuscripts taken from his study came upon three pages which suggested a graver offence than that which he was charged with—'diabolical atheism'. They read them carefully and wrote on them: '12 May 1593: Vile Heretical Conceits, denying the Deity of Jesus Christ our Saviour, found among the papers of Thomas Kyd prisoner.'

Kyd, when he realised what they were, was terrified. Vehemently he denied that the three pages were anything to do with him. They must have been carelessly 'shuffled' with his own manuscripts by mistake and they in fact belonged to another dramatist, Christopher Marlowe.

Why should Marlowe's papers be confused with his? Because, a year or so ago, they were working together in the same room. Marlowe, then, was a friend of his? God forbid! It was quite impossible for a quiet, law-abiding, religious man like Kyd to be a friend of so irreligious a man as Marlowe. How irreligious? Completely. He was accustomed to jest at the Bible, to gibe at prayers and to repudiate the sayings of the saints and the prophets. Could Kyd give an example? Too many and he disliked even repeating the monstrous blasphemies in which Marlowe habitually indulged. One simple one sprang to mind. When Kyd told him that he intended to write a pious poem on St Paul, Marlowe suggested he ought to call it *Fast and Loose*, because Paul was only a 'juggler' like Moses. Thomas Hariot, Sir Walter Raleigh's man, who could do much better in that direction than either Paul or Moses, might, Marlowe said, give Kyd some advice how to treat it.

Apart from his blasphemies, the inquisitors asked, what kind of a man was Marlowe?

'Cruel-hearted,' said Kyd. 'And apt to do sudden injuries to men.'

'Yet your lord was happy to employ him?'

'My lord knew only his writings and, when he understood his blasphemous nature, could not bear to hear his name mentioned.'

'So you are not working together now?'

'No. It would be impossible.'

'But you will swear that these three pages are his?'

'On my salvation.'

They added to the note they had made on the manuscript: 'which he affirmeth that he had from Marlowe' and went to report the matter to the Privy Council.

The Privy Councillors were interested. Six days later, on May 18 they directed one of the Messengers of Her Majesty's Chamber, Henry Maunder, 'to repair to the house of Mr Thomas Walsingham, or to any other place where he shall understand Christopher Marlowe to be staying and to apprehend him and bring him to Court'.

21. Last Act

Marlowe's arrest came at a moment when he was facing crises of a different kind. In his new poem he had just written

> Love is not full of pity (as men say)
> But deaf and cruel where he means to prey.

And not only when 'prey' was in question, he reflected. Insensitivity and cruelty were of the permanent nature of Eros the enticing. The perfect setting of a home where, in a Kentish spring, he had hoped to spend with Tom days of timeless content, only emphasised the disillusion. All sweetness had turned sour. He had discovered the plan for the cozening of the Buckinghamshire country boy.

His enlightenment was due to an accidental meeting with Skeres who had visited Scadbury on a matter connected with the plan. When Marlowe asked him his business, Skeres told him with considerable relish, expressing surprise that Marlowe knew nothing about it and supposing that he would now want his 'cut'. Furiously Marlowe had taxed Tom Walsingham with it and when it was nonchalantly confirmed transferred his scorn to Frizer with whom, he was sure, the idea had originated. This, the last of their many quarrels about Frizer, led to an unprecedented breach between them. For several days Kit and Tom did not speak to each other. Marlowe saw the matter in terms altogether misleading in their simplicity, since he had never been able to divest himself of his original jealousy of Frizer. Blinded by this misapprehension, he faced Tom with an alternative. Either Ingram Frizer must leave Scadbury or he would.

Such a request betrayed Kit's innocence of the ways of the world. Faced with the choice between a temperamental lover and a trusted and trustworthy servant who saw to the smooth running of the house and estate and who tactfully superintended the provision of all creature comforts, no one was likely to hesitate long, certainly not anyone of Tom Walsingham's self-indulgent habits. Since Marlowe had given the ultimatum, Tom would not admit that affection, as such, was involved and he assumed that Kit would soon settle down as he had on previous occasions. Even if he did not, Tom would not be heart-broken. The early enchantment was gone. The recurring tensions were becoming unendurable. Besides, since the death of 'Uncle Francis', things had changed in so many ways. It was time that he looked for a wife and gave his house an heir.

The quarrel with Tom and his—to Marlowe—inexplicable behaviour in not discharging Frizer was the most pressing, but not the only, matter troubling Kit. There was also Poley. On May 8, before crossing from Deptford to The Hague, Poley had called on him at Scadbury. He told him that the Scottish-Spanish plot was ripe for the plucking. The Catholic peers in Scotland, having decided that King James was 'weak and un-trustworthy, with no religion or fixed purpose' had relinquished any idea of co-operating with him and had decided to kidnap him instead. In his place as heir to the throne of England, they would put Lord Strange who on his mother's side was descended from a younger sister of Henry VIII; King James derived his title from the elder sister. Lord Strange's cousin, Sir William Stanley, who commanded a regiment of seven hundred English and Irish Catholics which he maintained at his own expense in the Low Countries, was about to make a secret journey to London to sound him on the matter and to give the signal for the Scottish rising.

In the Low Countries, the Duke of Parma had died and his place as Governor of Flanders was to be taken (so the English exiles hoped and planned) by the Duchess of Feria, who as Jane Dormer had been the friend and confidante of Queen Mary Tudor and had made a love-match with the Count of Feria, King Philip's intimate during the time that Philip was in

England as King.* Should the Duchess Jane be appointed, it might be taken for granted that the measures for aiding the English Catholics would be pursued with greater energy than ever and Poley was returning to the Low Countries in his usual guise of a persecuted English Catholic to ascertain how far the plan had progressed. Also, to find out when the offer to Lord Strange was to be made.

'So you understand,' Poley had said to Marlowe before he embarked, 'why you are needed back in the Service. You still write for Strange?'

'No,' said Marlowe, 'I was with his men for only one play and his lordship did not condescend to visit us during the writing of it.'

'But you could go back if you wished?'

'Possibly. But I am Lord Pembroke's man now as far as I am anyone's, and I have no wish to return to Lord Strange.'

'Yet,' persisted Poley, 'it would be possible should it be required?'

'Required by whom?'

'The Service.'

'I thought I had made it plain last time we talked that I have done with the Service?'

'Unless, as I remember, I asked it of you as a favour and for good reason.'

'And do you?'

'Yes.'

Poley explained the situation to him at somewhat greater length and at the end said: 'There is no need to make up your mind immediately. I shall not be back for over a fortnight. Meet me at Mistress Bull's house at Deptford on May 30 and we can decide then. In the meantime, I will send Royden to Scotland.'

When, after Poley had left for Flanders, the pursuivants, armed with the Privy Council's Order, arrived at Scadbury, Marlowe's first thought was that this was one of Poley's manœuvres. It would be in line with his deviousness, Kit reflected, to have made the matter official so that he would have

* See *The Sisters*, which also contains a selection of de Feria's letters to King Philip pp. 168–76. The cutting-up of history into arbitrary reigns and 'periods' destroys the sweep and logic of events. The steward and trusted friend of Sir William Stanley, for instance, living with him in Brussels was Guy Fawkes. See *Guy Fawkes*, Chapter 1.

no option but to do whatever Robin asked on May 30. But, as he rode back to Westminster, plying Maunder with questions (which, for the most part, the pursuivant skilfully parried), he was increasingly perplexed because all that he was able to elicit was that the subject of the Council's inquiry was Thomas Kyd. What crime could the timid, careful, self-righteous Kyd have committed to have brought him within the reach of the law?

Marlowe's brief appearance before the Privy Council on May 20 was satisfactory enough. The Archbishop of Canterbury had already interfered in his favour in the matter of his Cambridge degree; the Lord Admiral counted him as the best of his company's playwrights; the Earl of Essex (who was a newcomer to the Council) knew of him as one trusted by Walsingham; Sir Robert Cecil had been his contemporary at Cambridge; Sir Thomas Heneage knew from Poley that he had been valuable in 'the Service'. They treated him courteously as a witness, not hostilely as a potential criminal, and asked for information about the incriminating pages found among Kyd's papers.

Marlowe explained to them what they were—a summary of the beliefs of the Arians, denying the divinity of Christ, from a book published forty-four years ago and dedicated to Queen Mary Tudor. They had been printed in the form of a convenient epitome of what the author had set himself to refute.

Why were they in Kyd's hand? Because Marlowe had asked him as a professional noverint to copy them for him.

Did they represent Kyd's beliefs? Not as far as Marlowe knew. Did they represent Marlowe's own beliefs? No. Then what was the object of having them copied? Marlowe reminded Their Lordships that, as a result of their own magnanimous action, he had been privileged to study theology and philosophy at Cambridge and had been awarded his M.A. But in the six years since he had left the University, he had not abandoned his interest in these subjects and often discussed them with those of similar interests. This summary of Arianism was intended for such a discussion. With whom? Among others, Sir Walter Raleigh and his mathematical tutor, Thomas Hariot. Was Thomas Kyd at these discussions? Marlowe permitted himself a slight smile as he said: 'No, Your Lordships, I do not think they would have interested him.'

The questioning over, Marlowe was dismissed with the usual formula for witnesses in a case still *sub judice*—that he should 'give his daily attendance to Their Lordships until he should be licensed to the contrary', which meant no more than that he must stay within reach of Westminster until Kyd's case was decided. But at the suggestion of Essex, who hoped to uncover something to Raleigh's discredit supported by the Archbishop of Canterbury, who was suspicious of Marlowe's own religious beliefs, the Council set one of their spies, a shady young lawyer named Richard Baines, to shadow Marlowe and pick up what information he could about him.*

Marlowe went immediately to tell Raleigh what had happened, but Sir Walter, now that Parliament was no longer sitting, had gone down to his manor of Sherborne in Dorset, which had been the Queen's last gift to him before his disgrace, and Marlowe dared not disobey the Council's order by leaving London.

The day after Marlowe appeared before the Privy Council, John Penry was brought to trial before the King's Bench. He was arraigned as one 'had not the fear of God before his eyes but was seduced by a devilish impulse to devise and intend not only the overthrow of religion and the destruction of the honour of the Queen, by whose care it had been established; but also to move the people to rebellion and insurrection'. The case against him was based on certain passages selected from a book, *Reformation No Enemy*, which he had written while he was in Scotland the previous November.

'The last days of your reign', he wrote, addressing Queen Elizabeth, 'are turned rather against Christ Jesus and His Gospel than to the maintenance of the same.' Of the bishops, he averred: 'You shall find among this crew nothing but a troop of bloody soul-murderers and sacrilegious church-robbers.' And

* As Baines did not deliver his report until after Marlowe's death, it could have no bearing on subsequent Privy Council action; and, as Dr Boas has pointed out, there is no reason to suppose that Baines knew Marlowe personally as 'the assertions are such as might have been made by anyone moving in London Bohemian circles and collecting the gossip'.

'as for the general state of the Magistracy, of the Ministry, or of the Common People, behold nothing but a multitude of conspirators against God'.

The result of the trial was a foregone conclusion,* if only because most people believed that Penry was 'Martin Marprelate' himself and Archbishop Whitgift was determined on vengeance. When the trial was over Penry appealed for mercy to Burleigh himself, knowing that, in this matter at least, the old Lord Treasurer was on the side of moderation. But it was of no avail. Whitgift had his way.

Penry, awaiting execution in 'the Bench' prison in Southwark, was suddenly at eleven o'clock in the morning of Tuesday, May 29, told that he was to die between four and five that afternoon. He was to be allowed no farewells and no last speech at the gallows.

The Southwark place of execution was St Thomas à Watering, a little short of the second milestone on the Canterbury road from the Tabard Inn where there was a stream at which the pilgrims to the shrine of St Thomas of Canterbury used to water their horses. The gallows was erected 'near the Green Man' where there was 'only a very thin company attending'. It had been so arranged by authority 'for fear Penry might have raised some tumult either going to the gallows or on the ladder'.

Marlowe was among that 'very thin company'. He had been dining in Southwark to pick up gossip from some of the lesser actors at *The Rose* who had not gone on tour. Here he had met Nashe, on the point of leaving London, who had shown him his new poem on the plague, of which Kit had particularly approved the stanzas:

> Beauty is but a flower
> Which wrinkles will devour:
> Brightness falls from the air,
> Queens have died young and fair;
> Dust hath closed Helen's eye;
> I am sick, I must die!
>> Lord, have mercy on us!

> Haste, therefore, each degree
> To welcome destiny.

---

* 'A trial', according to Sir Thomas Phillips, Q.C., 'which disgraces English justice.'

Heaven is our heritage,
Earth but a player's stage.
Mount we unto the sky!
I am sick, I must die.
Lord, have mercy on us!

The slow ringing of a death-knell from St George's at an unaccustomed hour had prompted him to ask the reason. A special burial of plague victims, Marlowe's companions agreed —a sound too familiar to notice. Marlowe, however, continued curious and went out into the street to make further inquiries. When he found that it was a knell rung during the last journey of a criminal from prison to the gallows, he did not go back to the inn but made his way as quickly as he could to St Thomas à Watering.

He did not think that Penry, scanning the faces of the by-standers in search of some of his followers, recognised him. If he did, he gave no sign of it. Once he realised that he was to be deprived of the last privilege of every executed criminal—a dying speech from the scaffold—Penry devoted himself to prayer. Though this Puritan martyrdom was outwardly poles apart from the Catholic martyrdom of Gennings, Marlowe was aware that the blaze of belief and the certainty of the Glory-to-come united them in a dimension of which he had no experience. Logic about *Ens entium* shrivelled into irrelevance. As Penry was swung off the ladder to death, he found himself saying: 'Lord, have mercy on us all.'

Marlowe arrived early at Deptford next morning. Though Poley had set the time of meeting for noon and there was always the chance that a stormy crossing might delay the packet, Kit was at Mistress Bull's house by ten o'clock. To his surprise he found Ingram Frizer and Nicholas Skeres waiting for him. When he asked why they were at Deptford Skeres gave a coarse laugh and Frizer said with unconcealed bitterness: 'We have come to find the apple of my master's eye!' He explained that Tom Walsingham had expected Marlowe to return to Scadbury after the meeting of the Privy Council and had become increasingly anxious as the days passed and there was no sign of him. They did not even know if he was alive or dead. 'What with the plague and riots and other acts-of-God,' said Skeres, 'death to-day is at any corner.'

'But if you were alive and free,' said Frizer, 'we knew you would be here at noon today to meet Robin Poley.'

'And now you have found me?'

'You will I hope be my guest at dinner,' said Frizer, 'and afterwards we can get back to Scadbury to ease Master Thomas's mind.'

'I shall not go back to Scadbury today or ever,' said Kit.

'That is as may be,' said Frizer, 'but you will not refuse to take salt with me?'

'Would you honour it?' Marlowe flared. The atmosphere was murderous. Frizer shrugged. Skeres reverted to his remembered habit of cleaning his bitten nails with his dagger.

Poley arrived about half-past eleven and showed some annoy-ance at the presence of the other two. 'I came to speak to Kit privately,' he said.

'The garden is yours,' said Frizer. 'Nick and I can play tables.'

During the afternoon Marlowe and Poley wandered round the garden engrossed in conversation, Poley by turns persuasive and hectoring, Marlowe increasingly determined that he would have nothing to do with 'the Service'. In this the Privy Council order seemed to be his ally. He was bound, at least for the time being, to remain within call of the Star Chamber. Poley laughed the excuse aside. He would deal with it tomorrow when he went to report to Sir Thomas Heneage on his recent mission. In any case, Marlowe would not be required to leave London. All that he had to do was to attach himself again to Lord Strange's company and try to win his confidence. Surely this was little enough to ask!

'Little?' said Marlowe, remembering Babington. 'How many lives?'

'Not a single innocent one,' said Poley.

Kit did not say: 'By whose judgment?' but it was as if Poley had read his thoughts when he added: 'Unless your loyalty has withered as much as your obedience.'

The venom in his voice gave it a ring of finality. Marlowe

realised, with an involuntary shudder of fear, that Poley was now an enemy who would destroy him without pity if occasion arose. A broken tool, according to one of Poley's precepts, was best thrown away.

After supper Frizer suggested that they might have a last round of tables. He himself would not take part, as he had lost enough money to Skeres in the afternoon. Poley could play Marlowe and Skeres could adjudicate. Frizer, whose lame leg was paining him, lay on a couch behind the bench on which the other three were sitting, Marlowe in the middle.

In the first few moves the temperaments of the players revealed themselves—Poley playing the calculated 'running game', Marlowe the reckless 'back game'. But the dice were against Kit and after seven throws Skeres said over his shoulder to the recumbent Frizer: 'Our poet has as good as lost.' Frizer got up and made his way to the door.

'Where are you going?' said Marlowe.

'As the game is nearly over', answered Frizer, 'I am going to get the reckoning from Mistress Bull. You remember that we agreed that I should make the payment.' Kit did not see the meaning glance he threw to the other two. Skeres said provocatively: 'You need not trouble yourself. *He* will come back.'

At this reference to Babington's flight from the *Grapes* under pretence of going for the reckoning which had never lost its power of haunting him, Kit's control broke. He shouted: 'I never thought to hope so greatly in what I do not believe—the reckoning of God's judgment on you all.' At this he felt the knees of the men each side of him press against him, holding him like a vice. As he put his hands on the table to lever himself upright, they caught his wrists and held him helpless.

Frizer returned. 'The reckoning!' he said and with all his force drove his dagger into Marlowe's eye.

EPILOGUE

Deptford: Friday, 1 June 1593: Afternoon

The Verdict

Epilogue. The Verdict

Poley had one principle above all which had crystallised from years of experience: 'Always see that your lie adheres as closely as possible to the truth.' In this case only a slight deviation was necessary. By saying it was Marlowe who was reclining on the couch instead of Frizer and by giving Frizer some light flesh-wounds about the head to lend verisimilitude to the version agreed on by the three murderers, the jury could easily be cozened into accepting the plea of self-defence. And as they were all in 'the Service', they could rely on the Queen's Coroner giving them the benefit of any doubt. It was fortunate for them that the crime had been committed 'within the verge'. A local coroner might have probed more deeply than William Danby was likely to.

They were not disappointed. The verdict was as satisfactory as it could be. The findings were that on Wednesday, 30 May 1593 Marlowe, Poley, Frizer and Skeres 'about the tenth hour before noon met together in a room in the house of a certain Eleanor Bull, widow, and there passed the time together and then dined and after dinner were in quiet sort together there and walked in the garden until the sixth hour after noon and then together and in company supped; and after supper Ingram Frizer and Christopher Marlowe uttered one to the other divers malicious words for the reason that they could not agree about the payment of the sum of pence, that is *le recknynge*, there. Christopher Marlowe then lying upon a bed in the room where they supped and moved with anger against Ingram Frizer and Ingram, sitting with his back towards the bed where Christopher Marlowe was lying and with the front part of his body towards the table and with Nicholas Skeres and Robert Poley sitting on either side of him so that he could in no wise take flight, it so befell that Christopher Marlowe on a sudden and of his malice against Ingram maliciously drew the dagger of the said Ingram, which was at his back, and with the same dagger gave him two wounds on his head; whereupon Ingram, in fear of being slain and sitting between Nicholas Skeres and Robert Poley so that he could not in any wise get away, in his own defence and for the saving of his life then and there struggled with Christopher Marlowe to get from him his dagger, in which affray Ingram could not get away from Marlowe; and it so befell that in that affray Ingram in defence of his life, with the dagger aforesaid to the value of 12*d*., gave Christopher a mortal wound over his right eye of which wound Christopher Marlowe then and there instantly died.

'And so the jurors say upon their oath that the said Ingram Frizer killed and slew Christopher Marlowe aforesaid on the thirtieth day of May in the thirty-fifth year of the reign of our Sovereign Lady Queen Elizabeth at Deptford Strand within the verge in the room aforesaid within the verge, in the manner and form aforesaid, in the defence and saving of his own life. In witness of which thing the Coroner as well as the Jurors have interchangeably set their seals.'

Because of the plague the body of Christopher Marlowe was buried that afternoon, immediately the inquest was over, in the churchyard of St Nicholas's Church in an unmarked grave.

POSTSCRIPT

Marlowe and Shakespeare

Postscript. Marlowe and Shakespeare

This book is called 'an informal biography' in deference to the warning of the great Marlowe scholar, Dr C. F. Tucker Brooke: 'Formal biography is in this instance more than usually futile.' I have used the method of historical writing which I have been practising for the last twenty years or so in an effort to revivify the past—that is to say, to research and prepare as if for an academic thesis and then only, hedged by that knowledge, to use the historical imagination to try to bring the subject to life. All I claim for *Kind Kit* is that what I have narrated *could* have happened as I have reported it.

History is what actually did happen. That is why it is impossible to write. Academic history is a selection of facts chronicled without imagination. This is known as History—the History of which Tolstoy wrote that it would be excellent if it were true and which the dying Walpole refused to have read to him on the ground that it was bound to be false. Academic historians endeavour to maintain the pretence that 'History' is a 'science' and that it has a 'method' of interpreting 'facts' which justifies it in offering certain 'conclusions'.

But, in reality, 'History' can record less than a millionth part of the relevant facts of a situation,* is unable in consequence to draw any conclusions which can by any stretch of vocabulary be termed 'scientific' and has no 'method' other than that which applies equally to any form of investigation from designing an aeroplane to solving a murder—that is to say, finding out as

---

* It has been said that, with the enormous increase and accessibility of information, it would take a lifetime to 'study the sources' available for a single day's events and that the use of the telephone ensures that much vital information is never available anyhow.

much as possible, using and expressing that knowledge honestly, testing the tentative conclusions but admitting that, at any moment, something new may be discovered which will invalidate them.

The assumptions underlying academic claims that 'History' is anything but a department of national myth or a branch of political propaganda rests on three assumptions—that everything that has happened has been recorded and that if it has not been recorded it must be presumed not to have happened and that the record is not only accurate but must take precedence of any other kind of evidence. The absurdity of this is, I should have thought, self-evident.

If 'to know' is taken to mean 'to have indisputably authentic documentary evidence of', all we know of Christopher Marlowe's life could be comfortably written on one sheet of writing paper. We do not even 'know' that he wrote *Tamburlaine*, since there is no direct contemporary reference to him as author and his name is not on the title-page of the first published edition of the play during his lifetime in 1590.

Also, as there are several contemporary Christopher Marlowes both at Cambridge and in London, it is difficult to be sure when the poet-playwright is actually referred to or when certain actions should be ascribed to 'another man of the same name'. The disentanglement is not made easier by the chaotic spelling of the family name, varying between Marlowe, Marlow, Marloe, Marlo, Marle, Marlen, Marlin, Marlyne, Marlynge, Merlin, Marley, Marlye, Morle and Morley. He himself in the one specimen of his signature extant (discovered as late as 1939) uses 'Morley'.

A selection from even the apparently documented references to Marlowe has thus had to be made and I must confess that I have rejected one which is conventionally attached to him—that which one of his biographers, using a romantic rather than an historical imagination, has described: 'Roaring drunkenly homeward in the month of May 1592 Christopher Marlowe collided with Allen Nicholls, constable of Shoreditch, and Nicholas Helliot, under-constable. Perhaps he assaulted them. Frowsy heads of queans popped from the doors and windows of Holywell Street—behind them, peering hard, their soldier or actor clients. They saw the celebrated poet in the toils of the law—again.'

This purple piece is based on the recent discovery of a recogni-
sance entered into by a 'Christopher Marle, gentleman, of
London' to keep the peace. Apart from the improbability of its
reference to our Marlowe at this time in his life, there were at
least five other Christophers to whom 'Christopher Marle of
London' might apply. In his *Christopher Marlowe in London*,
Dr Eccles points out that the other most likely candidate lived
as far away from Holywell as Fleet Street. But that is not very
far and presumably the denizens of Fleet Street paid visits to
The Theatre and *The Curtain* in Holywell. The fracas sounds like
one of the usual theatrical brawls and if Marlowe was at any
theatre that particular week, it would surely be at *The Rose*
where both *Harry the Sixth* and the *Jew* were on. It seems to me
that, even with the number of facts so few, it is pointless to add
doubtful ones based on nothing but an identity of name in the
hope that it will enlarge our knowledge of Marlowe. I have
preferred to accept the little that is known and, for enlightenment, set it carefully and chronologically against the known
background of his life and the self-revelation of his writings.

One point, however, must be explained. Shakespeare does not
appear in the story because there is no reason to suppose that he
ever met Marlowe or, indeed, that he arrived in London before
Marlowe's murder on 30 May 1593. The exact date of his
arrival will probably never be known. His first play, *Titus
Andronicus*, an atrocity-drama, much *à la mode*, with rape,
tongue-cutting, three amputated hands and fourteen killings,
was first played at *The Rose* on 24 January 1594. The first
documented reference to him as an actor is in the Chamber
Accounts for the Christmas festivities at Court where he made
two appearances with Richard Burbage in the December of
1594. And his first poem, *Venus and Adonis*, which was indebted
to Marlowe's *Hero and Leander*, has '1593' on its title-page,
though as the year ran from March 25 to March 24, the '1593'
included what is now called January 1 to March 24, 1594.

The summer or autumn of 1593 is thus the most probable
date for the arrival of Shakespeare in London.

Unfortunately, the officially accepted date is 'well before the
autumn of 1592 and possibly as early as 1590'. This is based on
one contemporary quotation and on that alone—Robert Greene's
last plea to his fellow-dramatists: 'There is an upstart Crow

beautified by our feathers that with his *Tiger's heart wrapped in a Player's hide* supposes he is as well able to bombast out a blank verse as the best of you and, being an absolute *Johannes fac totum*, is in his own conceit the only Shake-scene in a country.'

The actor 'Shake-scene', who is so obviously Edward Alleyn, is said by academics to be Shakespeare and the *Tiger's heart wrapped in a Player's hide* (which is an allusion to the line '*O Tiger's heart wrapped in a woman's hide*' that opened one of Alleyn's most memorable speeches in the popular *True Tragedy of Richard Duke of York*) is attributed to another place where it also occurs—a subsequent revision of the *True Tragedy* called *The Third Part of King Henry VI* which was printed in the First Folio as Shakespeare's (who never claimed it) seven years after his death.

The mistaken identification of the 'Shake-scene' actor, the 'Crow', the Jack-of-all-Trades, as being Shakespeare, and the consequent misdating of Shakespeare's career does not concern this book, though it is only fair to point out that it is the conventional Eng. Lit. theory, accepted by generation after generation of writers, repeated in every textbook and encyclopaedia and too firmly embedded in Shakespearian criticism to be popularly dislodged, despite its demolition by Dr C. F. Tucker Brooke in *The Authorship of 2 and 3 Henry VI* (1912) and Dr Allison Gaw in *The Origin and Development of I Henry VI* (1926). It is, indeed, a 'source' which one accepts without question—as I must confess I did in *The Day Shakespeare Died*—until one approaches the story from the point of view of Marlowe.

The immensity of Shakespeare's genius makes his overshadowing of Marlowe inevitable for posterity and few are likely to question the critic who, suggesting that Cleopatra's dying: 'Give me my robe, put on my crown' is derived from Bajazeth's wife's mad farewell: 'Make ready my coach, my chair, my jewels', comments that 'Shakespeare never quite forgot the touch of the vanished hand that had guided him as a raw and youthful beginner'.

Yet, even admitting the similarity of the quotations,* the accuracy of the picture leaves something to be desired, because

*

* Which I do not. I should have thought it was nearer to Ophelia's mad 'Come, my coach.' One can, of course, play the professorial game *ad infinitum*:

Shakespeare was exactly eight weeks younger than Marlowe. He arrived in London at the age of twenty-nine with nothing to his credit, to make his name on a stage dominated by the reputation of the twenty-nine-year-old Marlowe with his *Tamburlaine*, his *Doctor Faustus*, his *Rich Jew of Malta*, his *Edward II*, his *Massacre at Paris*, his *Contention* and his *True Tragedy*—to say nothing of his M.A.(Cantab.)!—to demonstrate what could be achieved by the age of twenty-nine.

The young man from Warwickshire drifted into the opposite political camp as well as into the rival theatrical company to the young man from Kent. Whereas Marlowe was the friend of Raleigh, Shakespeare became the propagandist of the Essex set and in what has been so rightly described as his 'very bad juvenile play',* *Love's Labour's Lost*, satirised Raleigh with bitter relish. He started with the supreme insult of representing Raleigh as a Spaniard, Don Armado, but he left no doubt in anyone's mind who was intended by the knight who spent his time writing poetry, who addressed his servant with a West Country 'Chirrah', who was noted for the magnificence of his dress and his tales of travel ('I protest I love to hear him lie!'), who was always chronically short of money and whose 'humour is lofty, his discourse peremptory, his tongue filed, his eye ambitious, his gait majestical, and his general behaviour vain, ridiculous and thrasonical'. To underline the identity, if that were necessary, the dramatist quoted a popular reference to Raleigh as 'the Fox, the Ape and the Humble Bee', a tripartite character in which the fox represented his Machiavellianism, the ape his flattery, and the humble bee his buzzing about the Court.

As regards theatrical rivalry, Marlowe was an 'Admiral's man'; Shakespeare became a 'Chamberlain's man'. Marlowe wrote for Edward Alleyn under Henslowe's management at *The Rose*; Shakespeare wrote for Richard Burbage under the Burbages' management at *The Theatre* and at their new house, *The Globe*, built practically next door to *The Rose* as a competitor to it.

In the earlier years of Shakespeare's career, this posthumous

I arrest you of high treason (*Edward II* 1, 1924)
I arrest thee of high treason (*Henry V* II. ii. 145)
I do arrest thee, traitor, of high treason (*2 Henry IV* IV. ii. 107).

* The description is by Mr Milton Waldman. Today it has become the sport of very bad juvenile producers.

rivalry was expressed by imitation. *The Rich Jew of Malta* was still crowding *The Rose* when *The Merchant of Venice* appeared, with Shylock as an obvious version of Barabas and made up, with huge nose and red wig, in imitation of Alleyn in the part. And *Edward II* was the admitted model for *Richard II*. In his next plays, Shakespeare, having successfully survived comparison, went into the attack. He invented the character of Pistol, gave him an identifying reference to the most famous *Tamburlaine* tag

> Shall packhorses
> And hollow pampered jades of Asia
> Which cannot go but thirty miles a day
> Compare with Caesars and with Cannibals
> And Trojan Greeks? Nay, rather damn them with
> King Cerberus; and let the welkin roar!

and developed Pistol's entire vocabulary from play scraps and misquotations from *Tamburlaine* and other *Rose* plays until the character became a walking parody of Alleyn and the ranting style, hitherto so popular with playgoers, but now beginning to appear a little ridiculous to the younger generation. Having found this rich vein of laughter, Shakespeare pursued it mercilessly to its climax in *Hamlet* where he burlesqued Marlowe's *Dido Queen of Carthage* in the speech delivered by the First Player in answer to Hamlet's request for 'Aeneas' tale to Dido and thereabout of it where he speaks of Priam's slaughter. It begins with Pyrrhus.'

Marlowe's original needed only, as one critic has remarked, 'very slight heightening to give it a burlesque turn'.

> At last came Pyrrhus, fell and full of ire,
> His harness dropping blood, and on his sword
> The mangled head of Priam's youngest son,
> Who ran into the palace of the king
> And, at Jove's altar finding Priamus
> About whose wither'd neck hung Hecuba,
> He, with his falchion's point raised up at once,
> Treading upon his breast, struck off his hands

could be recalled with laughter as the First Player evoked the 'rugged Pyrrhus':

Head to foot
Now is he total gules, horridly tricked
With blood of fathers, mothers, daughters, sons;
With eyes like carbuncles the hellish Pyrrhus
Old grandsire Priam seeks. Anon he finds him.
Pyrrhus at Priam drives; in rage strikes wide
But with the whiff and wind of his fell sword
The wounded father falls.

There is no need to labour the point. Shakespeare's attitude to Marlowe is exactly what, the theatre being timelessly what it is, one would expect it to be. And the one direct reference to Marlowe in *As You Like It* epitomises it:

Dead Shepherd, now I find thy saw of might:
'Whoever loved that loved not at first sight?'

Far from this being, as one pious commentator has expressed it, 'a note of unmistakable tenderness' or, according to another, 'a tender salutation in homage', it is a deliberate 'send-up' intended to make the audience laugh, a quotation put into the mouth of Phebe to vindicate her sudden infatuation for Rosalind masquerading as a man.

And it is, given all the circumstances, exactly how an aspiring dramatist, with his finger on the public pulse, might have been expected to react to the inhibiting reputation of a great predecessor. Once Marlowe and Shakespeare are but considered as human beings instead of Eng. Lit. names and studied in their historical perspective in the theatre, the relationship between them is clear enough.

London
New Year's Day 1972

Index